CW01272231

THE HISTORY OF COCKFIGHTING

OTHER BOOKS AVAILABLE

Understanding Old English Game — Large and Bantams
Dr. J. Batty

Royal Pastime of Cockfighting
Robert Howlett
(Reprint of 1709 classic)

Bantams and Miniature Fowl
W.H. Silk

Cockfighting and Game Fowl
Herbert Atkinson

Cockfighting All Over the World
C.A. Finsterbusch

The Old English Game Fowl
Herbert Atkinson

King of Fowls
Mark Marshall

Understanding Modern Game
Dr. J. Batty and J.P. Bleazard

Understanding Indian Game
K.J.G. Hawkey

Poultry Diseases Under Modern Management
C.S. Coutts

THE HISTORY OF COCKFIGHTING

BY

GEORGE RYLEY SCOTT

F.Z.S., F.Ph.S.(Eng.), F.R.A.I.

Produced and published by:
TRIPLEGATE LTD.
1 Royal Parade
Hindhead, Surrey GU26 6TD

Distributed by:
SAIGA PUBLISHING CO. LTD.

© Learnex (Publishers) 1983

ISBN 0 86230 0606

Previously published by Charles Skilton Limited

Second Edition 1983

This book is copyright and may not be reproduced in whole or *in part* (except for review) without the express permission of the publishers in writing.

Produced and Published by Triplegate Ltd.

Distributor:
SAIGA PUBLISHING CO. LTD.

CONTENTS

		PAGE
	INTRODUCTION	9

CHAP.
I	THE ORIGIN OF THE GAME FOWL	15
II	BREEDS AND VARIETIES OF GAME FOWL	20
III	BREEDING AND REARING GAME FOWL	29
IV	SELECTION, TRAINING, PREPARATION FOR BATTLE AND CARE OF THE FIGHTING-COCK	37
V	THE GENESIS AND DEVELOPMENT OF THE ARTIFICIAL SPUR	51
VI	THE COCKPIT	57
VII	THE COCKFIGHT	71
VIII	THE ORIGIN AND ANTIQUITY OF COCKFIGHTING	87
IX	HISTORICAL ASPECTS OF COCKFIGHTING IN THE UNITED KINGDOM	93
X	HISTORICAL ASPECTS OF COCKFIGHTING IN THE UNITED STATES OF AMERICA	121
XI	COCKFIGHTING IN OTHER COUNTRIES	126
XII	THE WAR ON COCKFIGHTING	137
XIII	THE CASE FOR AND AGAINST COCKFIGHTING	151
XIV	COCKFIGHTING AND THE LAW	168

APPENDICES

I	STANDARDS OF PERFECTION FOR THE OLD ENGLISH GAME	179
II	A GLOSSARY OF TECHNOLOGIC AND JARGONIC TERMS	188
III	BIBLIOGRAPHY	194
	INDEX	199

LIST OF ILLUSTRATIONS

THE TRIMMED COCK (MARSHALL)	*Frontispiece*
	Opposite Page
THE COCK IN FEATHER	16
A GOLBURN PILE	17
HECTOR, A NOTABLE HEN-COCK	24
COCKFIGHTING (ALKEN)	25
WEIGHING IN THE COCKS AT HAVANA, CUBA	32
A BALINESE FEEDER TAKING FOUR BIRDS FOR AN AIRING	32
COCKS FIGHTING IN BALI	33
TRIMMING A COCK AT THE GALLERIA CHINCHINAGUA, GUIRA, CUBA	48
A HAITIAN WAITS FOR THE DUEL	49
MUFFLES OR MUFFS	54
SPURS AND SHEATHS	54
ARTIFICIAL SPURS	54
A COCK HAS FIGHTING-SPURS FIXED BEFORE A CONTEST IN BALI	55
COCKPIT IN THE YARD OF THE "HAWK AND BUCKLE" INN AT DENBIGH	58
A ROUGH OUT-OF-DOOR COCKPIT NEAR WINDERMERE	58
AN OLD COCKPIT AT HEVERSHAM, WESTMORLAND	59
COCKPIT WITH TWELVE RINGS OF SEATS AT GWENAP, REDRUTH, CORNWALL	59
RULES AND ORDER OF COCKING, AT ST. JAMES' PARK, WESTMINSTER	64
THE TRADE CARD OF A SILVER COCKSPUR MAKER	65
POSTER ADVERTISING A WELSH MAIN	65
THE ROYAL COCKPIT (ROWLANDSON)	74

ILLUSTRATIONS

	Opposite Page
THE COCKPIT (HOGARTH)	75
THE COCKFIGHT (GÉRÔME)	88
TREGONWELL FRAMPTON, THE FATHER OF THE TURF	89
THE CELEBRATED GILLIVER SPURRING A FIGHTING-COCK	102
A TANDEM COCKING CART	103
THE AFTERMATH OF A COCKFIGHT	124
WATCHING A COCKFIGHT IN HAITI	125
COLONEL MORDAUNT'S COCK MATCH AT LUCKNOW	128
SPECTATORS AT A COCKFIGHT IN CO. DONEGAL	129
CANTON BARGEMEN, FIGHTING QUAILS	129
A COCKFIGHT IN THE AUSTRIAN TYROL	132
COCKFIGHTING IN THE EAST INDIES	133
A MID-AIR BATTLE BETWEEN TWO COCKS IN PAKISTAN	144
COCKS FIGHTING IN PAKISTAN	145
ADMIRAL ROUS WATCHING A COCKFIGHT AT MALACCA	152
THE TRIMMED COCK (SARTORIUS)	153
OLD TROGDON	153
COCKFIGHTING IMPLEMENTS SEIZED NEAR CHESTER	168
EAGER SPECTATORS IN HAITI	169

The pictures opposite pages 16, 25, 74 and 75 are reproduced by courtesy of the Trustees of the British Museum; those opposite pages 33, 49, 55, 132 and 169 come from the *Picture Post* Library; those opposite pages 32 (top), 48, 144 and 145 are by arrangement with Messrs Paul Popper Ltd; and those opposite pages 58 and 59 are by arrangement with The London Electrotype Agency Ltd.

The National Museum of Wales (Welsh Folk Museum) kindly lent two of the photographs appearing opposite page 54 and one opposite page 65; the Co. Donegal Historical Society performed a similar service in respect of one appearing opposite page 129, and the City Museum, Bristol, gave assistance in respect of the photograph opposite page 64. From the Mansell Collection were secured the pictures opposite pages 17, 32, 88, 89, 102 and 153. Batchworth Press Ltd made available the picture opposite page 103 and the National Humane Review, Denver, lent the photograph appearing opposite page 124. We are obliged to the R.S.P.C.A. for the photograph opposite page 168.

INTRODUCTION

I

WHATEVER advantages may be incidental to the policy expressed in the popular notion respecting one who fights and runs away, it never applied in respect to the fighting-cock of the days when cockfighting was the national sport of England. The cock who ran away certainly did not live to fight another day—he was promptly killed and eaten!

It is a fact, however, that few Gamecocks of the real fighting kind ever did run away in those days or indeed ever do run away now. The courage of this particular type of fowl is proverbial. What is more, it is also a fact that, whether one witnesses a cockfight oneself or whether one gets a vicarious impression of such a combat through pictorial representation or a descriptive account, one cannot fail to be impressed. One is horrified at the gory sight, one is staggered at the barbarities of the "Battle Royal" and the "Welsh Main"; but one cannot fail to admire and to marvel at the stupendous courage displayed by the battling birds.

In most sports it is a case of the hunted and the hunter; the pursued and the pursuer. In cockfighting there is no such spectacle. The participators do not run, and will not run. They enter into battle with an intensity, an eagerness, a determination that are unsurpassed in sporting annals. It is this distinctive feature that has led so many persons to defend cockfighting against the allegations of cruelty and barbarity levelled at it.

II

The concept of cruelty presents numerous inconsistencies and anomalies. In many instances the most vigorous denouncers of one form of cruelty applaud some other form of cruelty. It always was so. It probably always will be so. Butler admirably expresses this curious and persistent inclination of the average man to support and excuse those forms of cruelty

> "He is inclined to,
> By damning those he has no mind to."

Prominent among the lessons which history provides is a conviction that there can be no suppression of cruel sports or practices in any wholesale way. The elimination of cruelty in a complete or an adequate sense must be a very gradual process. This gradualness is part and parcel of the campaign against cruelty. The supporters of sports which are considered cruel by those outside the fold become diminished in number in consequence of the fact that, luckily, these sportsmen exercise their propagandist powers in support and in justification of those particular forms of cruelty in which they are specifically interested, and those *only*. Had they, from the beginning and at all times, fought for the retention of *all* kinds of cruel sports, the task of the suppressors would have been much more difficult. Just as the members of a democracy or an oligarchy are in danger of losing their freedom through failure to strive for the retention of liberty as a general objective, leaving minorities to fight a losing battle on behalf of specific forms of freedom ; so the practitioners of blood sports, by their policy of denouncing, or at any rate taking an apathetic attitude towards, all types of cruel sports other than the ones they themselves practise, are, too, fighting a losing battle.

In the existence, so universally and so predominantly, of this trait in mankind, and the persistence of the policy arising out of it, lie the only hope for the *eventual* suppression of most forms of cruelty to animals and birds. I fear it is too much to hope that *all* such cruelty will or can be done away with. But the elimination of many of the more blatant forms seems reasonably certain. History shows what progress has already been made. In particular, the prohibition of cockfighting in Britain and many other parts of the world is peculiarly significant in this respect. Also, it points, perhaps more than any other factor, to the possibility that the success of the general campaign against cruelty may in time be realised. For the sport of cockfighting has been prohibited in the face of arguments in its favour which are perhaps more potent than those in favour of any of the other sports that have been prohibited on the ground of cruelty; and, what is most significant of all, many more sports that have not yet been declared illegal.

III

How far the prohibition of cockfighting constitutes interference with the freedom of the individual (granted the extension of the concept of freedom to non-humans!) is a point of some significance. And how far the deliberate training of fighting-cocks, and the act of placing them in circumstances where a battle to the death is almost inevitable, represent incitements to commit acts of unpremeditated brutality, is debatable. But no disinterested and impartial observer can fail to admit that, although the point is no justificatory one, the argument in favour of the prohibition of cockfighting must apply, equally in most cases and with additional relevance in some, to many other practices which are tolerated or approved in modern civilisation, to wit, stag and otter hunting, hare coursing, deer and fox hunting, salmon fishing, *et al*.

The case against cockfighting, with one important point of difference, is the case against every other form of blood sport. The choice of whether to fight or not lies with the bird itself, and the threat of death as a penalty for failing to fight has neither weight nor purpose. The case against so many other sports is that the *hunters only are willing*. In this connexion, the contention of the member of the Belgian Chamber of Deputies, when recently introducing a Bill to ban professional boxing matches, that fights between human beings should be punished in the same way as cockfights, is not without interest.

The most unholy feature of cockfighting, however, has nothing whatever to do with the birds taking part in it. It is concerned exclusively with those who encourage the sport, and who witness the contests. This is no puritanical argument along the lines of Macaulay's much quoted statement. Nor does the purely commercial aspect constitute the main ground for objection. The reason for it lies in the fact that cockfighting, because of its sanguinary features, appeals to, arouses, and develops brutality and savagery in the minds of the spectators. Hogarth and Rowlandson both succeeded in conveying to a remarkable degree, this aspect of the sport.

IV

It would be a pity if the passing of cockfighting were to be coincident with the virtual extinction of that truly handsome and remarkable breed of poultry, the Old English Game.

It is undeniable that the rise and development of this breed were coincident with, and largely the result of, the popularity which cockfighting enjoyed in the sixteenth, seventeenth, eighteenth and nineteenth centuries. These facts emerge in the pages which follow.

When the sport became illegal in Britain, although the extent of the breeding of the Old English Game was considerably curtailed, it by no means came to an end, and the survival of the breed was not seriously threatened. There were two reasons for this. The first was the continuance of cockfighting in a surreptitious form throughout the country, leading to a foreign demand for specimens of this universally acclaimed great fighting breed. The second reason was the cult of poultry breeding for purely exhibition purposes, which reached great heights of popularity in the latter half of the nineteenth century and the early decades of the twentieth. According to lovers of the fighting-cock, pure and simple, this concentration on the breeding of specimens suitable for the show bench has not been altogether an unmixed blessing. It is contended that exhibitors of Game have been a good deal more concerned with fine points of shape and colour than with the qualities so essential in a fighting-cock, and it is held in some quarters that there has been a consistent decline in the breed. On the other hand, breeders of exhibition Old English Game proclaim with equal force and certitude that present-day specimens equal in every respect the finest birds ever bred by the old-time cockers.

In this connexion, there is however no justification for the argument that cockfighting should be legalized in order to rescue the Old English Game Fowl from oblivion on the one hand or degeneracy on the other. Even were such efforts at rescue indicated (which is extremely dubious), and even were this the only method available, the price would be too big a one to pay, and the time when the breed became as extinct as a dinosaur might well be awaited with eagerness. But, in my opinion, despite the prohibition of cockfighting, the Game Fowl should continue to flourish, and hold a deservedly high position among the breeds of domestic poultry. The qualities for which it is so justly famed are not only retainable but are being retained in other ways. The presentation and elucidation of these methods constitute one of the objects I have in view in writing this book.

GEORGE RYLEY SCOTT.

LIST OF COLOUR PLATES

Plate		*Facing page*
1.	PAIR OF HENNY GAME	16
2.	TRUE OLD ENGLISH PIT GAME	
3.	TRIO BLUE OLD ENGLISH GAME	17
4.	COCKFIGHTING	
5.	PRESENT-DAY BROWN RED STAG	28
6.	BLUE HENS — OLD ENGLISH	
7.	AMERICAN SILVER DUCKWING STAG	29
8.	AUSTRALIAN GAME COCK	

ACKNOWLEDGEMENT FOR SECOND EDITION

We offer thanks for permission to reproduce the new colour plates to those named at the foot of each plate.

CHAPTER I

THE ORIGIN OF THE GAME FOWL

MUCH has been written concerning, and controversy has been fierce respecting, the origin of the Game Fowl, the bird which Buffon termed the "English Fowl". In particular, there has been considerable argument as to whether or not all breeds of Game are descended from a common ancestor, many authorities subscribing to the opinion that the Malay was the ancestral fowl. Apropos of this, Ferguson, writing a century ago, said:

"We contend the Game Fowl, if purely bred, bears no affinity to the Malay, and that he is not related by blood even in the remotest degree, but assign his descent to a species of the *Gallus sonneratii*. Whatever differences in feather may present themselves from the alliance they are but small compared to general computations on this head, and still less at variance in shape, carriage and general conformity. We do not maintain all varieties and sub-varieties of the class recognised as such are directly descended from this stock, neither do we consider the present Indian breed of the same lineage—while the true bird's symmetrical form closely resembles the air and elegance almost invariably exhibited in pure primary breeds, many may be observed bearing the carriage and appearance of the Malay, some with the Polish lower mandible, and crest appendages in a diminutive form, and others possessing a development of the ordinary fowl's coarse features and feathery armour. We do not urge that these termed Game Fowls are similarly descended, but merely that their game properties are indicative of partial descent, and that the progenitors of those traits were in themselves typical of a primeval order. The existence of the practice of cockfighting on the peninsula of Malay, and in some parts of India, long before the introduction of the Game Fowl into this country, and its continued nationality in those parts, does not in the least countenance the idea that the birds thus brought into requisition were or are identical with our gallants. The owners or backers of Malays of the present day frequently stake their 'all' upon the chances of one battle, until their last coin is placed upon the head of their favourite bird. The wealthy, not exceptionally, risk personal property to enormous amounts upon their supposed invincible hero, whose merits have been previously tested, and whose prowess still remains in unequalled force. But these champions are much heavier and less agile than the British Game, being usually generated from the Malay, but occasionally from an admixture of a smaller indigenous species, or a favourite imported variety with that bird. Neither can the breed produced from the Malay, when mated with the immediate descendant of the *Bankiva* or Bantam race, be confounded. The issue thus bred have been by some recognised as progenitors of the Game class; such must be confuted, since improbable conjecture is all the evidence in its favour. Let but the single comb become permanent from the admixture, and it will command our attention. This feature by domestication is induced to duplicity, but never to become single. Without extending objections, in this feature alone lies ample evidence in support of the non-recognition of this absurd theory."*

There are, as will be apparent in the next chapter, many breeds of Game, and if the destructive characteristic of each of these breeds, particularly as regards shape and size, are compared with those of others, there is often observable a world of difference: thus the huge Malay, the sturdy Indian, the sprightly Old English, the stilty Modern, the small Black Sumatra, and a number of others. These several breeds vary as much in their fighting proclivities and methods, as they do in size and appearance. They have evolved and have been bred in various parts of the world: in many cases considerable alterations or developments have been effected by selective breeding.

Much confusion has arisen through the error, common among those with no knowledge of the various breeds of domestic poultry, of terming every cock that fights, irrespective of breed or variety, a Gamecock. George Wilson, an enthusiastic cocker, writing in 1607 says: ". . . there be divers and sundry kindes and sorts of Cockes, but for brevitie sake I will only intreat but of three sorts or severall kinds: that is, the Cockes of the game, the halfe-bred Cockes, and the Dung-hill or

* G. Ferguson, *Illustrated Series of Rare and Prize Poultry*, Culliford, London, 1854, p. 221.

Plate 1: Pair of Henny Game (Fig Puddings)
         (From *Our Poultry*, Harrison Weir)

Plate 2: True Old English Pit Game (Black Reds)
         (Harrison Weir, *ibid*)

Plate 3: Trio Blue Old English Game
   (Harrison Weir, *ibid*)

Plate 4: Cockfighting from an old print by Hy Alken.

craven cockes. The Cockes of the game are so-called, because they carrie the credite away from all other Cockes in battell, which is the onely cause they are so highly esteemed, and so much valued as they be; for it is generally and commonly seene, that the most heroicall and noble-hearted men, take greatest delight in those thinges which are of most courage, and greatest valour, and that of all others (in my opinion) is the Cockes of the game; as already I have sufficiently declared."*

It was this firmly planted belief that led the poet to declaim:

> "No Bird can with a well-bred Cock compare,
> No Creature less than Man shall with him share;
> The Honour bravely won by dint of sword,
> From fiercest Foes in open field where Blood,
> Flowing from dying Warriors' fatal wounds,
> Breeds richest Rubies in Bellona's Grounds."

Although, however, the males of many breeds of poultry will, on occasion, fight grimly, determinedly and to the death if need be, with others of their kind; only in rare circumstances does one find, even among the more pugnacious breeds, a rooster that can hold his own with, much less vanquish, a representative specimen of the real Game Fowl. It is just such a bird that is so well described by Thomas Bewick, in the following passage from his famous ornithological work: "The appearance of the Gamecock, when in his full plumage, and not mutilated for the purpose of fighting, is strikingly beautiful and animated; his head, which is small, is adorned with a beautiful red comb, and his chin and throat with wattles; his eyes sparkle with fire, and his whole demeanour bespeaks boldness and freedom. The feathers on his neck are long, slender, and pointed, and fall gracefully down upon his body, which is thick, muscular, and compact; his tail is long, and the flexile feathers which fall over it form a beautiful arch behind, which gives a grace to all his motions; his legs are strong, and armed with sharp spurs, with which he defends himself, and attacks his adversary; he lays hold with his beak, and strikes with the feet and wings. When surrounded by his females, his whole aspect is full of animation; he allows of no competitor, but,

---

* George Wilson, *The Commendation of Cockes, and Cockfighting.* London 1607.

on the approach of a rival, rushes forward to instant combat, and either drives him from the field, or perishes in the attempt."*

It was this truculent courage, audacity and quarrelsomeness that caused the Gamecock to acquire a reputation which in some respects was the reverse of commendable. I well remember, in the days of my youth, when Gamecocks were fairly plentiful and securable without difficulty, that it was not uncommon for anyone who was pestered by trespassing fowls led by an exploring male, to express the intention of putting a stop to these visitations by purchasing a Gamecock.

In other ways than by actual fighting with other fowls does the true Gamecock present evidence of his courage. Without the smallest hesitation he will attack and drive away in dire fear a cat intent on stalking a chicken; he will kill a marauding rat; he has been known to tackle a fox.

The female of the Game Fowl often displays some of the courageous and pugnacious qualities characteristic of the male. Indeed, it has been affirmed that she goes so far, on occasion, as to proclaim her triumph over an antagonist in the typical masculine manner. In this connexion, it may be worthy of record that although I have heard several fanciers tell of "crowing hens," so far as my own not inconsiderable personal experience with poultry goes, I have never come across any such specimen myself, despite the fact that I have had many females which have developed the feathering or the head appendages typical of the opposite sex. However, apropos of the subject, I think the following extract from Ferguson's book (in which he declaims on the importance of a Gamecock's crow, and comments at length on the phenomenon of the "crowing hen") is sufficiently interesting and amusing to merit reproduction here.

"Crow varies with the diverse strains, but averages a clear, but not by any means shrill, alto—loud, but not harsh, and of medium duration; some varieties pronounce their authority in defiant and abrupt strains. Their note of war should be very continuous, and reiterated often during the day and at early morn, accompanied by the warrior's defiant flapping of his feathery armour, proving thereby his right to hold the title 'merry bird'; a term indicative of peculiar

---

* Thomas Bewick, *A History of British Birds*, Vol. I, Bernard Quaritch, London, 1885.

THE COCK IN FEATHER

From the painting by B. Marshall

A GOLBURN PILE

By Charles Towne (1780–1850)

excellence. If the hen return from a victorious conflict, she too will occasionally follow the example of her lord, and strain a note or two of his ambitious song. Game-hens of notorious good quality are prone thus to aspire to regal rights. Some irritable masters of the domain will scare their bold mistresses for this public violation of submission, this indelicate assumption and breach of modesty. Others, with the wing extended to the ground, will take a circuit round and sweep the turf in gallant ecstasies to the honour of their modest dame's resentment to the intruding foe. Much has been said by nearly every writer or compiler of our poultry journals, respecting the demerits or ill luck connected with the crowing hen, the whistling woman, and the lass who prattles Latin.* Were the kind authors 'vice versa sexed' a virtue not a vice perhaps might be conceived existing . . . I contend the hen is equally estimable the day she nobly triumphs in crowing notes as the day before, and desire to know what physical process has been operating to render her valueless so soon. The fact is she has really proved a valiant and a Briton, and we, as lovers of Briton's birds, do much admire and show her all attention, inducing her at the same time to render us her like. It is evident the blood, the spirit of a valiant, could not be appreciated, and therefore was abused. If discord she produces among the chanticleers, or strife betwixt her compeers, remove her gently from the rest, but ruin not her name. Say you not she is sterile, for young pullets, prolific as the feathery Spanish aristocracy, have pleased me oft by boldly proclaiming their part conformity to the character of their lord. I repeat some of the most distinguished Gallic heroes of this noble race have been generated from such worthies. As a rule among practical men all such are recognised as the marrow, spirit, and sinew of the strain, from whence its primitive original vigour and nobility may be remodelled."†

---

* Obviously a variant of the old saying: "A whistling woman and a crowing hen, are good for neither beast nor man."
† G. Ferguson, *Illustrated Series of Rare and Prize Poultry*, 1854, p. 233.

CHAPTER II

BREEDS AND VARIETIES OF GAME FOWL

CONTEMPORANEOUS with the development of cockfighting in England, the Game Fowl reached its highest degree of perfection, and there gradually evolved the breed that was to be known to this day as the Old English Game.* It was generally recognised, at the time when cockfighting had reached its zenith, that the type of bird bred in Britain was superior to any of the various types flourishing in other parts of the world. In the East, for instance, where cockfighting was extremely popular, the birds bred for this purpose resembled somewhat a small brand of Malay, much inferior in strength and fighting spirit to the English breed.

The typical Old English Game male bird is of medium size, averaging about 6 lbs. in weight, wide-shouldered and breasted, with a powerful neck, muscular thighs, strong well-set legs, his whole build and appearance indicative of power and quickness of movement. The head should be small and tapering; the beak short, hooked and strong; the eyes large and bright. The plumage should be glossy in appearance, and the feathering tight: both these qualities are indicative of the perfection of condition which is a primary requisite in this breed. Any signs of coarseness on the one hand or of delicacy on the other are bad faults. The typical female specimen should exhibit the same general qualities as the male, allowing for the facts that she is smaller and lighter, and that her plumage lacks the sheen and gorgeous colourings of the male.

The Old English Game exists in many varieties, distinguished by variations in the colour of the plumage. Among the best known of these varieties are the Black-breasted-Red, the Silver-Duckwing, the Brown-Red, the White, the Spangled, the Pile, the Birchen, the Dun, and the Henny.

* The Old English Game should be distinguished from the Indian Game on the one hand and what is known as the Modern Game on the other. The Indian Game (sometimes termed Cornish Game) as now bred is thick-set, heavy of build and short-legged; while the Modern Game is a long-legged bird bred purely for the show pen.

Perhaps the most famous of these varieties, so far as the annals of cockfighting are concerned, was the Black-breasted-Red. It was this variety that Lord Derby bred and fought with such success during the nineteenth century. These Black-breasted-Reds, known far and wide as the "Knowsley breed", were singularly handsome birds. As regards the male specimen, the back was rich red; the breast dense black; the hackle deep orange becoming of a particularly rich deep hue near the throat; the saddle rich orange; the wings maroon; and the tail deep lustrous metallic-black. Of especial importance was the deep black breast, and the presence of any feather of a foreign hue was enough to damn him both as a breeder and a fighter. Ferguson, commenting on this feature of the Black-breasted-Red cock says: "When clear, it forms a most striking relief to the eye, rendering the entire plumage rich, but toning down the otherwise gaudy suit to a subdued but splendid combination of handsomest hues, and a harmonious blending of richest shades." Of the female, this same authority says: "The plumage varies from a straw tint to a partridge-brown. Neck-hackle feathers, bright yellow and of considerable depth of tint towards the approach of the throat; the web pale brown or black, but in some instances white; saddle and wing-coverts of a rich straw or partridge-brown; primary wing feathers black; tail black, tinged with deep bay; breast clean roan or fawn, shading off towards the vent, which is of an ashy hue; beak, shanks, toes, and nails, white. In some hens may be observed a fine bright hair, running longitudinally through the centre of each feather of the entire suit, more especially in the wing-coverts and breast."* In further reference to the strain bred by Lord Derby, Ferguson goes on to say: "The merits of the Knowsley breed are unquestionable, and its prowess unsurpassable; one bird of this strain has been known, not exceptionally, to bring down two and sometimes three of his foes, and, according to well-authenticated record, no less than seven upon one occasion fell before the hero of the night."†

Members of another famous strain of fighting-Game were the Black cocks owned by Lord Vere. Of these birds Sketchley, the well-known authority on the Game Fowl, has this to say: "They were introduced

---

* G. Ferguson, *Illustrated Series of Rare and Prize Poultry*, 1854.
† Ibid.

by Mr. Thomas Wilson of Burton, Staffordshire, my place of residence, and I know of no amateur so eminently qualified as he was to do justice to any breed of cocks, however high in repute : few professors in those days were so systematic in their mode of breeding, nor were they likely to lose their former reputation in the transfer. They were a perfect jet black, gipsy-faced, black legs, rather elegant than muscular—lofty in their manner of fighting—close in their feather and well-shaped ; such was their established character, that wherever it was their lot to fight the odds always preponderated in their favour—in fact, level betting never followed their contest ; and for three years these cocks maintained a decided priority over most in the circuit they fought in. An opposite interest in some mains operated as a bar to our usual intimacy, which deprived me of being personally informed of the alteration of these cocks, that were very conspicuous the two years ensuing—a diminution in their appearance, their feathers long and dangling, their fire much abated, and so much unlike themselves, that they were more like crows than cocks. For reasons above stated I could not learn the cause from himself of these material changes in such valuable cocks, but if hearsay authority could be depended upon, Mr. Wilson had persevered in breeding from old stock—the result a certain consequence of derangement. That this error which had so frequently happened to others with all its train of mischief should have escaped the active penetration and vigilance of Mr. Wilson, who was sensibly alive to the refinements of breeding, has ever been a matter of surprise, for whenever it has crossed my ideas I have been at a loss, conclusively to account for it, otherwise than by a rooted infatuation, not easily to be conquered, of that too obsolete idea—that old favourite cocks may be continued for the use of propagation for a series of years, with the same propriety as the first year.* If analogy will bear me out with reason's aid—that a man of sixty and a woman of forty five shall produce as fine children as a man of twenty five and a woman of twenty two, then the impropriety falls at once, and that we have to refer to the catalogue of other causes enumerated in this work."†

* My own long and varied experience in breeding exhibition birds bears out Sketchley's opinion. I proved repeatedly that the power to produce progeny of high quality in regard to physique, stamina, perfection of colour and markings, diminishes after the second breeding year. This applies to both male and female breeding stock. No doubt there are variations in different breeds, especially in relation to the ability to perpetuate the finer shades of colour and the more distinctive markings.

† W. Sketchley, *The Cocker*, London, 1814, pp. 42-43.

Many were the controversies in the Press and heated were the discussions wherever breeders foregathered, as to the effect of colour on fighting prowess and stamina. Markham, writing in the seventeenth century, says, "the grey pyle, the yellow pyle, or the red with the black breast is esteemed the best; the pied is not so good; and the white and dun are the worst." Ferguson, in his *Illustrated Series of Rare and Prize Poultry*, gives high praise to the Dun. John Harris, the famous Cornish cocker, whose views are worthy of the most serious consideration, is of opinion that although the dark-coloured and dark-legged cocks are perhaps the hardier and more tenacious, the lighter-coloured birds are said to make up for any deficiencies in these respects by the deadliness of their heels and the wary manner in which they fight. On the whole, Harris is "inclined to think the happy medium may be found between the two," and in support of this opinion instances the "success of the Holford, Bellyse, Lowther, and Derby strains, all of which owe their origin to crosses with the darkest and lightest blood."*

Not alone the colour of the plumage but also that of the bird's legs was said to be of importance. Thus Sketchley affirmed that black-legged cocks are the best fighters; Richard Stamp, another cocker of note, preferred yellow-legged specimens; and although white-legged cocks have been eschewed by many authorities, it is a fact that some of the greatest fighters of all time have had legs of this disdained type, notably those of Downey and Bullock, and many of the Knowsley warriors.

Now, with all respect to the opinions of these famous breeders, I think they err in placing such importance on colour, and even so great an authority and so skilled a breeder as John Harris appears to have attributed the results of cross-breeding to the mixing of colours rather than of varieties. Cross-breeding, provided it is skilfully carried out, does undoubtedly increase strength, vigour and vitality in the progeny; but these results are obtainable by the crossing of two dark-coloured or two light-coloured varieties just as surely as by crossing a dark one with a light one. Even the intermingling of two different *strains* of the *same* variety may, in certain circumstances, provide this result.

Nearly two and a half centuries ago, Robert Howlett stated that colour was of relatively small importance; a view to be substantiated later by

* *The Life and Letters of John Harris, the Cornish Cocker*, by H. A. Privately printed, 1910.

other authorities. There have been, and no doubt always will be for the finding, tip-top fighting specimens of every existing colour of Game Fowl. The evidence, through the centuries, bears out this view. There were the famous Grays of Frampton; the redoubtable Grays and Duckwings of Lord Mexborough; the Grays and Yellows Birchens which Nunis bred with such success; the Duns of Sir Francis Boynton; the white-legged Duckwings and Piles which vied with the world-famed Black-reds in securing for Lord Derby so many victories; the notable Piles of Walker and of Faultless. And in the U.S.A. the Whites, known as "Connecticut Strawberries", of Patrick Duff were reputed to be unbeatable; as were, in their day, the Irish Grays of Uncle Pete.

In fact there was no special colour that could claim precedence in the matter of courage, skill and staying power. The points that counted were strain, training and the handler's skill. At one time and another every variety of fighting-Game has produced its champions.

Strangely enough, considering its appearance, the Henny or Hencock earned for itself a great reputation as a fighter. The male bears a striking resemblance in the matter of plumage to the female, being devoid of sickle-feathers, of hackle and saddle. Mr. W. B. Tegetmeier, a nineteenth-century authority on poultry, writes:

"The most important abnormal variation hitherto described in the covering of birds is the assumption of male plumage by females; this is common in the ordinary pheasant, and is always connected with diseased or abortive ovaries. The hens exhibiting this change are consequently always sterile. The same change of plumage, arising from a similar cause, also occurs occasionally in the hen of the common domestic fowl (*Gallus domesticus*), although a barren hen more commonly assumes merely the comb and wattles of the male without changing the appearance of the feathers. Some very well-marked specimens of this latter change were deposited by me in the museum of the Royal College of Surgeons two or three years since. The variation illustrated by the specimens exhibited by me to the members of the Zoological Society, March 26, 1861, is the converse of that which has been mentioned, it being the assumption of the female plumage by the adult male.

"It is well known that there are certain breeds of domestic fowl the males of which are always more or less hen-feathered; the most remarkable of these is the Sebright bantam. In this breed, however, the variation is hereditary, and the young cocks are as hen-feathered as their progenitors. Under the title of hen-cocks, certain Game Fowls acquired a high degree of notoriety for their prowess in the cockpit. I have an engraving, representing a bird of this description, that was formerly the property of George Edwards, the jockey who rode 'Phosphorus' and 'Variation' when they won the Derby and the Oaks. He is represented as trimmed for fighting, and is described as 'Hector, a hen-cock'. The late Mr. Caldwell informed me that he perfectly remembered the bird, and that he was notorious as having won a Welsh main—the most trying test of courage and endurance to which a Gamecock can be subjected. The peculiarity of plumage was hereditary in this variety of fowls.

"The specimen that I exhibited to the Society was bred by myself, and had never been out of my possession, consequently I was able to describe with great certainty the remarkable changes that it underwent; and as I have been breeding from the strain some years, I can speak without doubt as to there being no cross of any description introduced. The cock, whose portrait in his hen-feathered condition was engraved from a photograph, was hatched in the Spring of 1859, his parents being of a variety known as Brown-breasted Red Game bantams. When seven months old he assumed the full male plumage at his autumnal moult, and I preserved him as my best stock bird for the next season.

"During the year 1860 I bred some very good chickens from him. At the autumnal moult of that year, however, he lost all his cock-feathers; those of the neck, of the saddle, and the streaming sickle-feathers of the tail, alike disappeared, their places being supplied by feathers which, both in form and colour, were the exact counterpart of those of a hen of the same variety. This wonderful change was attended with slight increase of size, a great increase of combativeness, and certainly did not depend on any loss of generative power, as in the early part of the next year I sent him with a couple of hens to a run removed from other fowls, and hatched several strong healthy broods from the eggs.

"Some of the cocks were full male-plumage birds of very superior character; a pen exhibited by Mr. Angel took the second prize at the Crystal Palace show that year. Others of the cocks subsequently bred from him were as hen-feathered as their parent, and retained their hen-like plumage after several months. Nothing would have been easier than to have established a permanent breed or variety of hen-feathered Brown-Red Game bantams, had it been considered desirable to do so. The old bird died in 1864, retaining his hen-feathered plumage till the last. His disposition did not at all accord with his feminine appearance: he was combative and courageous to an extreme degree, and as he possessed the sharpest natural spurs I ever felt, he was a dangerous opponent for cocks many times his weight. In fact I had great difficulty in getting a run for him, as he had a troublesome habit of blinding cocks five or six times his weight."*

Apropos of the celebrated hencock "Hector", referred to by Mr. Tegetmeier, the following interesting account of this bird is culled from the pages of *The Sporting Magazine* (March, 1832): 'This sprightly creature, bred by and the property of Mr. G. Edwards of Newmarket, is as true a bred Game Fowl as ever flew between a pair of wings. . . . He is by one of Mr. Nash's dark red 'all eights'; his dam, a hen by Diggery; his grandam, by Mr. Fleming's old hen-cock, from the famous Tribe hen. Hector is nearly a black, and has all the properties of a cock, with the plumage of a hen—no saddle feathers on the back, nor streamers in the tail—and is certainly neither mule nor hermaphrodite, but is like, among his brethren the cocks—from his *lightness*, *elegance*, and *grace*— what Apollo appears to have been among the gods. Many have thought that the hen-cock, from possessing a more gentle carriage, and presenting a more delicate appearance, is less hardy than his Herculean-looking brothers: this happens however, not to be the case; as Hector fought three battles the day before he stood for his picture (the first a severe one), and won them all by real stoutness, courage, and fine fighting. It is a generally-received opinion that they are good heel cocks; but there is little doubt that they are as good as others in every point; and the difference when at equal weights and condition, from what we have seen, is in imagination only; and if these good judges would have the goodness to discover to us why Nature puts on these freaks of character, and fun in decoration, they would do much towards enlightening us. The Flemings, both father and son, men of the most extensive experience, say they have occasionally met with it in 'certain strains of cocks', but

---

* W. B. Tegetmeier, *The Poultry Book*, Routledge & Sons, London, 1867.

HECTOR, A NOTABLE HEN-COCK

From *The Sporting Magazine*, 1833

COCKFIGHTING

From H. Alken, *National Sports of Great Britain*, 1821

how it happens they do not know, unless it came from China. The Nash's, father and son, do not know enough about it to hazard an opinion. There are some very good sportsmen in England who have never seen this curiosity; and not a few, far from ignorant, that have never heard of such a thing."

As regards the fighting prowess of these Hennies, a correspondent of the *Field* (in which periodical Mr. Tegetmeier's descriptive account originally appeared), writing under the signature "Outright", mentioned that "the hen-cock, in colour like the ordinary Brown-breasted-Red hen, with short plumage and partridge hackle", was never a favourite in the Royal Pit of Westminster. Although lacking the size and the imposing appearance of the cock-feathered fighters, they usually had large and sharp spurs, dangerous enough properties in themselves, but rendered doubly so by the fact that the owners of these deadly spurs looked exactly like hens. It was not so much a matter of the spectators being deceived by the bird's hen-like appearance, but the hen-cock's opponent was often deceived as well, and before he discovered that the seeming female was in reality a powerful fighter, might easily receive a death blow. Says this correspondent: "I had a pair of these birds (brother and sister, cock and hen) given to me by the late William Stradling, probably the best handler that ever went into a pit. I never could get a bird more than 3 lb. 10 ozs. from them. The hen was small. The cock fought at 4 lbs. while in my possession, and crippled a very fine cock (who, in all probability, otherwise would have made short work with him) by being mistaken for a hen, and getting the first blow. The only difference in the plumage of these two birds was in the length of the tail, which, in the male bird, was something longer than that of the hen, and exactly resembled the drawing of Mr. Tegetmeier's specimen. I afterwards crossed the hen with a Black-Red of my own breeding; the result was, that these chickens, which had the usual feather of the Gamecock, were never more than tolerable, although the brood cock was of as good blood as any cock then bred. On the other hand, the only chicken which turned out to be a hen-cock proved to be a very good one, and fought a terrible battle as a stag, but lost by an accident."*

Jack Stobart (nicknamed "Auckland Jack"), professional cocker for

* Quoted from the *Field*, by W. B. Tegetmeier in *The Poultry Book*, Routledge & Sons, 1867.

over sixty years, when asked by J. Fairfax-Blakeborough what breed, according to his experience, produced the best fighting specimens, said that he had possessed "good uns of all sorts", but that, in his opinion, the hen-feathered cocks were "about the best", being the "fastest fighters" and able to take the "most punishment."*

In the East, and in other countries, the Malay was for centuries the principal breed used in cockfighting. A large powerfully-built bird, it would appear at first sight well-equipped for battle, but it lacks the agility of the smaller English breed.

Among other fighting breeds is the Sumatra Game Fowl, a small, long-bodied, profusely feathered, agile bird. This fowl never at any time figured in the British cockpit. It was, however, bred and exhibited under the name of Black Sumatra Game.

---

* J. Fairfax-Blakeborough, *Country Life and Sport*, Philip Allan & Co., London, 1926, p. 97.

Plate 5: Present-day Brown Red Cock
   (Dr and Mrs J. Batty)

Plate 6: Blue Hens — Old English Game
   (Dr and Mrs J. Batty)

Plate 7: American Silver Duckwing Stag
(W.E. Harris, USA)

Plate 8: Australian Game Cock
(Mr and Mrs P. Sultan, Eastern Creek, Australia)

CHAPTER III

BREEDING AND REARING GAME FOWL

I HAVE no intention of dealing in any exhaustive way with the practical aspects of breeding and rearing fowls: these are thoroughly and competently dealt with in the numerous books on poultry generally. All that I am concerned with here are such details of historical and practical interest as are concerned specifically with the breeding and rearing of fighting-Game.

It is strange that at the time when cockfighting was at the acme of its popularity in Britain, and the greatest care was taken in breeding as it was then understood, there should have persisted so fallacious a notion as that everything depended upon the female side of the mating, so much so indeed that it was held that a Game-hen of pedigree would produce first-class fighting-cocks if she were mated to any mongrel male that was selected for her or which through chance she became mated with. Gervase Markham, whose writings on the breeding of Gamecocks were held in high repute, had this to say:

"Now for the breeding of these Cocks for the battail, it is much differing from those of a dunghill, for they are like Birds of prey, in which the female is ever to be preferred and esteemed before the Male, and so in the breeding of these Birds, you must be sure that your hen is right, that is to say, she must be of a right plume, as gray grissel, speckt or yellowish, black or brown is not amiss; she must be kindly unto her young, and of large body, well poked behind for large eggs, and well tufted on the crown, which shows courage: if she have Weapons she is better, but for her valour it must be excellent, for if there be any sort of cowardice in her, the chickens cannot be true. And it is a Note among the best breeders, that the perfect Hen from a Dunghill Cock, will bring a good Chicken, but the best Cock from a Dunghill Hen can never get a good Bird; and I have known in mine own experience, that the two famousest Cocks that ever fought in these days, the one called *Noble*, the other

Grissel, begot on many ill Hens very bad Cocks; but the most famous Hen *Jinks*, never brought forth ill Bird, how bad soever her Cock were."*

Now although much of this was rank nonsense, the idea that the cock was of small importance in breeding persisted until, in 1744, a well-known Yorkshire poultry breeder named Thomas Dixon, who was one of the first advocates of scientific inbreeding, not only pointed out the advisability of breeding from selected stock on both sides, but gave an explanation for the importance which had hitherto been given to the female side of the mating. He drew attention to the fact that the life led by a fighting-cock, in time, inevitably sapped his constitution and vitality, whereas a hen, not being subject to the hazards of battle, and being permitted to remain in her natural habitat, was in much the better condition for carrying out the process of breeding.

It is true, as the old breeders realised, that the importance of the female cannot be overestimated, but it is equally true that the male plays a prominent part. The selection of breeding stock is therefore a matter of the utmost consequence. All the attributes of the perfect fighting-cock: the strong limbs, the broad chest, the wide back, the alert eye, must be looked for when choosing not only the hens but also the cock from which to breed. It has often been said that the male bird constitutes half the breeding pen, however many females are included in it.

As regards scientific inbreeding, or linebreeding as it is often called, its function is to fix and perpetuate the points already secured. There is nothing *creative*, in the sense of introducing new qualities or extending existent ones, associated with it. To do this it is necessary to resort to *outbreeding*, the antithesis of *inbreeding*. Fanciers who are desirous of producing a large proportion of birds conforming to a carefully defined standard of perfection, find inbreeding essential, some breeders going so far as to mate together brothers and sisters. The customary plan, however, is to mate father to daughter, or son to mother. Both methods of mating, provided care is taken to select strong, healthy, full-sized specimens of both sexes, can be adopted successfully and without causing the slightest form of degeneration. I can say this without hesitation as a result of my own practical experience.

It is a debatable point, however, whether, in the days when the

* Gervase Markham, *Country Contentments*, eleventh edition, London, 1675.

Game Fowl was bred purely on account of its fighting propensities, any form of inbreeding would have given better results than outbreeding, so long as both male and female breeders were Game Fowls and were selected with an eye to the physical qualities desired in a fighting-cock. With such an objective, niceties of colour and markings were of no importance, and in view of this I should think outbreeding gave the better results.

Today, however, when the Old English Game is destined to compete for prizes on the exhibition bench instead of battering an opponent to death, the matter takes on quite a different aspect. Perfection, in accordance with a carefully outlined standard, is the goal aimed at by breeders ; niceties of shape, colour and markings are of great importance. These points can be duplicated and perpetuated by inbreeding and by inbreeding alone. At the same time the physical qualities upon which the fighting prowess of the Old English Game Fowl are based, must be preserved.

The effects of environment should not be overlooked. Neglect to take into full and proper account this important factor may well nullify years of careful breeding. There are cases where a change of environment may bring about results similar to those caused by outcrossing. In this sense, a change of environment can work in two ways : it can be beneficial on the one hand and in some cases ; it can prove harmful on the other hand and in certain circumstances. The use as breeding stock of specimens of *one's own strain* that have been *reared in another part of the country* sometimes leads to physical invigoration or reactivation without the loss of those fine points of colour or markings that have been secured by years of linebreeding. These results are, however, by no means certain, and it may very well be that the experiment proves a failure. I well remember a case that fell within my own experience. Some forty years ago I purchased in Westmorland practically the whole flock of exhibition Rhode Island Reds bred from an imported American trio. These youngsters were from five to seven months old and, of their day, were remarkably fine specimens. So pleased was I with them that I tried, without avail, to purchase the parent birds. Some six months later however the owner died suddenly, and his widow, who was leaving the place, offered me the original American trio, an offer which I accepted. Because of the excellence of the progeny I decided to breed from this same trio once more, adding only three additional females, all daughters of the male bird, selected for their size and health as well as colour and shape. The result was exceedingly disappointing. Out of the large number of birds bred and reared not one was comparable, from an exhibition point of view, with the *average* of the birds resulting from the previous year's breeding. The only difference was that the first year's batch of youngsters was bred and reared in Westmorland; the second year's batch was bred and reared in Yorkshire. True the male bird and two of the females were a year older, but as they were still young and vigorous it seems unlikely that this point *in itself* could have had such a devastating effect on the progeny.

Apropos of this inability of certain birds to breed specimens of a quality equal to themselves, the remarks and experience of so celebrated a breeder as Sketchley are of value and interest. He says: "Many attempts have been made in different parts of the kingdom, to cross the Cheshire Piles with similar feather, but I never yet learnt that they were equal to the original Cheshire. I have taken much pains to establish what I have ever esteemed valuable cocks, but they never produced anything equal to themselves, notwithstanding the hens that were put to them were the Beverley Piles, and by no means inferior to the Cheshire. Perhaps their local situation may be more conducive to their constitutions than any other country, and I am fully persuaded that circumstance contributes very much to their excellency. . . . This idea does not arise from a solitary instance with myself for I have experienced a degeneration to a greater extent than that of the Cheshire Piles. In the years 1785 and 1786 I bought of the Rev. Mr. Brooks, of Shifnal, Shropshire, thirty pair of cocks that were brought from thence to Loughborough, and I believe no cocks ever gained a higher reputation than they, through the whole contest of three days, with advantage of nine a-head; the cocks pitted against them were selected from the first amateurs surrounding Loughborough. Our cocks had sustained an injury which we believed at the time to be serious; but Beastal's never-failing cordial (which might be called a grand specific) renovated all their finer faculties, and spurred them on to victory. Many were the applications for the purpose of breeding, and on that year as well as the following I never bred more, having put them to hens my reverend friend had sent

WEIGHING IN THE COCKS AT HAVANA, CUBA

A BALINESE FEEDER TAKING FOUR BIRDS FOR AN AIRING

COCKS FIGHTING IN BALI

me with the cocks, as well as to my own that were similar in feather, &c. The whole of these bred in 1785 and 1786 kept up their character, and we had every flattering hope of enjoying all we could wish for in these cocks; but to our great surprise and disappointment, those bred in 1787 and fought in 1789, exhibited such a falling off, that very much deranged our future breeding—nor could we ever recover their pristine excellence—as there was no prognostic of any fade or change in constitution, to rouse us to any trial, or anything to disturb that high confidence reposed; so of course they were fought without any trial, but I am well aware that we ought not to be governed by the most flattering appearances, or past merit, but give them a fair trial. . . . It may be thought superfluous to give a detailed account of our proceeding with these fowls—except briefly to say that every practicable attention in all the various departments in breeding were bestowed to hold them to their original excellence—but proved unavailing. Our endeavours then to develop this extraordinary deviation were unremitting, and every inquiry and investigation were made use of to elucidate and aid our opinions, what might be the cause which had wrought so serious a change in such valuable fowls—the aggregate of which only afforded a solitary surmise that a removal to distant country was the cause."*

In the rearing of the youngsters the old cockers took elaborate precautions to ensure that the male specimens developed no preventable defects that would mar their chances in battle. For instance there was the matter of perching. But here let us see what Master Markham has to say.

"You must also have an especial care to the Perch whereon your cock sitteth when he roosteth, for if he be too small in the gripe, or crooked, or so ill placed that he cannot sit but he must straddle with his legs, any of these faults will make him uneven heel'd, and whatsoever he was naturally, yet by this accident he will never be a good striker, for the making of the Perch either maketh or marreth the Cock. Therefore to prevent this fault, the best way is to have in your roost a row of little Perches, not above seven or eight inches in length, and not a foot from the ground, so that your Cock may with ease go up to them, and being set, must of force have his legs stand neer together.

* W. Sketchley, op. cit., pp. 30-32.

It is a rule, that he which is a close sitter, is ever a narrow striker. Let the footstool of the Perch be round and smooth, and about the bigness of a man's arm. Yet for your better knowledge, because words cannot so well express these quantities, it shall not be amisse for you to go to some famous Cockmaster's house, and view the Perches which are within his feeding Pens, and according to those proportions frame your own; for the Perch is the making and spoyling of any Cock whatsoever. Again, you must be careful, that when your Cock doth leap from his Perch, that the ground be soft whereon he lighteth, for if it be hard or rough, it will make your Cock grow gowty, and put forth knots upon his feet."*

It was customary for breeders to put out prospective fighting-cocks in what were termed "walks", which were so situated as to enable these selected birds to be free from exposure to disturbances likely to be created by other fowls. The selection of these "walks" was extremely important, as Sketchley points out: "Your utmost care and attention must be exerted to procure good 'walks', for half-bred fowls in a well-furnished 'walk' will beat the best Game when starved or pined; and hand-strewed 'walks' generally bring on an inactive sloth. To send fine stags that have enjoyed every indulgence to bad 'walks', is one of the most flagrant errors a breeder can commit, and it is undoing all you have done before. Cocks, from so sudden a deviation, experience a change in their systems, and it checks their growth—frequently a gradual decline ensues. Therefore the procuring of good 'walks' is absolutely necessary and conducive to the well-doing and constitution of your cocks. All town 'walks', except here and there a few, are not worth having, and there are few in villages where towns are near to each other, but may be ranked in the same class. The best are those whose situations are distant, and where plenty of corn and water abound. Grass 'walks' with corn are to be preferred to clay-bound fields, the latter defacing the birds' glossy plumes. Where a great number of 'walks' are wanted, the practice of running stags with cocks is unavoidable, and with some to a late period; even if he fights a long main early in the spring he may fall short of the whole of his stags being got out, and of course many are sacrificed. If you have much yard-room, or two yards belonging to the same dwelling, let the younger brood be accustomed to occupy the one, with a proper roost distinct from the other,

* Gervase Markham, *Country Contentments*, 1675.

seldom interfering with the older branch. Gentlemen who command any number of 'walks', have infinitely the advantage of those whose 'walks' are few and limited : the advantages over the latter are preeminently great, for many are so beautifully situated that even the crow or the sight of a cock seldom comes across them ; they are neither fretted nor teased, which ever causes them to lose much of their flesh and destroys their martial fire and spirit, when so habituated, added to the annoyance of stags—that when exhibited upon the pit, his raging pride is so far abated, it frequently makes him tardy and slow to action. Those who fight for considerable sums cannot be too scrutinizing in the choice of their stags, when they are to be sent out to clear 'walks', to see that they are in all respects free from ocular imperfections ; for the occupying 'walks' with any deficit is not only an increase of expense, but a great disappointment, as it frequently happens for want of such nice observation, that they are reckoning upon more fine cocks than they are possessed of."*

These various imperfections, the recognition of which is of such vital importance, include flat sides, short legs, thin thighs, a crooked breast, a short or thin neck, defective eyesight, a duck-foot, and any state of poor or imperfect health.

Before the Gamecock arrived at maturity a most important matter had to be attended to. He had to be dubbed. All the male birds were dubbed, irrespective of whether or not they were intended for fighting. It was, and is, just as important that the Gamecock intended for breeding should be dubbed as the one destined to figure in the cockpit. Gamecocks will fight with each other or with any other males they come across at every opportunity. Because of this fighting propensity, they are continually receiving injuries, and if an undubbed male comes into conflict with another of the same breed or variety that is dubbed, he is at a great disadvantage, and the injuries inflicted are likely to be of an exceptionally severe nature. Even if the undubbed Gamecock meets in battle a strong, pugnacious bird of a small-combed or flat-combed breed, the Gamecock may well receive severe injuries because of the large comb and wattles presented to his adversary. For this and other reasons dubbing has been customary in the case of Gamecocks, whether intended for

* W. Sketchley, *The Cocker*, pp. 13-14.

breeding or exhibition, just the same as it was in days gone by in the case of the fighting-cocks.

The operation is best performed when the bird has reached something approaching maturity, in other words when he has donned his full male feathering. It is advisable that for a whole day preceding the operation no food should be given to the bird. An assistant holds the bird in a firm grip, while the operator, using a pair of surgical scissors, sterilized by immersion in boiling water containing carbonate of soda (one per cent), removes first the wattles, and then the comb.

CHAPTER IV

SELECTION, TRAINING, PREPARATION FOR BATTLE, AND CARE OF THE FIGHTING-COCK

We have only to dip into the books devoted to cockfighting to see the importance that old cockers attached to the selection of a fighting-cock. It is true that every bird destined to fight for his life in the cockpit, and incidentally win fame and money for his owner, had to go through a course of training, just as a horse which is intended to enter a race must be trained, and a boxer before he is thought fit to enter the ring. But in every case, training, though of great importance, is not everything. No amount of training will turn a Minorca cockerel into a fighting-bird, a carthorse into a racer, or a clumsy youngster into a champion boxer. There are certain fundamental qualities or characteristics which are essential, and these are looked for with the keenest of eyes by the person who does the selecting, whether he is seeking potential champions in the cockpit, on the racecourse, or in the boxing ring.

In selecting a fighting-cock, not unnaturally much attention was paid to signs of strength and agility. Size was taken carefully into account, as whatever the bird's weight he had to be matched in the cockpit with an opponent of similar weight. Abnormally small or unusually large birds were difficult to match, and for this reason were rarely selected for training. Many of the early writers on the subject paid great attention to colour, as already noted. Markham says, *inter alia*: "If he be red about the head, like scarlet, it is a sign of lust, strength and courage; but if he be pale, it is a sign of sickness and faintness."* Signs of courage, says the same authority, are "his walk, his treading, the pride of his going, and his oft-crowing."

The importance of these points is stressed by Sketchley, thus: "Cocks that are well-formed and lofty have an amazing advantage over the disproportioned; the latter carrying with them much useless weight. High-

---
* Gervase Markham, *Country Contentments*, 1675.

bearing fowls will always have the odds in their favour over low-setting cocks. Cocks when they are justly formed, rise in their fight with more agility and force, are better heelers than those that carry their make equal to the extreme; and your dry-heeled cocks are generally of the latter description, the weight being too far from the centre of action, and once overpowered they are always under a cock, that is not alike defective—their legs are thrown out of the line of the body, and of course they are never close hitters. Cocks that do not bear cone-like shapes, are for the most part wide and straddling in their walk, and as they walk they fly—whereas in the cone-like shape the legs are more inverted and narrow, and are more terrible in their spur."*

The experienced cocker gave a good deal of attention to the thighs. For whether the bird was destined to fight with naked heels or with metal spurs, the power behind the strokes he made and his ability to keep on his legs in a long-drawn-out battle were dependent to a very large degree on the strength of his thighs. Development in this particular was to some extent connected with age. Thus maturity was a factor of considerable importance. Especially was this so in naked-heel fighting. Says Markham: "A cock should not be put to the battel before he be two years old, at which time he is perfect and compleat in every member; for to suffer him to fight when his spurs are but warts, you may well know his courage, but never his goodnesse."† It is worth noting that Lord Derby's famous fighters never appeared in the cockpit until they were two years of age.

Before the introduction of artificial spurs great attention was given to the weapons provided by nature. Here again Markham's observations are of interest. He writes: "For the sharpness of his heel, or as Cock-masters call it, the narrow heel, it is only seen in his fighting, for that Cock is said to be sharp-heel'd or narrow-heel'd, which every time he riseth hitteth, and draweth bloud of his adversary, gilding (as they term it) his spurs in bloud, and threatening at every blow an end of that Battail. And these Cocks are surely of great estimation, for the best Cockmasters are of opinion, that a sharp-heel'd Cock, though he be a little false, is much better than the truest Cock which hath a dull

* W. Sketchley, op. cit., p. 14-15.
† Gervase Markham, op. cit.

heel, and hitteth seldome; for though the one fight long, yet he seldome wounds, and the other though he will not endure the uttermost hewing, yet he makes a very suddain and quick despatch of his business, for every blow puts his adversary in danger. But that Cock which is both assuredly hard, and also very sharp-heel'd, he is to be esteemed, and is of the most account above all other, and therefore in your general election chuse him which is of a strong shape, good colour, true valour, and of a most sharp and ready heel."*

In regard to this important matter of selection, William Machrie, in his book on Cocking, which is considered to be a classic, says: "There are several other qualities no less necessary than that of true courage, to wit, rising well and carrying a bloody heel: and were I to make choice of a cock for Battle (I do not say for Brood) I would prefer one that riseth well and carries the bloody heel, to a great many of the true and hardest Cocks without these qualities; for altho the one fights long, yet seldom wounds or cuts his adversary: whereas the other never rises but he makes the blood to spring, endangering his adversary's life at every blow; these last are called by Cockers, narrow sharp or bloody-heel'd Cocks, as the former are call'd dull or flat-heel'd ones. But if you would have such a Cock as carries all these Properties of hardness, well-rising and a bloody heel, since such, according to all, are best either for Battle or Brood, for your better help in choosing of these, take what follows as certain Rules for knowing them right.

"First, a well-rising Cock no sooner catcheth hold with his Beak, but he riseth with a blow, and sometimes two or three, and the oftener he with one grip or hold repeats his stroakes, it is the better. And then secondly, if he direct his stroaks chiefly at the Head, Neck and Throat of his adversary, it is a clear and sure Mark of a prime, high-metall'd, and well-rising Cock. It's true, a cut or blow on the Pinion, Wing or Thigh may make a Cock lose his Battle, as well as those on the Head or Neck; yet this so rarely falleth out, that it cannot be reckoned a sure mark of a well-rising Cock: wherefore I conclude that a Cock that doth strike more at the Head and Throat, than at the Body, is certainly the best, by reason one blow or two at these parts are more dangerous, and sometimes kill outright; whereas in any other part it taketh many, even

* Gervase Markham, op. cit.

to disable."* Machrie gives explicit instructions for recognising the narrow and bloody-heeled cock, which he says is known from a dry and flat-heeled one by "the narrow walking," by "his wide or narrow standing when he feeds," by "his wide or narrow sitting when he perches," and by "the narrowness of the points of the two little bones" just below his rump.†

Writing a century later, Sketchley says: "Cocks vary much in their mode of fighting; some are hasty and fiery; others cautious, wary, and close hitters; some wide and generally dry-heeled; whilst many are lofty and darting. Those that are low and fluttering are seldom dangerous in their heels; the latter description are those that are destitute of that tapering shape that so eminently distinguishes them in their superior mode of fighting. Cocks that are as broad behind as before, have their legs thrown out of the line of the body, and of course are wide in their fly and dry-heeled. To judge well of a battle requires much attention—a quick, discerning eye—a knowledge of those parts of the cock most liable to sudden and destructive fate, and which turns the fluctuating tide of odds against them; others that are more slow in their efforts, yet fatal to their victory—many are momentarily crippled and yet not immediately detected: variously are the heels directed, and many parts are perforated with little injury in the heat of battle, although felt when cold—these are not alarming to the adept, and they take advantage of those who are: a cut throat is for the most part very conspicuous."‡

A cock having been selected, the next step was to prepare him for battle. This involved a special course of training carried out by an expert, for an untrained or a badly-trained bird would stand little chance against a well-trained one.

Each bird was confined in a roomy pen, or in a compartment of a range of pens. It was important that the birds did not see each other. To this end the back and sides of the pen consisted of boards, the front alone being constructed (in the old days) of wooden bars, or (more recently) of wire netting.

---

* William Machrie, *An Essay upon the Royal Recreation and Art of Cocking*, Edinburgh, 1705, pp. 12-13.
† Ibid.
‡ W. Sketchley, op. cit., p. 48.

The general method of feeding adopted by the early cockers is indicated in the following paragraph from Markham's book: "When your Cock is put up into his Penne, you shall for three or four dayes feed him only with old manchet [white bread], the crust pared away, and cut into little square bits, and you shall give him to the quantity of a good handfull at a time, you shall feed him three times in a daye, that is to say, at sun-rise, at highest noon, and at sun-set; you shall ever let him have before him the finest, coldest, and sweetest spring-water that you can get."

One of the most important parts of the training of Gamecocks has always been the special feeding they were given. No expense was spared, no trouble was considered too much, in this connexion. Special bread was baked for the purpose of keeping the birds in perfect physical condition. Each of the famous cockers had his own particular recipe to which the bread or cake was made, and these recipes were closely guarded secrets. But here let us again dip into Markham's book:

"Now you shall understand, that the bread which you shall give him at this time, and at all other times during his dieting, shall not be manchet [white bread], but a special bread made for the purpose, in this manner. You shall take of wheatmeal half a peck, and of fine oatmeal flour as much, and mixing them together, knead them into a stiff paste with Ale, the whites of a dozen Eggs, and half a pound of Butter, and having wrought the dough exceeding well, make it into broad thin cakes, and being three or four dayes old, and the blisterings of the outside cut away, cut it into little square bits, and give it the Cock. There be some others that in this bread will mix Liquorice, Aniseed, and other hot Spices; and will also in the Cock-water steep slices of Liquorice; but it is not commendable, for it is both unnatural and unwholesome, and maketh a Cock so hot at the heart, that when he comes to the latter end of a battle, he is suffocated and overcome with his own heat; therefore I advise men of judgment to take that for the best diet which is most natural, and least contrary unto the fowl's ordinary feeding."

Bourne's recipe for bread, as given in Rees' *Cyclopædia*, was: 3 lbs. fine flour, 2 whole eggs, 4 whites of eggs, yeast, and water. Of this bread each cock was given a teacupful of small pieces per day, as well as barley. Water was given very sparingly.

William Machrie gives a recipe for what in his opinion is the best cock-bread known: "Of the best and finest Wheatmeal I take three quarters of a peck, and one quarter of Oatmeal of the purest sort, and first of all mix these well together; then add the whites of twenty new laid Eggs, four Yolks, an Ounce of the best extract of Liquorice, and as much of the fine powder of brown Sugar candy, a quarter of an ounce of Aniseeds, and Carroway-seeds grossly bruised, with a lump of good sweet Butter as big as your fist at least, and a quarter of a Pint or more of the best White-wine that can be bought for Money, with three or four spoonfulls of Syrup of Clove-gilliflowers put into it, and a Date or two, with some Candyed Eringo Root cut very small so that it may be scattered into every part, and let these ingredients be all well worked together, in some Tub, or Pan fit for that purpose, with your hands, until you are satisfied that they are thoroughly incorporated. Then take Wood-sorrel, Ground-ivy, Featherfew, Dandelion, and Burrage, of each a like quantity, and distil them in a cold still, and add three or four spoonfuls of the pure juice of Lemons to every pint of distilled water; and add as much of this Julip as will serve to make all into a good stiff paste: let this be wrought quick, and made into little flat loaves, which ought to be a day or two old before you spend them, and then being well rasped, or pared, so that none of the burned or brown outside remains, they may then be cut and given to the cocks, as aforesaid."*

Markham advocates steeping the bread in urine, a practice adopted for centuries by cockers, and more recently by breeders of Game Fowls when preparing their birds for exhibition. I well remember a famous exhibitor telling me some thirty years ago that the secret of getting birds into perfect show condition was to feed them on wheat which had been steeped in urine.

After a four days' course of special dieting, says Markham: "sparring" exercises were started, one cock being matched against another. As it was of the utmost importance that the birds should suffer no injury of any kind, their spurs were covered with soft pieces of leather, known in the cocking vernacular as "hots"; while the heads and combs were protected by means of hood-like contrivances made of linen or cloth.

* R. Howlett, *The Royal Pastime of Cock-fighting*, 1709, pp. 58-59.

Alternatively, leather or string muzzles were used to prevent the infliction of any damage by the birds' beaks.

From the accounts of the early cockers it would appear that the "sweating" process which followed each morning's "sparring" was considered an essential part of every Gamecock's training.

For a description of this process let us once again turn to the pages of Markham's treatise. Thus: "You shall take him into a fair even green Close, and there setting him down, having some Dunghill cock in your arms, you shall shew it him, and so run from him, and entice him to follow you, and so chase him up and down half an hour at least, suffering him now and then to have a stroke at the Dunghill cock. And when you see that he is well-heated and panteth, you shall take him up and bear him into your Cock-house, and there first give him this scouring: take of Butter, which hath no Salt, half a pound, and beat it in a Mortar with the leaves of Herb of grace, Hyssop, and Rosemary, till the Herbs cannot be perceived, and that the Butter is brought to a green Salve, and of this give the Cock a roll or two, as big as your thumb, and then stove him in a basket till Evening,* and then feed him as formerly declared. The next day you shall let him rest and feed, and the next day after, you shall spar him again: and thus every other day for the first fortnight, you shall either spar or chase your Cock, which are the most naturallest and kindliest heats that you can give him, and after every heat you shall give him a scouring; for this will break and cleanse from him all grease, glut and filthiness, which lying in his body, makes him pursie, faint and not able to stand out the latter end of a battel. Having fed your Cock thus the first fortnight, the second fortnight you shall also feed him in the same manner, and with the same food, but you shall not spar him, or give him heats above twice in a week at the most, insomuch that thrice or four times in the fortnight will be sufficient, and each time you shall stove and scour him according to the nature of his heats, that is to say, if you heat him too much, you shall stove him long, and give him of your scouring the greater quantity; if you find

---

* Markham describes the method of scouring thus: "You must have a deep straw basket made for the purpose, with sweet soft straw to the middle." After removing his 'hots', put in the bird, "cover him with sweet straw up to the top of the basket, and then lay on the lid close, and there let the cock stove and sweat till the evening. . . . You may in time of necessity, for want of these straw baskets, stow your Cock in a Cock-bag, by laying straw both under and above him, but it is not so good, because the air hath more power to pass through it. After four of the clock in the evening, you may take your Cock out of the stove, and licking his head and eyes all over with your tongue put him into his Pen."

that he is in good breath, and needeth but slight heats, then you shall stove him the lesse while, and give him the lesse of the scouring. Now to the third fortnight, which maketh up the six weeks compleat (being a time sufficient to prepare a Cock for the battail) you shall feed him as aforesaid, but you shall not sparre him at all, for fear of making his head tender or sore, neither give him any violent exercise, but only twice or thrice in the fortnight, moderately let him run and chase up and down, to maintain his wind, and now and then cuffe a Cock, which you shall hold to him in your hands; which done, you shall give him his scouring well rounded in the powder of Sugar-candy, white or brown, but brown is the better, for the Cock then being come to perfect breath, and having no filth in his body for the scouring to work on, it will work and cause operation upon the vital parts, and make the Cock sick, which the Sugar-candy will prevent, and strengthen Nature against the medicine."*

It seems obvious that such treatment must have been a severe strain upon any bird, however strong, and there are grounds for wonder that such a system of "sweating" was favoured by cockers, not only of Markham's day, but for many years afterwards. It would appear however that early in the eighteenth century these rigorous measures were abandoned in favour of a much milder method of training. True, "sweating" was considered essential, but the period was shortened to occasional bouts of three or four hours' duration, and the whole training period was shortened to two or three weeks instead of the six weeks held to be necessary in the earlier days of cocking. As time went on more changes were introduced. From an article contributed to Rees' *Cyclopædia* by a famous cocker named Thomas Bourne, it appears that by the end of the eighteenth century the "stoving" system had been abandoned altogether.

The bird having been fed, sparred and prepared in every way possible so that he was, on the day of battle, in the pink of condition, the important question of matching him with a suitable opponent cropped up. But let us hear what Markham has to say:

"Now when you bring him into the Pit to fight, you must have an especial care to the matching of him, for in that art consisteth the

* G. Markham, *Country Contentments*, eleventh edition, 1675.

greatest glory of the Cockmaster, for what availeth it to feed never so well, if in the matching you give that advantage which overthroweth your former labour ? Therefore in your matching there are two things to be considered ; that is, the length of Cocks, and the strength of Cocks ; for if your Adversary's Cock be too long, yours shall hardly catch his head, and then he can never endanger eye nor life ; and if he be the stronger, he will overbear your Cock, and not suffer him to rise, and strike with any advantage ; therefore for the knowledge of these two rules, though experience be the best tutor, yet the first, which is length, you shall judge by your eye, when you grip the Cock about the waist, and make him shoot out his legs, in which posture you shall see the utmost of his height, and so compare them in your judgment. Now for his strength, which is known by the thickness of his body (for that Cock is ever held the strongest, which is the largest in the garth) you shall know it by the measure of your hands, griping the Cock about from the points of your great finger, to the joynts of your thumbs, and either of these advantages by no means give to your adversary ; but if you doubt loss in the one, yet be sure to gain in the other : for the weak long Cock will rise at more ease, and the short strong Cock will give the surer blow ; so that because all Cocks are not cast into a mould, there may be a reconciliation of the advantages, yet by all means give as little as you can."*

From what has been said in the foregoing pages it will be seen that the selection, feeding and training of the bird destined to fight for his life and incidentally for the money dependent upon his prowess, were all of the greatest importance. Ergo, the feeder or trainer was a most important person. How important will be apparent from the following passage culled from Pierce Egan's *Life in London* :

"On their way to the Cockpit, Jerry advised the Corinthian and Logic to back the Countryman designated Tommy the Sweep. 'That won't do,' replied the Oxonian, 'the yokels have always been beat in London !' 'Never mind', answered Hawthorn, 'I'll give you that in, but Tommy will take the shine out of the Cockneys this time. He is a capital feeder, and an excellent judge of Cocks ; he is, I understand, familiar with

* G. Markham, op. cit.

all the various breeds, and well acquainted with the properties of the right S.....n-winged colour, the Shropshire Reds, the Staffordshire Jet-blacks, &c.' 'I think we may as well, Bob,' said the Corinthian, 'yield to Jerry's judgment upon this occasion'. 'It shall be so, then,' said Logic. Hawthorn was no novice at cocking, and the interior of the Pit afforded him but little variety for observation: the confusion of voices; the bettings of 2 to 1, 5 to 4, &c.; the poundage; the anxiety displayed by the backers, on the telling out of the Cocks, were exactly the same as Jerry had previously witnessed in the Country; but the singularity of the remarks, and the knowing looks of the visitors, both high and low, did not fail in making an impression on his mind. It is rather singular to remark, it was the first time a London feeder was beaten on his own ground; and Tom and Logic 'won their blunt', in consequence of backing the opinion of Hawthorn."

As it was of the utmost importance that a feeder should be conversant with the foods most suitable for the particular birds in his charge, as well as with any peculiarities of constitution, the engagement of a fresh feeder, who had not the essential knowledge of and experience with these specific birds, was not to be lightly entertained. Sketchley's interesting book contains some observations on this very point: "A prior knowledge to what extent they can bear reducing, and to what degree of facility they are raised, are beneficial acquirements, and must preponderate over an entire stranger. It is not much to be wondered at, that a feeder under such a disadvantage should fail in his first attempt with an antagonist who has been in the habit of feeding the same cocks for years. These failures frequently take place, and are as frequently the consequence of changing feeders. In the six great mains which I fought with ---- Cussans, Esq. at Loughborough and Derby, John Beastal fed for me, whereas Mr. Cussans had a fresh feeder every main: the result was that Beastal won five mains out of six—from 11 to 7 a head. Here not a feeder but David Smith had any previous knowledge of their cocks—cocks too of his own breeding, and were the well-known Greys; but my Black-Reds under the many year's experience of their feeder, seldom or ever failed of success. A propensity to change under these circumstances (more particularly if your feeder ranks as an able professor) should not be encouraged, because he has failed in his first attempt: but let him feed your trial cocks with as much attention as for the main; give him all the local knowledge of them that you can, and let him be acquainted with every character of your fowls, and you will find him superior to any change you generally can adopt. You will not find yourself much at a loss, on his progressive fighting, to determine your future choice; he will either exhibit some trait in favour of your initiation, or he may drop into mediocrity."*

The bird having been trained, he had to be prepared for battle. A cock in full feather would have been at a grave disadvantage in combat with one whose hackle and wings had been clipped. The trimming of the hackle was however allowed within specified limits only, as a fighting-cock is in the habit of seizing his adversary by the hackle, and therefore trimming was not allowed to an extent which would prevent any hold at all. On this point, Machrie, that celebrated authority on cocking, says: "When you Poll your Cock, leave a little mane or small ridge of short cut feathers from the root of his Comb, along the hinder part of his head, for a cock to hold by. As for the rest of the feathers of his Neck (called his Hackle) this ought to be much longer than the Ridge: all which is reckoned a *Fair Hackle*; but if otherwise cut so bare that there's no hold to rise by, a *Foul Hackle*. Next, poll or pluck bare all the feathers away below his Rump towards his Belly, then cut his Tail pretty short; which done, cut the upper part of his Wings. If he be a small cock and riseth too high, an inch and a quarter shorter than his Body; but if a large cock, not so short; for the latter needs a longer Wing than the former, in respect of his weight. As to the underpart of the Wing, six or seven of the foremost feathers thereof must be cut sloping, and a great deal shorter than the rest; still polling a day or two before they fight; and what Bloody feathers you find about your Cock's Head, Neck, Rump or Tail, pull them out by the root four days before battle. And notice that the upper part of your Cock's Beak be but a little longer than the lower; otherwise in Fighting he'll neither Mouth nor hold well."†

Seeing that the rules of the cockpit allowed the clipping of certain

---

* W. Sketchley, op. cit., p. 28.
† W. Machrie, *An Essay Upon the Royal Recreation and Art of Cocking*, 1705, p. 53.

parts of the plumage, every fighting-cock was prepared for battle in the same manner. The foregoing comments, culled from Machrie's work, are borne out by the anonymous writer responsible for *The Sportsman's Dictionary* (1778), in which he gives the following detailed instructions : "To prepare a cock to fight : (1) with a pair of fine sheers cut off all his mane close to his neck, from the head to the setting on of the shoulders ; (2) clip off all the feathers from the tail, close to his rump ; the redder it appears the better is the cock in condition ; (3) spread his wings by the length of the first rising feather, and clip the rest Slopewise, with sharp points, that in rising he may therewith endanger an eye of his adversary ; (4) scrape, smooth and sharpen his spurs with a penknife ;* (5) and lastly, see that there be no feathers on the crown of his head for his opponent to take hold of them ; moisten his head all over with your spittle, and turn him into the pit to try his fortune." During the four days immediately preceding the fight, says the same authority, "give the Cock hyssop, violet and strawberry leaves, chopt small in fresh butter ; and in the morning he is to fight put down his throat a piece of fresh butter, mixt with powder of white Sugar candy."

Although in these particular instructions, no mention is made of it, from the various recipes for cock-bread given earlier in this chapter it will have been noted that alcohol in the form of ale or wine was considered to be an important part of the diet of birds which were being prepared for the cockpit. It was considered equally if not more essential immediately before the actual combat. So much so indeed, that at this juncture the customary procedure was to use liquor of even stronger alcoholic content in the shape of rum or other spirit. In many countries where cockfights are still staged, whether openly or surreptitiously, there is evidence that the practice persists.

To conclude this chapter we must give some attention to the care bestowed on the bird *after* the battle, presuming that he was fortunate enough to survive. Often his plight was indeed a sorry one. Let us see what that fount of cocking lore, Markham's *Country Contentments*, has to say on this important matter :

"When the battail is ended, the first thing you do, you shall search his wounds, and as many as you can find, you shall with your mouth suck

* This applied only to a bird which fought with naked heels.

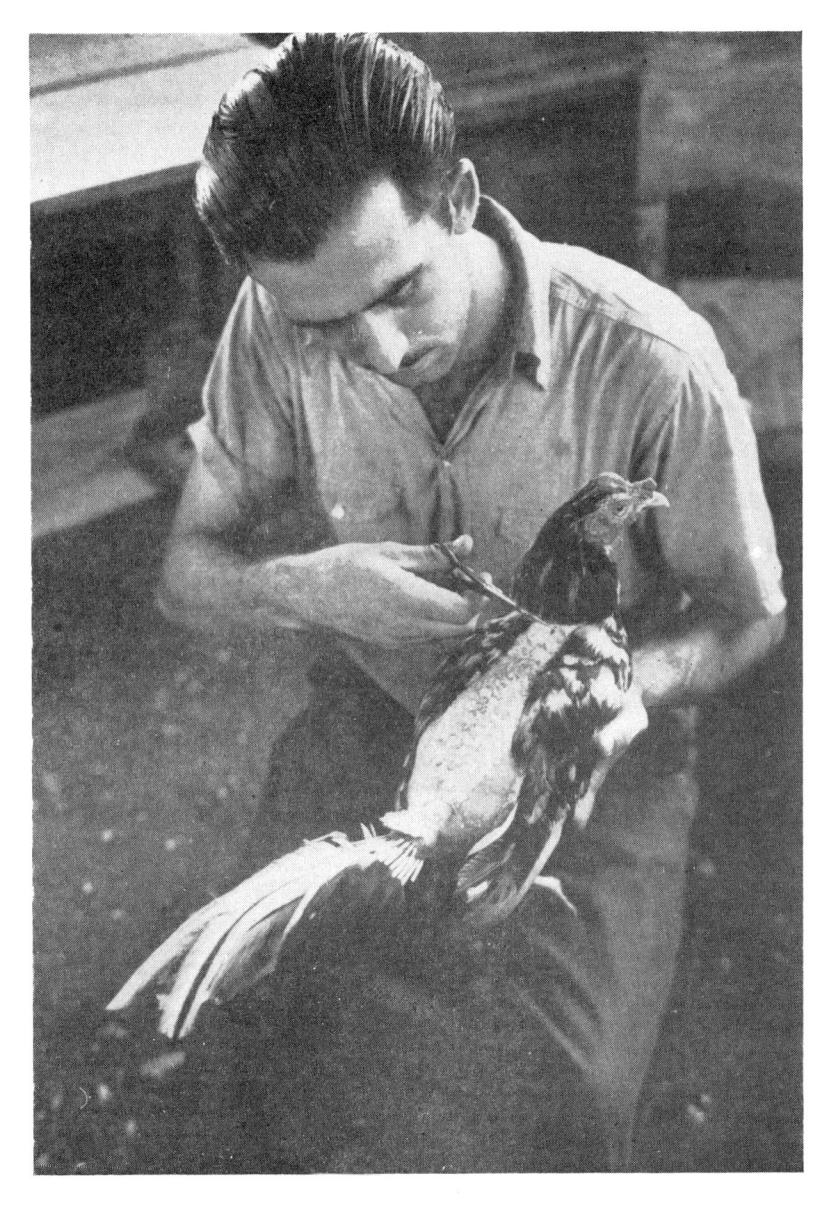

TRIMMING A COCK AT THE GALLERIA CHINCHINAGUA, GUIRA, CUBA

A HAITIAN WAITS FOR THE DUEL IN WHICH HE WILL ENTER HIS FANCIED FIGHTER, MEANWHILE HOODED

the blood out of them, then wash them very well with warm urine, to keep them from rankling, and then presently give him a roll or two of your best scouring, and so stove him hot as you can, both with sweet straw and blanketing, in a close basket for all that night; then, in the morning take him forth, and if his head be much swell'd, you shall suck his wounds again, and bath them with warm urine, then having in a fine bag the powder of the herb *Robert*, well dryed, and finely sierst, pounce all the sore places therewith, and then give the Cock a good handfull of bread to eat, out of warm urine, and so put him into the stove again, in the same manner as before mentioned, and by no means let him feel the air untill all the swelling be gone, but twice a day suck his wounds, dresse him and feed him, as is aforesaid. But if he have received any hurt, or blemish in his eye, then you shall take a leaf or two of right ground Ivy (not that which runneth along the ground, and is of the ignorant so-called, but that which grows in little tufts in the bottome of hedges, and is a little rough leaf), and having chewed it very well in your mouth, and suckt out the juyce, spit it in the eye of the Cock, and it will not only cure it of any wound, or any blow in the eye, where the sight is not pierced, but also defend it from the breeding of Films, Hawes, Warts, or any such other infirmities which quite destroy the sight: oberving that you do not cease to dress the eye therewith so long as you shall perceive any blemish therein. Now if your Cock have in his fight veyned himself, either by narrow-striking, or other cross blow, you shall find out the wound and presently bind thereunto the fine soft down of a Hare, and it will both staunch it and cure it. . . . After you have put forth your wounded Cocks to their walks, and come to visit them a month or two after, if you find about their heads any swollen bunches, hard and blackish at one end, you shall know that in such bunches are unsound cores, therefore presently with your knife you shall open the same, and crush out the cores with your thumbs, then with your mouth suck out all the corruption, and then fill the holes full of fresh Butter, and it will cure them. And thus much for the nature of the Cock, and how to keep him for his best use."

I have given these somewhat lengthy extracts because of the light they throw upon the curative methods in vogue among seventeenth century poultry breeders, and not because I am convinced of, or would care to subscribe to, their efficacy. It so happens that I have had considerable experience in ministering to the injuries suffered by male birds which, despite the greatest care as regards the provision of adequate fencing, managed to invade the domain of others of their kind. Sometimes I was able to bring the fight to an abrupt termination by picking up one of the contestants before much harm had been done, but there have been occasions many and often when one of or both the birds suffered grievous damage before I became aware of the fact that a fight was in progress. In all such cases prompt attention is necessary if the bird is to live to crow again. Even where the injuries appear to be of the most superficial character immediate treatment is advisable, and in every instance the mouth should be washed thoroughly with an antiseptic solution.

CHAPTER V

THE GENESIS AND DEVELOPMENT OF THE ARTIFICIAL SPUR

The male domestic fowl, as all poultry-keepers and a good many persons who are not poultry-keepers know, possesses a pair of spurs, one on each leg. The size, strength and length of these spurs vary considerably in different breeds, in different specimens of the same breed, and in the individual bird at different stages of its existence. For instance, in a young fowl the spurs are short, with little or no points; and it is not until the second year of the bird's life that they become strong, bony, sharp-pointed, deadly fighting instruments.

Cockfighting has become so associated in the popular mind with wicked-looking steel spurs that few people realise that male birds of certain breeds of poultry, notably the Game Fowl, will on occasion fight to the death without anything other than the weapons nature has given them. Many are the fierce and sanguinary combats which I have witnessed, not only between Gamecocks but between pugnacious specimens of other breeds, notably Rhode Island Reds. It is true I have never actually witnessed a battle of this character where the victor crowed over his dead adversary, but this is merely because I invariably interfered. Occasionally, as a result of such interference, I got a blow from the heel of one of the combatants: hence I can personally testify to the damage for which a naked spur alone can be responsible.

In all countries, when first fighting-cocks were pitted against one another, I think it may be taken as certain that the birds fought with heels innocent of any form of metal spur. The use of the artificial spur must surely have followed a period during which naked-heel fighting was in vogue. Also no doubt in many instances battles in which the cocks were armed with artificial spurs were contemporaneous with others in which the combatants fought with naked heels, as, from historical records, we know was the case in ancient Rome.

For naked-heel fighting it was of course imperative that the spurs should be sharp-pointed and clean. Hence, it was customary to scrape them carefully with a knife until they were smooth and sharp. To ensure that no unfair practices were attempted by unscrupulous cockers, it was customary in connexion with some fights that the spurs should be thoroughly cleaned immediately before the battle in full view of the spectators, and in some cases, to prevent the use of poison, that the trainers should lick the spurs.

In most countries artificial spurs have supplanted the natural weapons, but there are still a few where naked-heel fighting or some variant of it persists. In Spain, for instance, the natural spur is still supreme, even to the extent of spurs removed from dead cocks being fitted to fighters which, because of their youth, have not grown spurs long or sharp enough to be of any use for fighting purposes. West Indian cockers affix the peculiarly hard and keen pointed spurs which sometimes grow on hens.

The real object of arming the birds with metal spurs appears to have been to make the contest more equal. It is well-nigh impossible, in naked-heel fighting, to ensure that the opposing champions meet on equal terms. One or other invariably starts out with an advantage: his spurs may be longer, they may be more pointed, they may be curved in a way which adds to their lethal power. As I have already mentioned, birds of different breeds and even specimens of the same breed, show considerable variation as regards the size and character of the spurs with which nature has provided them. Age, in particular, as already mentioned, has a good deal to do with size. Most male birds, before they are two years old are badly equipped for fighting with their naked spurs, which could do little harm to an opponent. On the other hand, many birds, aged two and a half or three years, have spurs reaching a length of at least three inches; and in a few cases even this length is exceeded. There is a tendency for the spurs to curve, too.* The massive-chested Indian Game, on the other hand, never develops very long spurs, and his comparatively short legs are a handicap when it comes to speed. Again, a battle is usually far more prolonged where natural spurs are the weapons

---

* It is customary to remove spurs which have become long and sharp-pointed, especially from male birds used for breeding purposes, otherwise serious injuries may be inflicted on the females. Then again long curved spurs may impede the movements of the bird himself.

used, and the victor as well as the vanquished (in battles where no mortal blow is struck) are likely to bear severe wounds which heal slowly and often lead to incapacitation. The steel spur, on the other hand, makes a clean wound, which, where it does not kill, usually heals in a short time and leaves the bird in a state where he can fight again. So, too, the silver spur. But that made of nickel, according to no less an authority than John Harris, is an exception: the wound which it inflicts is a deadly one, healing slowly or not at all.

It is contended, by those favouring naked-heel fighting, that victory is the more likely to go to the bird which shows the greater power of endurance and is the gamer of the two. It is by no means unusual for a fight to continue for as long as two hours, and on rare occasions, even longer. Moreover, it is seldom that a combatant ends the battle with a lucky lethal stroke, as not infrequently happens where metal spurs are worn.

There seems to be no authentic record as to when the first artificial spurs were devised, or in what country they were first used. Many writers have discussed the matter, and made supposedly authoritative pronouncements, but these, on investigation, would appear to be little more than guesswork. There is, however, Aristophanes' oft-quoted reference to their use in ancient Greece. Apparently this early form of artificial spur, which was termed a *telum*, consisted of a cap made of bronze or other metal which was placed over the cock's own spur. Among ancient Roman remains discovered at one time and another in various parts of England have been included spurs of iron, bronze and silver, in some instances attached to the leg-bones of cocks. In Atkinson's interesting and authoritative book there is an illustration of a Roman cock-spur found in Cornwall: it is made of silver.

Some writers and historians are of opinion that artificial spurs were unknown in Britain before the seventeenth century, but the evidence upon which the supposition is based seems to me dubious. Granted the use of metal spurs by the Romans there seems no reason why they should not have been used in later centuries. It is true that what are apparently the oldest spurs of English manufacture now in existence would appear to be the pair which Charles the Second presented to his mistress Nell Gwynn about the middle of the seventeenth century;

but it is highly probable that these silver spurs were preceded by specimens of the conical type, made of iron or brass.

However this may be, in the early decades of the nineteenth century, in England, the silver spur seems to have ousted all its rivals, at any rate so far as the fashionable cockpits were concerned. For in the rules and regulations pertaining to cockfighting at the more famous venues we find it stated that the battle must be fought by cocks wearing silver spurs. In those days, only at the lower-class cockpits, where battles for small stakes were customary, could one find birds armed with spurs made of iron and steel. The main reason for this preference for silver spurs was apparently the fact that the fight was likely to last much longer than would be the case if the keener and sharper-pointed steel weapons were used. With the abandonment of the hollow conical spur devised to fit over the natural spur, the silver weapon consisted of a solid piece of metal, shaped like a spur and slightly curved.

The silver spur is no longer in use even in those parts of the world where cockfighting is openly practised. There is a very good reason for this. The making of silver spurs was a more or less secret process, which now ranks among the lost arts. Similarly with the making of gold spurs, which it is said were at one time used. These metals, silver and gold both, had to be tempered, and apparently there is no one living today who knows how this was accomplished.

Wherever Gamecocks meet in combat today (apart from the relatively few places where naked-heel fighting is practised) they are armed with steel spurs. Because of the extreme secrecy surrounding cockfighting in Britain, little information is available respecting the spurs now used, but most of them probably follow the pattern of the silver spurs so famous in the eighteenth and early nineteenth centuries. In the United States, however, there is no such secrecy observed. Steel spurs are bought and sold openly; illustrations of them appear in sections of the Press in which they are advertised for sale at prices ranging from ten to twenty dollars a pair. The blade of the spur is perfectly round, it tapers from socket to point, and is slightly curved. It is made in various sizes, ranging from $1\frac{1}{4}''$ to double this length.

A variation of the orthodox round spur is that known as the "slasher", a wicked-looking razor-edged broadish blade terminating in a point. This

SPURS AND SHEATHS (BORNEO)

MUFFLES OR MUFFS

ARTIFICIAL SPURS

A COCK HAS FIGHTING-SPURS FIXED BEFORE A CONTEST
IN BALI

type of spur is deadly in execution, and a battle in which the combatants are armed with "slashers" is sure to have a lethal end. The blades vary in length. In most cases where this type of spur is used one leg only of the cock is armed. It is perhaps some slight tribute to the scruples of American and British cockers that the use of the "slasher"* is prohibited. It seems to be restricted to Mexico, the Philippines, and certain of the republics of Central and South America.

The fixing of artificial spurs to a cock's legs is by no means a simple affair to be entrusted to a novice. On the contrary it calls for considerable skill and not a little experience. The early writers on cockfighting stressed the importance of this preliminary preparation of the fighting-cock. There was no hard and fast rule in the matter of where exactly or how precisely to fix the artificial spurs. So much depended upon the individual bird, and only after careful and prolonged observation of his method of fighting and manner of using his natural spurs, could the expert cocker decide these points; points which could mean all the difference between victory and defeat. For this reason the artificial spur was not always fixed in the exact place where the natural spur grew: the precise position and direction depending upon the cock's method of striking, as observed during his sparring exercises. Because of this, too, there was a risk, if an error should be made in fixing the spurs, of the cock being at a grave disadvantage in actual battle. Apropos of this danger, Ferguson says: "A Gamecock's object in fighting is to seize his foe by the hackle, hold him down and spur him on the head: to do this he must kick, or spur close past his own head; and hence, if the spur is not set at the proper angle, is apt to dig it into his own head."†

In the old days, silver spurs were affixed to the stubs on the cock's legs (the natural spurs having been removed or shortened) with strips of leather, pigskin or buckskin. This practice has survived through the centuries and in most cases, "leathering", as it is called, is still the method

---

* It seems probable that the 'slasher', or something closely resembling it, was used, on occasion, in England. The following quotation, which is taken from John Ashton's *Social Life in the Reign of Queen Anne* (page 301), would appear to indicate as much: 'Note that on Wednesday there will be a single battle fought with Sickles, after the East India manner. And on Thursday there will be a Battle Royal, one Cock with a Sickle, and 4 Cocks with fair Spurs. On Friday there will be a pair of Shakebags fight for 5£. And on Saturday there will be a Battle Royal, between a Shakebag with fair Spurs, and 4 Matchable Cocks which are to fight with Sickles, Launcet Spurs, and Penknife Spurs, the like never yet seen. For the Entertainment of the foreign Ambassadors and Gentlemen.'

† Article on cockfighting by the Worshipful Chancellor Ferguson, in *Transactions of the Cumberland and Westmorland Antiquarian & Archaeological Society*, Vol. IX, 1887.

favoured, narrow strips of kid or other soft material being used. There are some places, however, notably in the U.S.A, where the use of leather is prohibited, the spurs having to be tied on with string.

With artificial spurs there would appear to be less risk of one of the combatants being at a disadvantage, unless the individual responsible for fixing the heels bungles the job. The fixing of the spurs too tightly, or too slackly, may easily make all the difference between victory and defeat. Then again, there is a possibility, even where the fixing of the spurs is accomplished with the highest skill, that the bird may react badly to the presence of artificial heels. True, it is rare for a cock to attempt to free his legs from these appendages, but there is no means of knowing what inhibiting effect they have, or whether indeed they have any effect at all of this nature.

CHAPTER VI

THE COCKPIT

Cockfighting was practised both indoors and outdoors. In the earliest times the fights were invariably staged in the open. Later, when cockfighting became the sport of royalty and of the aristocracy, the indoor cockpit was favoured.

The outdoor cockpit of the ancients was a simple affair, easily constructed. A circular space of ground perfectly level and covered with short grass was selected and enclosed by a board wall about a foot high. In some cases seats were erected around the enclosure; in other instances the spectators stood.

Atkinson is of opinion that Gwenap Pit, near the Cornish town of Redruth, was "probably the largest and most ancient open-air Pit in England."* This same authority considers that it was pre-Roman, and gives a number of interesting details concerning the Pit. The fighting arena was "some 13 feet in diameter". There was a platform providing accommodation for judges and referees, while the needs of the spectators were taken care of by twelve rows of seats. There is evidence that this cockpit was in full blast in 1743: John Wesley had to postpone an oration pending the holding of a cockfight there. Atkinson refers to other outdoor pits at Chislehurst in Kent, at Holcombe in Somerset, and at Dolgelley in North Wales.

It is probable that numerous outdoor meetings were held through the ages, even when indoor venues were there for the finding in all parts of the country, but they enjoyed a new lease of life in Britain after cockfighting was prohibited by statute, and in the North of England and North Wales, under conditions of the strictest secrecy, cockpits were improvised in various little known or seldom frequented spots among the hills (see page 170). Today, the majority of the surreptitious contests are held in similar out-of-the-way spots.

* Herbert Atkinson, *Cockfighting and Game Fowl*, George Bayntun, Bath, 1938, p. 69.

The indoor cockpits, not unnaturally, were far more elaborate affairs. True enough, they failed in one particular: the combatants could not fight in their natural habitat. In some cases the floor of the pit was covered with sods in an attempt to provide environmental conditions as nearly as possible approaching what was natural. This, however, was not always practicable, and in such cases matting was laid on the floor in place of turf. One of the most famous and elaborate of the London cockpits was the one erected in Tufton Street, Westminster. An excellent description of this particular pit is given by Edward Herbert, thus:

"The cockpit is a large, lofty and circular building, with seats rising, as in an amphitheatre. In the middle of it is a round matted stage, of about eighteen or twenty feet diameter, as nearly as my eye can measure it, and rimmed with an edge eight or ten inches in height, to keep the cocks from falling over in their combats. There is a chalk ring in the centre of the matted stage, of, perhaps, a yard diameter, and another chalk mark within it much smaller, which is intended for the setting-to, when the shattered birds are so enfeebled as to have no power of making hostile advances towards each other. This inner mark admits of their being placed beak to beak. A large and rude branched candlestick is suspended low down, immediately over the mat, which is used at the night battles."*

The Tufton Street cockpit was not the only one in London town. Nor was it by any means the first. The eighth Henry of amatory fame was responsible for what, if the historians do not lie, was the earliest London cockpit. He had it built in the purlieus of Whitehall Palace, and it was to this particular cockpit that James the First hied himself on two occasions in each week.

An equally celebrated rendezvous for cockers was the royal pit of Birdcage Walk, where many celebrated fights were staged annually. It was, in fact, with the destruction of this pit in 1816 that the Tufton Street place came into its own. And there were many other famous places where Gamecocks battled to the death. Among the best known were the one in Shoe Lane, visited by Pepys; another in Drury Lane; and yet another in Pickled-Egg Walk. Others were to be found in

---

* *The London Magazine* (November, 1822) Vol. VI. No. XXXV. p. 398.

COCKPIT IN THE YARD OF THE "HAWK AND BUCKLE" INN AT DENBIGH, NORTH WALES. THIS PIT, SCHEDULED AS AN ANCIENT MONUMENT, HAD A SPECTATORS' GALLERY

A ROUGH OUT-OF-DOOR COCKPIT NEAR WINDERMERE; MANY OF THESE STILL EXIST

AN OLD COCKPIT AT HEVERSHAM, WESTMORLAND, BEHIND THE RUINED GRAMMAR SCHOOL WHERE SCHOLARS PAID THEIR "COCK-PENNY"

COCKPIT WITH TWELVE RINGS OF SEATS AT GWENAP, REDRUTH, CORNWALL

Bainbridge Street; in Jewin Street; in Cripplegate; in Old Gravel Lane, near Blackfriars; in St. Georges-in-the-East; in Gray's Inn Lane; at the New Vauxhall Gardens, and in Little Grosvenor Street, Westminster. In many cases the cockpit was combined with some other form of amusement. Thus Malcolm says: "The Bowling-green and Cockpit behind Gray's Inn Gardens were advertised for sale or to let in 1710; but, though the public seem thus to have lost one place of resort, Punch's Opera, under the direction of Powell was opened at the same time at the end of Lichfield Street, where the prices of admission were, boxes 2s., pit 1s., gallery 6d."* Two years before the time of which Malcolm writes this same cockpit had been seriously injured by fire. The circumstances in which this fire occurred were peculiar and tragic. According to a contemporary chronicler "There had been a great Match fought on *Saturday*, and the Weather being hard, two of the Feeders, *Crompton* and *Day*, would stay all Night with their Cocks; when by Negligence their Candle fell among the Straw, which took Fire. In the Morning one Mr. *Newberry*, a great Cocker, sent his two Sons to see his Cocks fed, who wonder'd they saw no Snow upon the Cockpit; when coming thither they saw a great Smoak, and before they cou'd make any Body hear, the place was all on Fire. One of the Feeders was found burnt, only some part of his Body remaining, and the other is missing."† The pit was repaired and reopened the following year. And there was the pit at Endell Street, Long Acre, where the last public cockfight to be held in London was staged. Timbs says:

"The Whitehall Cockpit, after the fire of 1697, was altered into the Privy Council Office—a conversion which has provoked many a lively sally. Hatton describes the cockpit as 'between the gate into King Street, Westminster, and the gate of the banqueting house', the former was designed by Holbein, and known as the Cockpit Gate. The old place had some interesting historical associations. Philip Herbert, Earl of Pembroke and Montgomery, from a window of his apartments in the cockpit, saw his sovereign Charles I, walk from St. James's to the scaffold. Monk, Duke of Albemarle, died here, 1669-70; and Villiers, Duke of

* James Peller Malcolm, *Anecdotes of the Manners and Customs of London During the Eighteenth Century*, second ed., 1810, Vol. II., p. 127.

† Quoted by John Ashton, *Social Life in the Reign of Queen Anne*, Chatto & Windus, 1882, Vol. I, p. 300, from *A Looking-Glass for Swearers*, etc., 1708.

Buckingham, 1673. And here, in the Council Chamber, Guiscard stabbed Harley, Earl of Oxford. The cockpit retained its original name long after the change in its uses."*

Evidence as to the number of cockpits in the London of the seventeenth and eighteenth centuries is provided by the names given to so many places in the metropolis. Gilbey affirms that on consulting a map of London, published in 1761, he found ten Cock Alleys, nine Cock Courts, eight Cock Yards, four Cock Lanes; also "Cock Hill, Cockpit Alley, Cockpit Buildings, Cockpit Street, Court and Yard, Cocks' Rents, and Cockspur Street."† There is evidence, too, that cockfights had at some time or other been staged in the theatres then existent in London. Timbs says: "The original name of the *pit* in our theatres was the cockpit, which seems to imply that cockfighting had been their original destination. One of our oldest London theatres was called the Cockpit; this was the Phoenix, in Drury Lane, the site of which was Cockpit Alley, now corruptly written Pitt Place."‡

Although most of the important mains were fought in the great London cockpits, there were many battles between famous Gamecocks in provincial towns, notably at Newmarket, York, and Carlisle. Of this last-named, we read: "It is said that he [The Earl of Surrey] and Sir James Lowther, in 1785, erected the cockpit, which up to 1876 stood in a court on the west side of Lowther Street, Carlisle. . . . It was octagonal, 40 ft. in diameter, the walls 12 ft. high, and it was 45 ft. in height to the top of the octagonal roof. In 1829, it was occupied by Messrs. Burgess and Hayton, as a brass and iron foundry, and afterwards was well known as Dand's Smithy."§

Atkinson refers to the cockpit opened on April 6, 1826 at Melton Mowbray as being "probably the best equipped cockpit in the provinces."‖ "Liverpool has many sites of ancient cockpits like Shaw's Brow (William Brown Street)."¶ Welshpool, in the county of Montgomeryshire boasted the possession of a cockpit. It was situated on the

---

* John Timbs, *Romance of London*, Bentley, London, 1865. Vol. II., p. 240.
† Sir Walter Gilbey, *Sport in the Olden Time*, Vinton & Co., London, 1912, p. 76.
‡ John Timbs, *Romance of London*, 1865.
§ *Transactions of the Cumberland and Westmorland Antiquarian & Archaeological Society*, Vol. IX.
‖ Herbert Atkinson, *Cock-Fighting and Game Fowl*, 1938, p. 70.
¶ *Liverpool Evening Express*, March 7, 1952.

site now occupied by the Post Office and the National Provincial Bank, and consisted of a brick building, octagonal in shape, and having a gallery containing seats for the principal spectators.

Many of these provincial cockpits were improvised or crudely constructed affairs. The outdoor pits were usually surrounded by a wall or a fence; the indoor arenas were housed in sheds or other outbuildings.

The modern cockpit, in any country where cockfighting is not a surreptitious affair, probably differs little from the London cockpit of the eighteenth century. The floor on which the birds fight is now, as it was then, a matter of primary importance. Where the fights are staged indoors, as they mostly are, a hard floor is made by pounding down a mixture of earth and clay to make an even surface. Sometimes the floor is carpeted or covered with matting as in the old days.

As was to be expected, a rigorous set of rules and regulations governing cockfighting had to be devised and enforced. It was, of course, necessary and advisable that every effort should be made to ensure that no cock had an unfair advantage over his antagonist, and to this end the birds were matched for weight, etc. Then it was essential that rules governing the conduct of the setters-to or handlers of the combatants should be clearly stated; that there should be precise stipulations respecting the duties of the person appointed to act as teller of the law or umpire, and that the mode of deciding the outcome of battles where there was room for dispute should be rigidly defined.

In the first half of the eighteenth century, as is apparent from the rules published by Reginald Heber in 1751, much attention was given to the conduct of the spectators. Whether the behaviour of these patrons of the cockpit improved in the decades that followed, or whether for some unexplained reason it was deemed advisable to deal with this matter in another way, is not clear, but in later regulations additional attention was given to the actual contests themselves. The following set of rules which may be taken as applicable at the leading London cockpits, are taken from the 1808 edition of Hoyle's *Games*:

"*General Orders and Rules for Cocking*: On the weighing morning, that person whose chance is to weigh last, is to set his cocks and number his pens, both main and byes, and leave the key of the pens upon the weighing table (or the other party may put a lock on the door), before any cock is put into the scale; and after the first pack of cocks is weighed, a person appointed by him that weighed first shall go into the other pens to see that no other cocks are weighed but what are so set and numbered, provided they are within the articles of weight that the match specifies; if not, to take the following cock or cocks until the whole number of main and bye cocks are weighed through. After they are all weighed, proceed as soon as possible to match them, beginning at the least weight first, and so on; and equal weights or nearest weights to be separated, provided by that separation a greater number of battles can be made; all blanks are to be filled up on the weighing day, and the battles divided and struck off for each day's play, as agreed on, and the cocks that weigh the least are to fight the first day, and so upwards.

"At the time agreed on by both parties, the cocks that are to fight the first battle are brought upon the pit by the feeders or their helpers; and after being examined to see whether they answer the marks and colours specified in the match-bill, they are given to the setters-to, who, after chopping them in hand, give them to the masters of the match (who always sit opposite to each other), when they turn them down upon the mat; and the setters-to are not to touch them, except they either hang in the mat, in each other, or get close to the edge of the pit, until they have left off fighting, while a person can tell forty. When both cocks leave off fighting, until one of the setters-to, or a person appointed for telling the law, can tell forty gradually; then the setters-to are to make the nearest way to their cocks, and as soon as they have taken them up, to carry them into the middle of the pit, and immediately deliver them on their legs beak to beak, and not touch them any more until they have refused fighting, so long as the teller of the law can tell ten, without they are on their backs, or hung in each other, or in the mat; then they are to set-to again in the same manner as before, and continue it till one cock refuses fighting ten several times, one after another, when it is that cock's battle that fought within the law. But it sometimes happens that both cocks refuse fighting while the law is telling; when this happens, a fresh cock is to be hovelled, and brought upon the mat as soon as possible, and the setters-to are to toss up which cock is to be set-to first, and he that gets the chance is to choose. Then the cock who is to be set-to last must be taken up, but not carried off the pit; next setting the hovelled cock down to the other, five separate times, telling ten between each setting-to, and then the same to that which had been taken up; and if one fights and the other refuses, it is a battle to the fighting-cock; but if both fight, or both refuse, it is a drawn battle. The reason of setting-to five times to each cock, is, that the ten times setting-to being the long law, so on their both refusing, the law is to be equally divided between them.

"Another way of deciding a battle, is, if any person offers to lay ten pounds to a crown, and no person takes it until the law-teller tells forty, and calls out three separate times, 'will any one take it?' and if no one does, it is the cock's battle the odds are laid on, and the setters-to are not to touch the cocks during the time the forty is telling, without either cock is hung in the mat, or on his back, or hung together. If a cock should die before the long law is told out, although he fought in the law, and the other did not, he loses his battle.

"There are frequent disputes in setting-to in the long law, for often both cocks refuse fighting until four or five, or more or less times, are told; then they sometimes begin telling from that cock's fighting, and counting but once refused, but they should continue their number on, until one cock has refused ten times; for when the law is begun to be told, it is for both cocks; and if one cock fights within the long law, and the other not, it is a battle to the cock that fought, counting from the first setting-to. All disputes about bets, or the battle being won or lost, ought to be decided by the spectators.

"The crowing and mantling of a cock, or fighting at the setter-to's hand before he is put to the other cock, or breaking from his antagonist, is not allowed as a fight."

Osbaldiston, writing at the close of the eighteenth century, gives four important cockpit laws, thus: "(1) In setting a cock, none are to be upon the clod but the two setters chosen for that office, and as soon as the cocks are set beak to beak in the middle of the clod, and there be left by the setters, if the set cock do not strike in counting 20 and six times 10, and 20 after all, then the battle is lost. (2) If he strikes, then they are to begin counting again. (3) In betting, if any offer a mark to a groat, or forty shillings to one, or ten pounds to five shillings, if any take the wager, then the cock is to be set, and they are to fight it out. (4) 'Done and done' is a wager, or sufficient betting, when the cocks are cast in the clod or in fighting."*

It was customary for an agreement to be signed by the owners of the contesting cocks, and duly witnessed before the fight took place. The terms of such an agreement varied slightly at different cockpits, but the one given below, which is taken from Sketchley's admirable little book, *The Cocker*, may be taken as the standard form.

"Articles of Agreement made the . . . day of 18. . . between W. S. and J. C. First, the said parties have agreed, that each of them shall produce, shew and weigh at the . . . . . Cockpit, on the . . . . day of . . . . . . next, beginning at the hour of seven o'clock on the said morning, ... cocks, none to be less than three pounds six ounces, nor more than four pounds eight ounces; and as many of each party's cocks as come within . . . . . ounces of the other party's cocks, shall fight for . . . . . . guineas a battle—that is, ... guineas each cock; in as equal divisions as the battle can be divided into, as pits or day's play, at the cockpit aforesaid; and that the party's cocks that win the greatest number of battle matches out of the number aforesaid, shall be entitled to the sum of . . . . guineas as odd battle money; and the sum is to be made stakes into the hands of Mr. . . . . before any cocks are pitted, in equal shares between the parties aforesaid; and the parties further agree to produce, shew, and weigh, on the said weighing day, ... cocks, for bye-battles, subject to the same as the main cocks before-mentioned, and those to be added to the number of main cocks unmatched; and as many of them as come within one ounce of each other shall fight for two guineas each battle, to be equally divided as can be, and added to each pit or day's play with the main of cocks— and it is also agreed, that the balance of the battle money shall be paid at the end of each pit or day's play, and to fight in fair reputed silver spurs, and with fair hackles, and to be subject to all the usual

* William Augustus Osbaldiston, *The British Sportsman*, London, 1792, p. 113.

The Rules and Order of Cocking

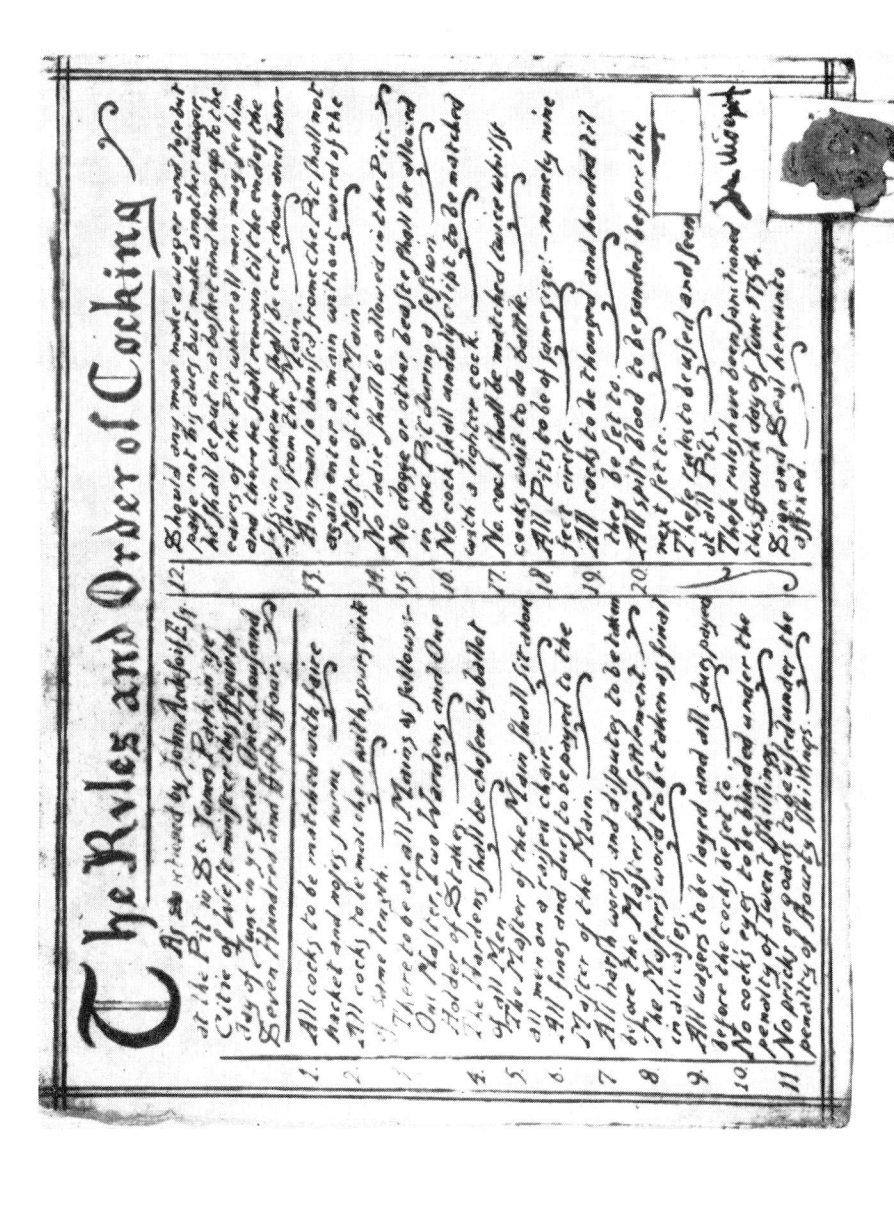

As reviewed by John Andsoll Esq. at the Pit in St. James Park in ye Citie of Westminster this fifteenth day of June in ye year Our Thousand Seven Hundred and fifty four.

1. All cocks to be matched with faire hackel and not shorne.
2. All cocks to be matched with spurrs gink of some length.
3. There to be at all Maines as followes:— One Master, Two Wardens, and One Holder of Stakes.
4. The Wardens shall be chosen by ballot of all Men.
5. The Master of the Main shall sit about all men on a raised chair.
6. All fines and duty to be payed to the Master of the Main.
7. All hard words and dispute to be taken before the Master for settlement.
8. The Master's word to be taken as finall in all cases.
9. All wagers to be layed and all duty payed before the cocks defight.
10. No cocks eggs to be blinded under the penalty of Twenty shillings.
11. No prick or gouch to be used under the penalty of fourty Shillings.
12. Should any man make a wager and ye cocks have not by dieing but make another wager it shall be put in ye other and hung up to ye edge of the Pit where all men may see him and then the fust cock to be won till ye end of the fifticen when he shall be cut downe and han-g'd from the Main.
13. Any man so handled from the Pit shall not againe enter a main without word of the Master of the Main.
14. No lodie shall be allowed in the Pit.
15. No clogge or other bruise shall be allowed in the Pit during fighten.
16. No cock shall unduly slipt to be matched with a higher cock.
17. No cock shall be matched twice whilst cocks waits to do battle.
18. All Pits to be of squarrige—namely nine feet circle.
19. All cocks to be charged and hooded e'er they be set to.
20. All spilt blood to be sanded before the next set to.

These rules to be dressed and sette at all Pits.

These rules above are mentioned this fourth day of June 1754.
Sign and Seal hereunto affixed

J. Wright

RULES AND ORDER OF COCKING, AT ST. JAMES' PARK, WESTMINSTER

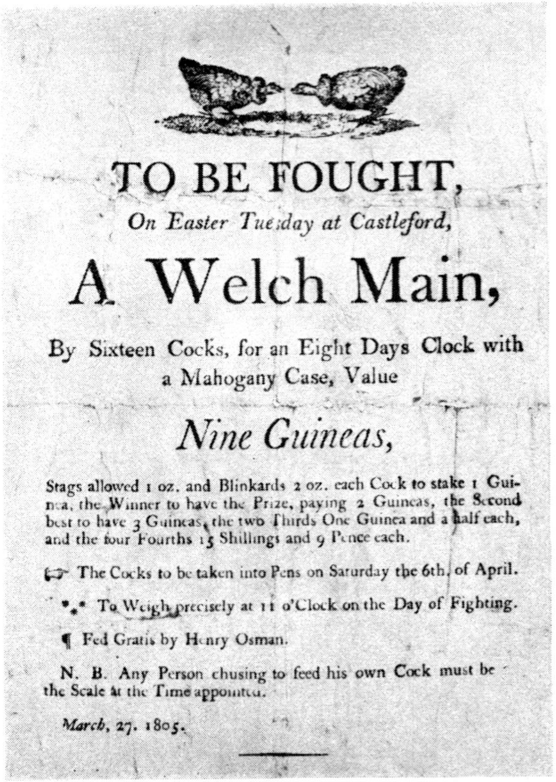

TO BE FOUGHT,

On Easter Tuesday at Castleford,

A Welch Main,

By Sixteen Cocks, for an Eight Days Clock with a Mahogany Case, Value

Nine Guineas,

Stags allowed 1 oz. and Blinkards 2 oz. each Cock to stake 1 Guinea, the Winner to have the Prize, paying 2 Guineas, the Second best to have 3 Guineas, the two Thirds One Guinea and a half each, and the four Fourths 15 Shillings and 9 Pence each.

☞ The Cocks to be taken into Pens on Saturday the 6th of April.

⁂ To Weigh precisely at 11 o'Clock on the Day of Fighting.

¶ Fed Gratis by Henry Osman.

N. B. Any Person chusing to feed his own Cock must be at the Scale at the Time appointed.

March, 27. 1805.

POSTER ADVERTISING A WELSH MAIN

THE TRADE CARD OF A SILVER COCKSPUR MAKER

rules of cockfighting as is practised in London and Newmarket—and the profit of the pit or day's play to be equally divided between the said parties, after all charges are paid and satisfied that usually are thereupon.

Witness our hands this . . . . day of 181. . .

W.S.
J.C.

Witness. . . . .

On some occasions, however, fights were staged in which there was no matching of the combatants as to weight, size, etc. In such instances the birds were often outsize cocks and there would probably have been difficulty in matching them. The birds which figured in these battles were termed "Shakebags", and apropos of the origin of this term Dr. Wilde says they are so termed from an old custom of certain cockers "who are great admirers of large Cocks, because they may be fought at a venture, without the trouble of Matching, and their way is to steep their own Brains in Brandy, till they are not only past judging of a Cock's size, but also past handling of him too, wherefore they neither see the Cock they are to fight with beforehand, nor lay a hand upon their own, after he is brought into the Pit, but take the Bag by the bottom, and shake the Cock out at the Mouth upon the Pit, and so let him go against his adversary, from which custom they are called 'Shakebags' here in England."*

The stakes in these battles between individual cocks were often high, at any rate for those days when the pound had suffered neither debasement nor devaluation. Even bigger money, however, changed hands when the "odd" battle, as it was termed, was fought. This particular fight concluded the main, which consisted of an "odd" number of individual battles. Thus two competing cockers would agree to match, say, 11 cocks each, the stakes to be ten guineas each battle, and twenty guineas the odd one, i.e. the eleventh. On other occasions the stakes agreed upon might be ten guineas a battle in a series of contests, and fifty guineas in addition to the winner of the main, i.e. the largest proportion of the ten battles.

* R. Howlett, *The Royal Pastime of Cock-fighting*, London, 1709, p. 21.

In the *Transactions of the Cumberland and Westmorland Antiquarian & Archaeological Society* (Vol. IX) we read that in the year 1768, "at York, during the Races, a main of Cocks was fought between Mr. Hardwick & Mr. Lord for ten guineas a Battle, and two hundred guineas the Main, which was won by the former by several battles." Again, in 1783, at Carlisle "during the Races a Main of Cocks was fought between the Earl of Surrey & A. R. Bowes, Esq., for ten guineas a Battle & one hundred guineas the Main, which was won by the latter."

Sir Walter Gilbey gives several instances. Thus in 1727, at Weston in Cheshire, a match between a Mr. Streatham and a Mr. Poole, in which each cocker staged 21 cocks, the stakes being 6 guineas each battle, and 20 guineas the odd; followed by a return match held at Leek in Staffordshire.* Pierce Egan tells of a match at Newcastle "for twenty sovereigns between Parker and Reed, feeders, and won by the latter, after a hard contest." The cock which Parker had put into the ring, he goes on to say, "came round so soon after that his party made a second match, to come off on the following Monday, for a like sum, which was again won by Reed, after a severe battle, a circumstance perhaps altogether unknown in the annals of cocking."†

An advertisement appearing in the *Northwich Chronicle* in the week preceding Chester Races, 1826, reads: "Cocking. A Grand Main of Cocks will be fought during the Five Race Days, between R. F. Benson, Esq., and J. Bellyse, Esq., for 20 gns. the Battle and 500 gns. the Main. Brown and Phillips, Feeders."‡ Also *The Birmingham Post* refers to a Whitsuntide match at Duddeston Hall, lasting three days, where "Forty-one cocks fought on each side at ten guineas a battle and 200 guineas the odd battle—and if this were not enough there were 21 cocks on each side for 'bye-battles' at two guineas each contest."§

Sometimes matches were arranged in which one town pitted a collection of its best fighting-cocks against those of another town; on other occasions counties challenged each other in a similar manner. Apart from exceptional instances, in these cases the stakes were higher than where the rivals were individuals. Gilbey gives a case where, in 1727,

---

* Sir Walter Gilbey, *Sport in the Olden Time*, p. 57.
† Pierce Egan, *Book of Sports*, p. 147.
‡ Quoted in the *Northwich Chronicle*, March 15, 1952.
§ *The Birmingham Post*, March 8, 1952.

the town of Preston matched its fighting-cocks against those of Wakefield, for ten guineas the battle and 180 guineas the odd; and as an example of one county challenging another, the main, fought in 1750, between Gloucestershire and Wiltshire, each staging 41 cocks, with stakes of ten guineas a battle, and two hundred guineas the main.*

A somewhat unusual contest, mentioned by Ashton, was held in the reign of Queen Anne, in which were pitted cocks owned by "'the Gentlemen of Essex against all the rest of Great Britain, for 10 Guineas a Battle and 500 Guineas the Odd Battle.' These," says this writer, "were the highest stakes ever publicly advertised in Queen Anne's reign, whatever might have been done at private matches—as, for instance, in the Tatler's Club (*Tatler*, 132), Sir Jeoffrey Notch, their chairman, would talk about his favourite old Gamecock Gauntlett, 'upon whose head, the Knight, in his youth, had won five hundred pounds, and lost two thousand'."†

In the pages of *The Sporting Magazine* there are for the finding numerous references to such contests. Thus, in the issue for July 1830, we read:

"The gentlemen cockers of the Isle of Wight and those of East Sussex fought a main of cocks at Halnaker on the 26th of May, twenty-one on each side, for four sovereigns a battle, and fifty the odd—Cook (with Hall) feeder for the Island, and Shaw (with Cobden) feeder for Sussex. In the first in-go Sussex won five out of six battles; but in the second the Island took the lead, and kept it till the last battle, which, after an hour's contest, was won by Sussex, and ended a tie main, each party gaining seven battles. The byes were all won by the Isle of Wight cocks.

A main of cocks was fought during Stafford Race-week, between the Gentlemen of Staffordshire (Jones, feeder) and those of Warwickshire (Hadley, feeder), for five sovereigns a battle, and 100 sovereigns the main."

Again in the June 1831 issue, appears the following entry:

"A grand main of cocks was fought at the New Royal Cockpit,

---

* Sir Walter Gilbey, *Sport in the Olden Time*, p. 59.
† John Ashton, *Social Life in the Reign of Queen Anne*, Vol. I, p. 301.

Little Grosvenor-street, Millbank, Westminster, on Monday the 25th of April, and five following days, between the Gentlemen of Northamptonshire (Fleming, feeder) and the Gentlemen of Kent (Shaw, feeder), for 20 sovereigns a battle, and 500 sovereigns the main.

A main of cocks was fought on the 27th and 28th of April at Weshampton, near Ellesmere, Salop, between the Gentlemen of Cheshire (Jones, feeder) and the Gentlemen of Shropshire (Hines, feeder)."

Turning the pages of this illuminating periodical, we find additional accounts which show how keen was the rivalry between the various counties. I cull the following from the issues of the magazine for the months of August and September, 1830:

"During the Race-week at Buxton, a main was fought between the Gentlemen of Staffordshire (Woodcock, feeder) and those of Nottinghamshire (Randle, feeder), consisting of thirty-one mains and eight byes.

A long main was fought during the Races at Newcastle, between the Gentlemen of Northumberland and Yorkshire for 10 guineas a battle and 200 guineas the main, which was won by the latter.

Stamford—During the races a main was fought between the Gentlemen of Lincolnshire and Nottinghamshire (Weightman, feeder), and those of Essex and Suffolk (Hardwick, feeder), for 5 sovereigns and 100 sovereigns the main.

Huntingdon—In the Race-week a main was fought between the Gentlemen of Huntingdonshire (Fleming, feeder) and those of Cambridgeshire (Shadbolt, feeder), for 10 sovereigns a battle, and 200 sovereigns the odds. Two in-goes each morning; thirty mains, eleven byes."

Finally, let me cite a report in the issue for September 1834:

"A main of cocks was fought at the Hotel Pit, Stamford, during the Race-week, between the Gentlemen of Lincolnshire (Weightman, feeder) and those of Northamptonshire (Shaw, feeder), for 10 sovereigns a battle, and 100 the odd; nineteen mains and five byes."

The *Walsall Times* (March 29, 1952) mentions an eighteenth century announcement of a cockfight reading: "This is to give notice that there will be a main of cocks fought at John Hancox's at the Star Inn, Stourbridge, between the Gentlemen of Stourbridge and the Gentlemen of Walsall for two guineas the battle, and forty the main." In the *Worcester Journal* (March 12, 1752) appeared the following announcement: "A Cock Match to be fought at Mr. Woodcock's, at the Hop-Pole, in the City of Worcester, between the Gentlemen of Herefordshire and Gloucestershire, on the one Side, and the Gentlemen of Worcester, on the other: To show Thirty-one Cocks, on each side, for Five Guineas a Battle, and Fifty Guineas the Main, and Twenty-one for Bye-Battles, for Two Guineas a Battle: To weigh on Monday the 16th instant, and fight the three following Days." Again, according to *The Birmingham Post* (March 8, 1952), there was an occasion when an advertisement appeared respecting a main which was to be staged "at Duddeston Hall between the 'Gentlemen of Warwickshire and Worcestershire' for four guineas a battle and forty guineas the main."

These contests, when not connected with Race-meetings, were usually held at the time of some festival or holiday. Thus Easter and Whitsuntide were favourite occasions. The following announcement, writes Langford,* appeared in a Birmingham newspaper dated June 1, 1747:

"Birmingham Cock Match, 1747—On Whitsun Monday, the 8th of June, will be shewn at Duddeston Hall, near Birmingham, in Warwickshire, Forty-one Cocks on each Side, for a Match to be fought the three following Days, betwixt the Gentlemen of Warwickshire, Worcestershire, and Shropshire, for Ten Guineas a Battle, and Two Hundred the Odd Battle; and also Twenty-one Cocks on each Side for Bye Battles, which Bye Battles are to be fought for Two Guineas each Battle."

Another advertisement was as follows:

"On Monday, the 11th of April, 1748, being Easter Monday, will be a match of Cocks weigh'd to fight the three following Days at Duddeston Hall, near Birmingham, each Party to weigh Forty-one

---

* John Alfred Langford, *A Century of Birmingham Life*, Birmingham, 1868. Vol. I., p. 43.

Cocks, for ten Guineas a Battle, and two Hundred the Main; and each Party to weigh Twenty Cocks for Bye Battles, for Five Guineas a Battle, each Cock to give and take Half an Ounce. The Gentlemen of Worcester and Herefordshire against the Gentlemen of Warwickshire and Staffordshire."*

This same authority states that in the middle of the eighteenth century notices and reports of cockfighting were more numerous and were given more space than most contemporary events; and it is to his interesting book that I am indebted for the following report of a cockfight and the anecdote attached to it.

"The second of the 7 Years Main subsisting between the Gentlemen of Birmingham and Bridgnorth was decided in Favour of the Birmingham Gentlemen, at Duddeston Hall, in the Whitsun Week, by 8 Battles ahead in the Main and 14 in the Byes: What was very remarkable, out of 61 Cocks weighed, 58 were matched. Next Year the 3rd Main will be fought at the Crown in Bridgnorth in Whitsun Week.

At the above Cocking, a gay young Fellow, of a very good Family near Bridgnorth, having lost all his Money (which was a considerable Sum) apply'd to a Recruiting Officer, and enlisted himself; but as soon as he had received the Advance-Money, he returned to the Cockpit, and again deeply engaged in the Bets, and being so fortunate as to win between nine and ten Pounds more than he had before lost, quitted the Pit, and immediately repaired to the Officer to whom he had enlisted, came to terms with him for a Discharge, and then returned home."†

---

* Langford, op. cit., p. 44.
† Ibid., p. 89.

CHAPTER VII

THE COCKFIGHT

The cockfight as it was known to eighteenth-century aristocracy was a development of the combat between two pugnacious male fowls with which every poultry-keeper or country-dweller is familiar. Were it not for this natural propensity for fighting which the male birds of many breeds of poultry possess, the cockpit would never have been created by man, and the cheers and cries of the spectators would never have punctuated the deadly blows of cocks meeting in mortal combat.

In its earliest stages, of course, a cockfight arranged and supervised by man was nothing more than the bringing together of two pugnacious male fowls. In the majority of cases they would fight, and in so doing provide a spectacle calculated to give pleasure to the majority of the onlookers. For, leaving aside the commercial aspects of organised cockfighting, it is a fact that in most cases where two male fowls happen, for any reason or in any circumstances, to engage in battle in the presence of a number of men or boys, no effort will be made by anyone other than the owner or owners of one or both birds, to stop the fight. I make this assertion as a result of my own experience. In my childhood days I witnessed many such combats, filling the role of spectator. In early manhood, when I was a breeder and exhibitor of poultry myself, and in a position to understand to the full the injuries and suffering which the combatants, both victor and vanquished, inevitably suffered, I observed, on occasions not a few, the expressions and sounds indicative of disapproval which followed my intervention and stoppage of the fights. These experiences have led me to believe that the majority of men have always enjoyed the spectacle of cocks fighting. This enjoyment was undoubtedly responsible for the genesis of commercial cockfighting and the popularity it achieved in Britain during the seventeenth, eighteenth and early nineteenth centuries, and which it enjoys today in America and other countries.

With the development of cockfighting as an organised sport, many changes occurred in the way in which the fights were conducted. Even where the battling birds used the weapons with which nature had endowed them, and fought in the open-air, rules were, as we have seen, devised for these contests. Birds were matched for size and weight, their wings and tails were trimmed, their combs dubbed; but, most important of all, various types of combats were arranged, which, in some cases, altogether changed the character of cockfighting as a natural characteristic of the Game Fowl, an aspect about which I shall have more to say in another chapter of this work.

The only persons allowed inside the pit itself were the teller and the two "setters", as they were called, who looked after the combatants to the extent allowed by the rules and regulations of the cockpit. For instance, these "setters" were allowed to disentangle the birds in the event of the spurs of one cock having got caught in the feathers of his antagonist, or in the matting or other covering of the floor; of placing them face to face with each other after the one or both had gravitated or retreated to the boundaries of the pit. Also, when the two combatants showed no inclination to fight, but danced around or stood and glared at each other for any inordinate length of time, after the teller had slowly counted up to a number prescribed in the rules, the "setters-to" could then seize their respective birds and place them beak to beak in the centre of the arena.

In every battle to the death, the bird which emerged on his feet or living was adjudged the victor, even if in every respect the dead warrior had proved himself the better or more courageous fighter, and had succumbed to a chance blow. On rare occasions only was a cock allowed to fight more than once a day. Nor did any owner of fighting-cocks permit two of his own birds to fight each other.

At all the cockpits it was usual to have what were termed long and short mains. By a main was meant a contest between a given number of cocks on each side, matched in pairs. It was customary for the number of these pairs to be an uneven one, so that however close the contest, it was certain that one of the rival competitors would win more battles than the other. Thus the minimum number of battles agreed upon would be three, and above this there was, within reason, no limit to the number. Stakes were competed for in each battle, and there was an additional stake or a prize for the winner of most battles, that is the winner of the main.

What was termed the "Devonshire Main" seems to have been peculiar to the south-western counties of England. Gilbey says: "In this the matches were fought by 'set weight'. A pair of birds each of 4 lbs. were matched, then a pair of 4 lbs. 1 oz., then a pair of 4 lbs. 2 ozs., and so on, each pair weighing an ounce each more than the last till the maximum 5 lbs. 3 ozs. was reached."*

A type of cockfight known as the Welsh Main, after the country of its origin, became very popular. It was this particular form which Pegge referred to as "a disgrace to us as Englishmen." Any number, ranging from sixteen to thirty-two fighting cocks, of approximately the same weights, were matched in pairs, and the fight began. It was a battle to the death in each case. Supposing the entries numbered thirty-two birds, the sixteen winners of the initial round were then pitted against each other; then the eight survivors once more entered the arena; following this series of battles, the four survivors fought to the death; after which there was one more battle which left the last cock to stand on his legs, bloody, battered and probably near to death himself, winner of the main and his owner richer by the stakes. The tale is told of one such famous contest in which the final battle between the surviving rivals resulted in the victor, immediately after dealing out a lethal stroke to his opponent, himself falling dead in the pit.

Another equally barbaric, and perhaps even more popular type of fight, was termed the "Battle Royal". Any number of fighting-cocks were placed in the pit simultaneously. There was no matching in regard to weight or anything else. The contest was open to all comers. The conflict can best be described as a free-for-all fight in which the birds attacked one another indiscriminately. As can well be imagined the scene was a sanguinary one, blood flowing freely as the wicked, savagely-wielded spurs found their marks. The fight went on until, with one exception, all the contestants were dead or dying. This survivor was adjudged the winner.

* Sir Walter Gilbey, *Sport in the Olden Time*, 1912.

There are for the finding in contemporary literature many accounts by eye-witnesses of the cockfights which occurred in the principal arenas of eighteenth or early nineteenth century England. These accounts are of considerable interest and value, as they enable us to get some idea of what actually took place. One of the best of these is to be found in *The London Magazine* (November 1822). It is a description (in the form of a letter to a friend, one Russell Powell) by Edward Herbert, of a scene in the famous London cockpit at Tufton Street, Westminster.

"When we entered there were very few persons in the pit; for, as the gentlemen of the match were not seated, the principal followers of the sport were beguiling the time at a public-house opposite the cockpit. A tall, shambling, ill-dressed fellow was damping the mat with a mop, which he constantly dipped in a pail of water, and sparingly and most carefully sprinkled around him. This was to make it soft for the birds, and to prevent their slipping. We took our seats at the foot of a flight of stairs, that went up into one of the coops—judging that that would be the best spot for seeing as much as was to be seen. There are two 'tiring rooms'—of course for the separate sides—one room, or more properly, coop, is up the flight of stairs I have mentioned; the other is beneath it, and has an entrance without the pit. At this time my friend Tom's friend Mr. D . . . . . arrived. . . . . I begged to know something of the rules and regulations of cocking. He turned-to them, in high feather, on the instant. The birds, Russell (I am saying after him) are weighed and matched—and then marked and numbered. The descriptions are carefully set down in order that the cock may not be changed; and the lightest cocks fight first in order. The key of the pens in which the cocks are set and numbered, is left on the weighing-table on the day of weighing; or the opposite party may, if he pleases, put a lock on the door. The utmost possible care, in short, is taken that the matched birds shall fight, and no substitutes be intruded. Mr. D . . . . . . next gave me a very particular description of the modes of setting-to, of terminating difficult battles, of betting, and of parting the entangled birds; but as I really could not very clearly follow his rapid and spirited explanation, and as I am about to relate to you a battle as I myself saw it, I will not detain you here with my imperfect detail of his very perfect description. . . .

THE ROYAL COCKPIT

From the aquatint by Rowlandson and Pugin in R. Ackermann, *The Microcosm of London*, 1808

THE COCKPIT, BY WILLIAM HOGARTH, 1759

The scene is probably laid at Newmarket, and in this motley group of peers, pickpockets, jockeys, gentlemen —gamblers of every denomination, Lord Albemarle Bertie is the principal figure

"I was continuing my enquiries into the characters around me, when a young man of very slang, slight, but extremely prepossessing appearance, passed me, dressed in tight kerseymeres, with a handkerchief round his knee, neat white cotton stockings, small shoes, a blue check waiter-looking jacket, short about the waist, and a gay 'kerchief knowingly tied on his neck. He was really a clean handsome-faced young fellow, with thin but acute and regular features, small light whiskers, and with his hair closely cut, and neatly and 'cutely combed down upon his forehead. He had scarcely passed me before I felt something rustle and chuckle by my elbow; and turning round, saw a stout plump old ostler-looking man carry a white bag past me, which by the struggle and vehement motion inside, I guessed to be one of the brave birds for the battle. The two men stepped upon the mat, and the hubbub was huge and instantaneous. 'Two to one on Nash!' 'A guinea on Nash!' 'Nash a crown!' Only sounds like these were heard (for the bets are laid on the setters-to), till the noise aroused a low muscular-brooding chuckle in the bag, which seemed to show that the inmate was rousing into anger even at the voice of man!

"From the opposite door a similar procession entered. The setter-to (Fleming by name) was dressed much in the same manner, but he appeared less attractive than young Nash (the name of the young man I have just mentioned). He certainly was not so smart a fellow, but there was an honesty and a neatness in his manner and look, which pleased me much. The chuckle of the cock in the one bag was answered deeply and savagely from the other—and the straw seemed spurned in the narrow cell, as though the spirit that struck it would not be contained.

"Nash's bag was carefully untied, and Nash himself took out one of the handsomest birds I think I ever beheld. I must have leave to try *my* hand at a description of a Gamecock! He was a red and black bird—slim, masculine, trimmed—yet with feathers glossy, as though the sun shone only upon his nervous wings. His neck arose out of the bag, snakelike—terrible—as if it would stretch upward to the ceiling; his body followed, compact, strong, and beautiful, and his long dark-blue sinewy legs come forth, clean, handsome, shapely, determined, iron-like! The silver spur was on each heel, of an inch and a half in length—tied on in the most delicate and neat manner. His large vigorous beak showed acquiline—eagle-like; and his black dilating eyes took in all around him, and shone so intensely brilliant, that they looked like jewels. Their light was that of thoughtful, sedate and savage courage! His comb was cut close—his neck trimmed—his wings clipped, pointed, and strong. The feathers on his back were of the very glossiest red, and appeared to be the only ones which were left untouched; for the tail was docked triangularwise like a hunter's. The gallant bird clucked defiance—and looked as if he 'had in him something dangerous!' Nash gave him to Fleming, who held him up above his head—examined his beak—his wings—his legs—while a person read to him the description of the bird from paper—and upon finding all correct, he delivered the rich feathered warrior back to Nash, and proceeded to produce his own bird for a similar examination.

"But I must speak of the senior Nash—the old man—the feeder. When again may I have an opportunity of describing him? and what ought a paper upon cocking to be accounted worth if it fail to contain some sketch, however slight, of old Nash? He wore a smock-frock, and was clumsily though potently built; his shoulders being ample, and of a rotundity resembling a wool-pack. His legs were not equal to his bulk. He was unconversational almost to a fault—and never made any the slightest remark that did not appertain to cocks and cocking. His narrow, damp, colourless eye twinkled with a cold satisfaction when a bird of promise made good work on the mat; and sometimes, though seldom, he was elevated into the proffer of a moderate bet—but generally he leaned over the rails of a small gallery, running parallel with his coop, and, stooping attentively toward the pit, watched the progress of the battle. I made a remark to Tom and Mr. D . . . . ., that I thought him extremely like a cock. Tom was intent upon Fleming, and could not hear me; but Mr. D . . . . . was delighted at the observation, which seemed to him one of some aptitude. Old Nash's beaked nose drawn close down over his mouth—his red forehead and gills—his round body—and blue thin legs; and his silver grey, scanty, feathery hair lying like a plumage over his head—all proved him cock-like! This man, thought I, has been cooped up in pens, or penned up in coops, until he has become shaped, coloured, mannered like the bird he has been feeding. I should scarcely have been surprised if Mr. D . . . . . had told me that old Nash crowed when the light first dawned over the ancient houses of Tufton Street, on a summer morning! I warrant me he pecked bread and milk to some tune, and perchance slept upon a perch!

"But Fleming lifted his bird from the bag, and my whole mind was directed his way. This was a yellow-bodied black-winged handsome cock—seemingly rather slight, but elastic and muscular. He was restless at the sight of his antagonist, but quite silent—and old Nash examined him most carefully by the paper, delivering him up to Fleming upon finding him answer to his description. The setters-to then smoothed their birds, handled them—wetted their fingers and moistened their bandaged ankles where the spurs were fastened—held them up opposite to each other—and thus pampered their courage, and prepared them for the combat.

"The mat was cleared of all persons except Fleming and young Nash. The betting went on vociferously. The setters-to taunted the birds with each other's presence—allowed them to strike at each other at a distance—put them on the mat facing each other—encouraged and fed their crowning and mantling until they were nearly dangerous to hold—and then loosed them against each other, for the fatal fight.

"The first terrific dart into attitude was indeed strikingly grand and beautiful—and the wary sparring, watching, dodging, for the first cut, was extremely curious. They were beak-point to beak-point—until they dashed up in one tremendous flirt—mingling their powerful rustling wings and nervous heels in one furious confined mass. The leap —the fire—the passion of strength, the *certaminis gaudia*—were fierce and loud! The parting was another kind of thing in every way. I can compare the sound of the first flight to nothing less than that of a wet umbrella forced suddenly open. The separation was death-like. The yellow or rather the ginger bird staggered out of the close—drooping— dismantled—bleeding! He was *struck*! Fleming and Nash severally took their birds, examined them for a moment, and then set them again opposite to each other. The handling of the cocks was as delicate as if they had been made of foam, froth, or any other most perishable matter.

F

Fleming's bird staggered towards his opponent, but he was hit dreadfully —and ran like a drunken man, tottering on his breast, sinking back on his tail!—while Nash's, full of fire and irritated courage, gave the finishing stroke that clove every particle of life in twain. The brave bird, thus killed, dropped at once from the 'gallant bearing and proud mien', to the relaxed, draggled, motionless object that lay in bleeding ruin on the mat. My heart sickened within me! Can this be sport? thought I! Is satisfaction to be reaped from this pampered and profligate butchery? I sighed and looked thoughtful—when the tumult of the betters startled me into a consciousness of the scene at which I was present, and made me feel how poorly timed was thought amid the characters around me.

"The victor cock was carried by me in all his pride—slightly scarred —but evidently made doubly fierce and muscular by the short encounter he had been engaged in. He seemed to have grown to double the size! His eyes were larger. The paying backward and forward of money, won and lost, occupied the time until the two Nashes again descended with a new victim; and then the usual noise—betting, clucking, and murder followed. I will not shock you with any further recital of battles, which varied in cruelty and duration, but invariably terminated in death to one side.

"Sometimes the first blow was fatal—at another time the contest was long and doubtful, and the cocks showed all the obstinate courage, weariness, distress, and breathlessness, which mark the struggles of experienced pugilists. I saw the beak open, the tongue palpitate—the wing drag on the mat. I noticed the legs tremble, and the body topple over upon the breast—the eye grow dim—and even a perspiration break out upon the feathers of the back. When a battle lasted long, and the cocks lay helpless near or upon each other—one of the feeders counted ten, and then the birds were separated and set-to at the chalk. If the beaten bird does not fight while forty is counted, and the other pecks or shows signs of battle, the former is declared conquered."

This description, it will be noted, was from the pen of one who was neither a cocker nor a poultry fancier; in other words, it presents the scene as depicted by the ordinary observer. Daniel Defoe, another independent observer, writing in the early days of the eighteenth century, has this to say:

"A cockfight is the very model of an amphitheatre of the ancients. The cock fights here in the arena, as the beasts did formerly among the Romans, and round the circle above sit the spectators in their several rows. It is wonderful to see the courage of these little creatures, who always hold fighting on till one of them drops, and dies on the spot. I was at several of these matches, and never saw a cock run away. However, I must own it to be a remnant of the barbarous customs of this island, and too cruel for my entertainment. There is always a continued noise among the spectators in laying wagers upon every blow each cock gives, who, by the way, I must tell you, wear steel spurs (called gaffles) for their surer execution. And this noise runs, fluctuating backwards and forwards, during each battle, which is a great amusement, and I believe abundance of people get money by taking and laying odds on each stroke, and find their account at the end of the battle, but these are people that must nicely understand it. If an Italian, a German, or a Frenchman should by chance come into these cockpits, without knowing beforehand what is meant by this clamour, he would certainly conclude the assembly to be all mad, by their continued outcries of 'six to four, ten pounds to a crown,' which is always repeated here, and with great earnestness, every spectator taking part with his favourite cock, as if it were a party cause."*

With a view to supplementing these accounts with another description of a cockfight as it appeared to the trained eye of the fancier, I present the following from the pen of W. B. Tegetmeier. The cockpit, in this instance, was not a public arena such as that in Tufton Street: on the contrary it was an improvised one in a large room of a private house.

"In the middle of Holcomb's room was unrolled a piece of matting; and all the visitors stood round in a large ring, which was cleared for the setters and the birds. On some pegs were hung ten or a dozen white canvas bags, with the bottoms filled with straw, each holding a cock ready trimmed and heeled. It was a strange sight to me to see the 'setter', Old Sam, take out one of his trimmed birds: it was a splendid red cock with a black breast; the feathers around his throat were cut

---

* Daniel Defoe, *Journey Through England*, London, 1724.

close, so that as he reached his serpent-like neck out of the bag it looked as fierce as that of a rattlesnake: his hard and horny beak was thick and massive at the roots: and his eye large, fiery, and expressive of savage courage. His wing-feathers were trimmed to less than half their length, and his tail docked, so as to be of a triangular shape, like that of a nick-tailed horse. The spurs natural to his firm, bony shanks had been cut short, and their places supplied by steel spurs nearly two inches in length; each of these had a ring to go over the bottom of the natural spur, and was fastened to a piece of leather which was neatly but firmly secured to the leg by a waxed thread, so artistically tied as not to impede the free motion of the limb. The other 'setter', young Gillingham, pulled out a red and white bird, which they called a 'pile'; this had been treated in the same manner, and was equally closely trimmed and heeled. As soon as the birds saw each other both uttered a chuckle of defiance, when, holding them near, the 'setters' permitted them to strike at each other with their beaks. The object of the trimming was evident, it being to prevent the opposing bird getting a ready hold of his opponent by the feathers.

"After stimulating their courage by these means, the 'setters' stooped down and placed the birds on the floor opposite each other. They rushed forward, and for a few moments stood with their beaks close touching, raising their heads together, each one trying to get the advantage of the first cut. In an instant they sprang together high up in the air, and for a moment nothing was to be seen but a confused mass of legs, wings and feathers. As they rebounded from the force of the blow the result of the struggle was evident. Gillingham's bird had been hit, the spur of the red cock had gone through the neck. 'He's throated', cried out young Green; 'two to one on the black-red'. The 'setters' caught up their birds in an instant, and smoothing their ruffled plumage, again placed them on the mat. But the contrast was striking. Old Sam's bird looked fiercer than ever, and was hard to hold. But Gillingham's 'pile' stood unsteady, and though he rushed forward with the courage of desperation, the red cock sprang above him, and the steel heels were buried up to their hilts in the body of his prostrate foe.

"The second fight was over in a few seconds; at the first fly the victor drove his spur through the centre of the back into the heart of his opponent, whose head sank, blood poured in a stream from his mouth, and he fell forward and died without a struggle. The third was a different sort of thing every way. Old Sam's bird was a strong beautiful duckwing, Gillingham's a birchen grey. The advantage, at first, was altogether with the duckwing, which was a stronger bird, and longer in the reach of the neck, but the birchen was of the highest courage, and fought without flinching; at last, when nearly overpowered, he struck the duckwing in the head, and the blow deprived his opponent of sight, either wholly or partially. It was a cruel sight to see these noble birds, the stronger blinded, but still trying to seize his adversary with his beak and hold him, whilst he struck him down with his spurs; the weaker, with his life ebbing rapidly away, but still fighting to the death against his blinded foe. At last the duckwing caught him by the throat, and leaping into the air above, brought down the spurs with a stroke that no living bird could have withstood."*

A famous descriptive account in verse is that given by Sir Richard Blackmore:

> 'Two Valiant Cocks in Albion bred,
> That from the insulting Conqueror never Fled:
> A Match in strength, in Courage, and in Age,
> And with keen Weapons Arm'd, alike engage
> Each other they assault with furious Beaks,
> And their twin'd Plumes distain with Bloody streaks,
> Each nimble Warrior from the Mat-ment bounds,
> And wing'd with death, their heels deal ghastly Wounds.
> By turns they take, by turns fierce strokes they give,
> And with like Hopes, and Fears for Conquest strive.
> Both obstinate maintain the Bloody Field,
> Both can in Combat die, but neither yield.
> Till with their Bleeding Wounds grown weak and feint,
> And choak'd with flowing gore they gasp and pant:
> Disabled on the Crimson Floor they lie.
> Both Honour win, but neither Victory.
> And now the Throng rush in, the Combat's done,

---
* W. B. Tegetmeier, *The Poultry Book*, 1867.

By neither Hero lost, by neither won,
And rending with their Shouts the tortur'd Air,
Back from the Pit the Combatants they bear.'

Then there is the description of a cockfight from the pen of George Wilson, an enthusiastic seventeenth-century cocker. A notable feature of this account is that although Wilson expounds on the courage displayed by the winning bird, he refers to the other cock as being *cruel*. Thus: "There was a cocke about Shrovetide last, which in the cockpit in the citie of Norwich, fought with a strong and a stout adversarie, untill such time as both his eyes were beaten out, his head sore wounded, and shrewedly battered, and all his bodie most pitifully bruised, and then with the sudden astonishment of a sound blow, which from his cruell adverserie he received, being beaten downe, and lying for dead, not stirring any whit, nor seeming otherwise (to the beholders) than to be stark dead, he suddenly started up, contrary to all their expectations (when there was offered twenty shillings, yea, twenty pounds to be layd to one, that there was no breath remaining in his bodie) and closed with his adversarie, at whom he stroke most violent blowes, and never gave over, untill (to the amazement of all the spectators) he had most valiantly slaine him."

Finally, there are the verses of Dr. Robert Wild, the seventeenth-century divine and poet. Here is presented some idea of the dogged courage and indomitable will to conquer which the Gamecock displays in battle.

"Go you tame Gallants, you that have a Name,
And would accounted be Cocks of the Game;
That have brave Spurs to shew for't, and can Crow,
And count all Dunghill breed, that cannot show
Such painted Plumes as yours: which think't no Vice,
With Cock-like lust to treat your Cockatrice
Tho' Peacocks, Woodcocks, Weathercocks you be,
If y'are not Fighting-Cocks y'are not for me.
I of two Feather'd combatants will write;
And he that means to th' Life to express their Fight.

Must make his Ink the Blood which they did spill,
And from their dying Wings must take his Quill.
No sooner were the doubtful people set,
The match made up and all that would had bet;
But straight the skilful judges of the play
Brought forth their sharp-heel'd warriors; and they
Were both in linen bags, as if 'twere meet
Before they died, to have their winding-sheet.
Into the pit they're brought, and, being there
Upon the stage, the Norfolk Chanticleer
Looks stoutly at his ne'er before seen foe,
And like a challenger, began to crow
And clap his wings, as if he would display
His warlike colours, which were black and grey.
Meantime the wary Wisbich walks and breathes
His active body, and in fury wreathes
His comely crest, and, often looking down,
He whets his angry beak upon the ground.
This done, they meet, not like that coward breed
Of Aesop; these can better fight than feed;
They scorn the dunghill, 'tis their only prize
To dig for pearls in each other's eyes.
They fought so nimbly that 'twas hard to know,
To th' skilful, whether they did fight, or no;
If that the blood which dy'd the fatal floor,
Had not bore witness of 't. Yet fought they more;
As if each wound were but a spur to prick
Their fury forward. Lightning's not more quick,
Or red, than were their eyes: 'twas hard to know
Whether 'twas blood or anger made them so.
I'm sure they had been out, had they not stood,
More safe, by being fenced in with blood.
Thus they vy'd blows; but yet (alas!) at length,
Altho' their courage were full try'd, their strength
And blood began to ebb. You that have seen
A watery combat on the sea, between

Two angry, roaring, boiling billows, how
They march, and meet, and dash their curled brow,
Swelling like graves, as tho' they did intend
T' intomb each other e'er the quarrel end;
But when the wind is down, and blust'ring weather,
They are made friends, and sweetly run together;
May think these champions such; their blood grows low,
And they, which leap'd before, now scarce can go;
Their wings, which lately, at each blow they clapp'd
(As if they did applaud themselves) now flapp'd.
And having lost th' advantage of the heel,
Drunk with each other's blood, they only reel:
From either eyes such drops of blood did fall,
As if they wept them for their funeral.
And yet they fain would fight; they came so near,
Methought they meant into each other's ear
To whisper wounds; and when they could not rise,
They lay and look'd blows int' each other's eyes.
But now the tragick part! After this fit,
When Norfolk cock had got the best of it,
And Wisbich lay a lying, so that none,
Tho' sober, but might venture sev'n to one;
Contracting, like a dying taper, all
His strength, intending with the blow to fall,
He struggles up, and having taken wind,
Ventures a blow, and strikes the other blind,
And now poor Norfolk, having lost his eyes,
Fights only guided by antipathies:
With him (alas!) the proverb holds not true,
The blows his eyes ne'er saw, his heart must rue.
At length, by chance, he stumbled on his foe,
Not having any pow'r to strike a blow.
He falls upon him with his wounded head,
And makes his conqueror's wings his feather-bed!
Where lying sick his friends were very charie
Of him, and fetch'd in haste a Pothecary

But all in vain his Body did so blister,
That 'twas incapable of any Glyster;
Wherefore at length opening his fainting Bill
He call'd a Scriv'ner and thus made his Will.
Imprimis, Let it never be forgot,
My Body freely I bequeath to th' Pot,
Decently to be boil'd, and for its Tomb
Let it be buried in some hungry Womb.
Item. Executors I will have none,
But he that on my side laid sev'n to one:
And, like a Gentleman that he may live,
To him and to his Heirs my Comb I give.
Together with my Brains, that all may know,
That oftentimes his brains did use to Crow.
Item. It is my will to th' weaker ones
Whose Wives complain of them, I give my Stones;
To him that's dull I do my spurs impart;
And to the coward I bequeath my Heart:
To Ladies that are light it is my will,
My feathers should be given; and for my Bill
I'd giv't a Taylor but it is so short,
That I'm afraid he'll rather curse me for't:
And for th' Apothecaries fee who meant
To give me a Glyster, let my rump be sent.
Lastly, because I feel my life decay,
I yield and give to Wisbich Cock the day."

There is evidence that at some of the cockpits the pugnaciousness of the fighting birds was matched by that of the spectators. Rough house tactics seem to have been frequently displayed. It would appear, too, that many of the losers were prone to clear off without paying their debts, so much so, indeed, that at one time it was thought well to include among the rules of the cockpit a special clause relating to these welshers. Thus among the regulations published by Heber in 1751 was one which read: "If any Man lay more money than he hath to pay, or cannot satisfy the party with whom he hath laid, either by his credit or some friend's word; the which if he cannot do, then he is to be put into a basket to be provided for that purpose, and to be hanged up in that basket in some convenient place in the Cockpit, that all men may know him during the time of play that day; and also the party so offending never be permitted to come into the Pit, until he hath made satisfaction." This practice of "Basketing" survived in some quarters until the close of the eighteenth century.

CHAPTER VIII

THE ORIGIN AND ANTIQUITY OF COCKFIGHTING

Long before the days when cockfighting became a regular pastime or sport, the fighting-cock was an object of the greatest admiration and respect. More, there is evidence, gatherable from the writings of ancient historians, that he was a subject for religious reverence. The Ancient Syrians, says Diodorus Siculus, worshipped the fighting-cock as one of their principal deities. So, too, say Athenaeus and Dioscorides, did the Ancient Greeks. He was dedicated to Apollo, Mercury and Mars. In Borneo, according to Magellan, the eating of the flesh of the Gamecock was prohibited on the ground that the bird was sacred. In South Canara cockfights are held, states Thurston, "with the object of propitiating various demons."*

Sumatra was another place where at one time the Gamecock was an object of worship. The inhabitants were famed for their valour, and, says Nicoli-di-Conti, the historian, much attention was given to cockfighting. He writes: "They annex stately buildings to their Temples, where they keep at public charge, divers fighting-cocks, which are brought forth, as the people come to worship, and are fought in a spacious court Eastward, on the right-hand of the door of the House of their Gods: after which a certain priest, skilled in cocking, and approved for his great ability in astronomy, and all natural philosophy, having a voluble ready way of speaking, first takes up the conquering cock after the battle is over, and presents him to their deities, and then comes and takes up the slain cock, and puts him into a golden cauldron, where he bathes his bloody limbs in Sankereen; and then, with rich gums and spices, burns his body upon an altar made for that purpose; after which his ashes are put carefully in a golden pot or urn, there to remain for ever. And then the Brammen or Priest, makes a long speech to the people,

---

* From a chapter written by E. Thurston in *Customs of the World*; edited by Walter Hutchinson; Hutchinson & Co., London, n.d.

showing the excellency of cocking, and the great use and benefit of it to all such as know how rightly to apply it, and expatiates much upon the present combat, drawing divers inferences from the various passages and transactions made use of by the late foughten cocks, showing also the great magnaminity, courage, skill and constancy of these warriors. And lastly, he applies it so pertinently to all that are present, in terms so fit and suitable, that it conduces greatly to their edification, grounding in them a firm and stable temper of mind, with an unshaken valour, whereby they are now truly said to be a people invincible; and verily I am of opinion that from hence at first came that saying so common among us still, viz. *He is gone to church to see a cockfight.*"*

In many countries the fighting-cock, if not actually deified, was honoured and idealised to a degree which to modern observers seems little short of remarkable. In ancient Rome, however, it possessed an influence and a power well nigh unbelievable, as the following passage from the writings of Pliny indicates:

"They are great Commanders, and Rulers, and are made for War and Fighting; and the Countries from whence they first came are grown into Name, being much renowned for their breed, as namely Tenagra and Rhodus in the first and highest Degree: in the second rank and place, be those of Melos and Chalcis. And unto these Birds (for their worth and dignity) the Purple Robe at Rome, and all magistrates of State disdain not to give Honour. These rule our great Rulers every Day: and there is not a mighty Lord or State of Rome, that dare open or shut the Door of his House, before he knows the good Pleasure of these Fowls: and that which is more, the Sovereign Magistrat in his Majestie of the Roman Empire, with the regal Ensigns of Rods and Axes, carried before him, neither sets he forward, nor reculeth back, without Direction from these Birds; they give order to whole Armies to advance forth to Battle, and again command them to stay and keep within the Camp. These were they that gave the Signal, and foretold the issue of all those famous foughten Fields, whereby we have achieved all our Victories throughout the whole World: In one word, these Birds command those Great Commanders of all Nations upon the Earth."

* Quoted from *History of Sumatra*, in *The Royal Pastime of Cock-fighting*, by R. H., London, 1709.

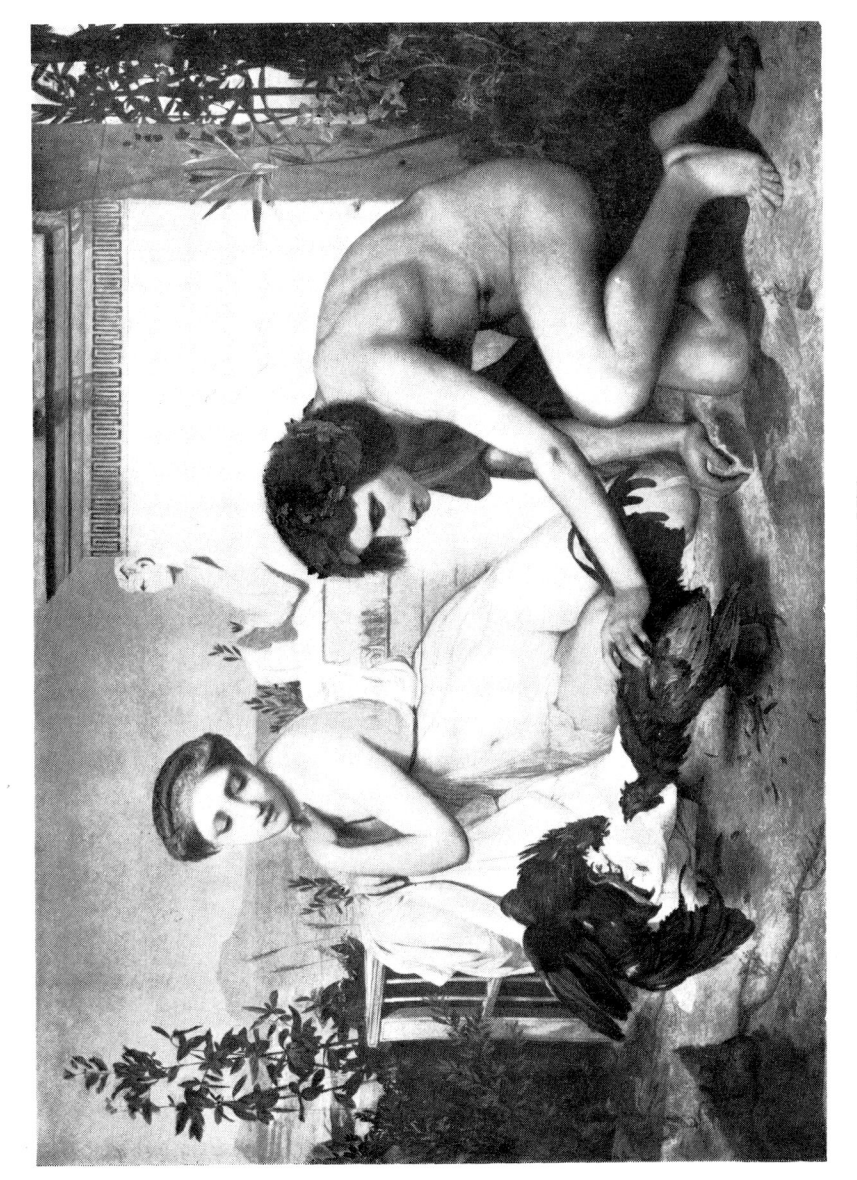

THE COCKFIGHT

By Jean Léon Gérôme
(Luxembourg)

TREGONWELL FRAMPTON, THE FATHER OF THE TURF,
WITH HIS COCK AND HOUND

By John Wootton (*c.* 1686–1765)

When opening the second Andra Regional Poultry Exhibition held at Vijayawede in May 1953, Dr. V. R. Rajagopalan, Director of Animal Husbandry, of Madras, stated that a fight between two cocks decided the fate of the Macharia Kingdom.*

In Samuel Pegge's interesting essay (*Archaeologia*, Vol. III, p. 135), we read: "The Dardanii, a people of Troas, had two cocks fighting upon their coins; and as they were neighbours, in a manner, to the Pergameni, cockfighting was probably a diversion among them; but then, as these coins are of a late date, the antiquity of this species of diversion among the Dardanians cannot be collected from them. Perhaps it might have been introduced both there and at Pergamus, from Athens; where the custom was instituted by Themistocles."

As regards the origin of cockfighting specifically as a sport or an amusement much has been written, and when the evidence, such as it is, has been sifted there appears to be no definite time when, and no specific country in which, the *sport* of cockfighting in any *organised* sense, originated. In any other sense cockfighting may be said to have existed from the beginning of time. It is natural for male fowls, whether wild or domesticated, to fight when they come together as *strangers* and in *rivalry*. It is necessary to make these qualificatory statements for, as every poultry breeder knows, there are occasions when male birds of even the most pugnacious breeds will live together in perfect harmony. It is customary for the male specimens to be reared together in flocks. A moment's thought will enable one to realise that it would be impossible for a breeder of poultry to rear each male bird in a separate pen: all that can be done is to confine specimens of approximately the same age and size in flocks. So long as they are kept together all is well: it is when a bird is removed from the flock for a few days and then returned to it that trouble starts. In the case of birds of a particularly pugnacious breed it is sometimes necessary or advisable to place an older bird with them to keep the youngsters in order.

Now it is well at this juncture to correct the fallacious notion that *all* cocks will fight whenever the opportunity arises. They will do no such thing. Pugnacity varies greatly in degree in different breeds of poultry. For instance a male Brahma or Cochin rarely shows any dis-

---

* *South China Morning Post*, May 22, 1953 (United Press report).

position to fight. Both these are what are termed heavy breeds. Turning to the other extreme, a male specimen of the light-weight Ancona or Leghorn seldom puts up much of a fight. In all these instances, and I could give numerous others, not only is there little inclination to fight among themselves, but there is usually even less desire to tackle a specimen of one of the pugnacious breeds. At the same time there are exceptional cases where a bird of a generally accepted pusillanimous breed will on occasion and in certain circumstances show fight. I mention this in case any reader may feel disposed to write and inform me or my publishers that he has seen or is in possession of a Cochin or an Ancona cock which is a champion fighter and has vanquished in combat a Rhode Island Red!

Now this much made clear, it may be stated that the finest fighting-cocks of today, as of all time, are specimens of the breed now known as the Old English Game. Other breeds of Game are great fighters too; as also are breeds of more recent evolution that have Game-blood in their ancestry. Here again, however, I must correct the widespread fallacy that every cock belonging to one or other of the pure Game breeds, or to any of the many modern breeds descended from Game, is necessarily a skilled and an inveterate fighter. This is not true. There are many such cocks which show no pugnacious disposition at all: they will use their legs and wings to some purpose in an endeavour to get out of the reach of any cock which approaches them with bristling hackle and open beak.

It may be taken as certain that it was to the fact that cocks displaying their pugnacity and courage were to be found in plenty among the fowls, wild or domesticated, of the early days of civilisation that the idea occurred of selecting powerful specimens and pitting them one against the other in fights to which spectators were admitted, and for which money or prizes went to the owners of the victorious birds. From this it was only to be expected that onlookers would lay wagers on the prospects of the birds they fancied as winners. The path to commercialized cockfighting was thus wide open.

According to that celebrated lexicographer, Nathaniel Bailey, who was responsible for the compilation known as *A Universal Etymological English Dictionary* (one of the most famous and most ambitious of the early lexicons), Themistocles, the celebrated Athenian general, was primarily responsible for the rise of cockfighting into a national sport, an amphitheatre for this express purpose being erected in the city of Pergamus. When the general was preparing to make war on the Persians, says Bailey: "In his march he espied two cocks fighting and immediately caused his army to behold them, and made the following speech: 'Behold, these do not fight for their household gods, for the monuments of their ancestors, for glory, for liberty, or the safety of their children, but only because the one will not give way to the other'. This so encouraged the Grecians that they fought strenuously and obtained a victory over the Persians, upon which cockfighting was by a particular law ordained to be annually practised by the Athenians."

"But others, as well as Themistocles," says Pegge, "have taken advantage of the sight of cockfighting, and from thence have drawn an argument for the incitement and encouragement of military valour. Socrates endeavoured from thence to inspire Iphicrates with courage. Chrysippus, in his book *De Justitia*, says 'Our valour is raised by the example of cocks.' We find Musonius also, in Stobaeus, drawing the like matter of instruction from the battling of quails and cocks; and, as is remarked by the excellent Perizonius, the young men were obliged to attend the exhibitions of the theatre for the sake of the instruction."*

When the Roman Emperor Severus decided to conquer Britain, he realised that his sons Antoine and Geta were in no state to embark upon an enterprise involving so many dangers, difficulties and hardships. They were at the moment, these two young men, soft and indolent through the life of gaiety and pleasure they had long been leading. To prepare them and also the principal officers of the army for sterner and more exacting work, Severus commanded that cockfighting should form part of their daily amusements, "not only to make them emulous of glory through the performance of great achievements, but also to be firm and unshaken in the midst of dangers, nay in death itself."†

Then, too, there was the high opinion of cockfighting held by Gustavus Adolphus. For he it was who informed the Danish king that

---

* Rev. Samuel Pegge, *A Memoir on Cockfighting* in *Archaeologia*, Vol. III. The Society of Antiquaries of London, 1786.

† R. Howlett, *The Royal Pastime of Cock-fighting*, 1709.

he had nothing to fear from the Germans now that they had devoted themselves to dancing and drinking instead of cockfighting.

Ferguson affirms that "the Persian breed of cocks appears to have been regarded as invincible, and was much sought after by all capable of paying the exorbitant prices demanded. The description furnished by Aldrovandi, on the authority of Florentius, of certain hens in Alexandria from which fighting-cocks were bred, bears close resemblance to our own; he moreover mentions their extreme incubating powers, and their general excellent qualifications as mothers and protectors. They were called *monositae* (i.e. one-mealers, or such as eat but once a day). There is nothing peculiar respecting this latter circumstance, for no close sitter of any breed should leave the nest more frequently than once in 24 hours; nature invariably contriving to relieve and replenish itself during the regular interval of a few minutes per day."*

The consensus of opinion is that the Romans followed the Greeks in taking up cockfighting as a sport, but the evidence in support of this seems to me to be of the slenderest, and the probability is that it became popular in both countries contemporaneously. It is said to have been prevalent in the Roman Empire at least 470 years before the Christian era. It appears that the Romans used quails as well as the Game Fowl for fighting purposes, and Herodotus asserts that it was owing to differences of opinion respecting the fighting propensities and abilities of quails and ordinary Game that Bassianius and Geta quarrelled.

Many writers are of opinion that the Romans introduced the sport into Britain. Others assert with equal confidence that it was already existent at the time of the Roman Conquest, pointing out the statement of Julius Caesar to the effect that the ancient Britons bred fowls for pleasure and diversion rather than food. At any rate it is probable that the Romans were responsible for the introduction of artificial spurs (see Chapter V) and the first form of *organised* cockfighting.

---

* G. Ferguson, *Illustrated Series of Rare and Prize Poultry*, 1854.

CHAPTER IX

HISTORICAL ASPECTS OF COCKFIGHTING IN THE UNITED KINGDOM

WE HAVE seen that while some authorities state that fighting-cocks were brought to Cornwall by the Phoenician traders who came to Britain for tin from the Cornish mines, others assert that the Romans, when they invaded Britain, introduced cockfighting to the inhabitants; while yet others proclaim with confidence that cockfighting was practised in these islands long before so much as a single Phoenician or Roman landed on its shores. Whatever may be the truth, certain it is that although the sport probably did flourish for a time early in the Christian era it must have had but a small measure of popularity, as a search of records and literature fails to reveal any reference to cockfighting until well into the twelfth century, when it was mentioned by William Fitzstephen in a tract dealing with the amusements of the English people at that time.

Surprisingly enough, this reference by Fitzstephen is to cockfighting as a sport of schoolboys, for it appears that for many years it was purely and exclusively a boy's amusement. Indeed it was not until the thirteenth century had gone to glory that grown men again showed any considerable interest in cockfighting.

It would appear that initially, at any rate, schoolboy cocking was an annual event. According to Fitzstephen "Every yeare on Shrove-Tuesday the schoolboyes doe bring Gamecocks to their masters, and in the forepart of the day, till dinner time, they are permitted to amuse themselves with seeing them fight."

The school itself was, in most cases, turned into a temporary cockpit by the removal of desks and forms so that a space was available for the combatants; though there were instances of pits being constructed outside and adjoining the school building. The schoolmaster supervised the fight, and in one way or another found the sport, from his point of view, a remunerative one. Not only did he receive as perquisites all birds that were killed in battle, but he also in many cases got a certain sum of money each year from every pupil. At schools with a large number of scholars this annual income, often enough, was not to be sneered at. Sir John Sinclair in his *Statistical Account of Scotland*, published in 1792, said these "cockfight dues" which accrued to the schoolmaster at Applecross in Ross-shire amounted to a sum equivalent to a quarter's scholastic fees. In a book entitled *Folklore of the Northern Counties of England*, published in 1879 by William Henderson, we read that the author was informed by a clergyman that during the years of his attendance at Sedbergh Grammar School the schoolmaster received 4½d. per annum from every boy for the purpose of purchasing fighting-cocks. Kendal Grammar School was, by regulation, free to all boys living in the parish, except for a "voluntary payment of a cock-penny." Similarly, in regard to Clitheroe Grammar School, although otherwise free, each scholar was expected to make an annual Shrovetide contribution towards the expenses in connection with cockfighting, the precise amount varying "according to the circumstances of the parents."* Apparently, some schoolmasters did much better out of the practice than did others. A particularly fortunate pedagogue appears to have been the dominie of Mauchline. According to the Rev. Dr. Edgar, author of *Old Church Life in Scotland*, in this particular case the schoolmaster was not called upon to purchase the fighting-cocks, which were provided by local breeders or owners, who "paid to the schoolmaster a small sum in name of entry money, and those who did not provide a combatant had to pay an extra sum for admission to the spectacle. It was a gala day in the schoolmaster's calendar, for not only had he the benefit of pocketing the entry and admission money, but he had the privilege of picking up the carcases of the slain and seizing the persons of the fugitives." The runaway cocks "were called fugees, corrupt, I suppose," says Brand, "for refugees."

Pegge, the archaeologist, quotes a description of one of these school cockfights from the pen of a historian, writing of the time of Henry the Second: "The theatre (cockpit) it seems was the school, and the master the comptroller and director of the sport. The master presides, having the names of the boys inserted in paper billets and huddled together

---

* John Harland and T. T. Wilkinson, *Lancashire Folk-lore*; John Heywood, Manchester, 1882, p. 219.

in his hat. The names of any two boys being first drawn and announced, their respective cocks were brought into the pit and fought until one of them was dead: a second couple was then drawn, then a third, and then a fourth, till such time as one half of the original cocks lay dead; when the remaining ones, in the same manner as before, brought to a second contest, till one only of the whole was left alive, the owner of which was distinguished by the glorious name of victor, with many privileges annexed to it, and never to be subjected himself, during the whole time of Lent, to the disgrace of flagellation; but, what was still more, when any other boy was on the point of undergoing that punishment, he was at liberty, if he pleased, to exempt him from it by only clapping his hat on the culprit's posterior, and thereby saving him from the lash."

Another excellent description of a cockfight at Cromarty Grammar School in the early part of the nineteenth century, is to be found in an interesting volume by Hugh Miller. The account reads: "The school, like almost all the other grammar-schools of the period in Scotland, had its yearly cockfight, preceded by two holidays and a half, during which the boys occupied themselves in collecting and bringing up their cocks. And such always was the array of fighting-birds mustered on the occasion, that the day of the festival, from morning till night, used to be spent in fighting out the battle. For weeks after it had passed, the school-floor would continue to retain its deeply-stained blotches of blood, and the boys would be full of exciting narratives regarding the glories of gallant birds, who had continued to fight until both their eyes had been picked out, or who, in the moment of victory, had dropped dead in the middle of the cockpit. The yearly fight was the relic of a barbarous age; and, in at least one of its provisions, there seemed evidence that it was that of an intolerant age also: every pupil at school, without exemption, had his name entered on the subscription-list, as a cockfighter, and was obliged to pay the master at the rate of twopence per head, ostensibly for leave to bring his birds to the pit; but, amid the growing humanities of a better time, though the twopences continued to be exacted, it was no longer imperative to bring the birds; and availing myself of the liberty I never brought any. Nor, save for a few minutes, on two several occasions, did I ever attend the fight. Had the combat been one among the boys themselves, I would readily enough have done my part, by meeting with any opponent of my years and standing; but I could not bear to look at the bleeding birds. And so I continued to pay my yearly sixpence, as a holder of three cocks—the lowest sum deemed in any degree genteel—but remained simply a fictitious or paper cockfighter, and contributed in no degree to the success of the *head-stock* or leader, to whose party, in the general division of the school, it was my lot to fall."*

"The credit of the school," avers George Roberts, "was without doubt often involved in the proper issue of the fight."† Says this same authority, "Sir James Mackintosh, when at school at Fortrose in 1776-7, had this entry in his account, in which books were charged 3s. 6d. :—'To cocks'-fight dues for 2 years, 2s. 6d. each, 5s.'"‡

According to Rogers, the Scots historian, towards the close of the seventeenth century, the Town Council of Dumfries issued certain regulations respecting the school's yearly cockfight. Thus: "That at Fastern's Even [the English Shrove Tuesday] upon the day appointed for the cocks' fighting in the school-house, the under teacher cause keep the door, and exact no more than twelve pennies (Scots) for each scholar for the benefit of bringing in a cock to fight in the school-house; and that none be suffered to enter that day to the school-house but the scholars, except gentlemen and persons of note, from whom nothing is to be demanded; and what money is to be given in by the scholars, the under teacher is to receive and apply to his own use, for his pains and trouble; and that no scholars, except who pleases, shall furnish cocks, but all the scholars, whether they have cocks or not, are to get into the school, such children as have none, paying two shillings (Scots) by way of compensation."§

In connexion with the Westmorland School of Wreay, near Lake Windermere, a silver bell was offered for competition each year. The following account appears in Carlisle's *Endowed Grammar Schools in*

---

* Hugh Miller, *My Schools and Schoolmasters, or The Story of My Education*, Thomas Constable & Co., Edinburgh, 1860, pp. 49-50.

† George Roberts, *The Social History of the People of the Southern Counties of England in Past Centuries*, Longmans, Brown, Green, Longmans & Roberts, London, 1856, p. 401.

‡ George Roberts, op. cit.

§ Rev. Charles Rogers, *Scotland Social and Domestic*, 1869, p. 197.

England and Wales (1818): "A singular donation was made by a Mr. Graham, of a *Silver Bell*, weighing two ounces, upon which is engraven '*Wrey Chapple*, 1655,' to be 'fought for annually on Shrove Tuesday by cocks.' About three weeks previous to that day, the boys fixed upon two of their schoolfellows for Captains, whose parents were able and willing to bear the expense of the approaching contest, and the Master on his entering the School was saluted by the boys throwing up their hats, and the acclamation of '*Dux, Dux*.' After an early Dinner on Shrove Tuesday, the two Captains, attended by their Friends and Schoolfellows, who were distinguished by blue and red Ribbons, marched in procession from their respective homes to the Village Green, when each produced three Cocks, and the Bell was appended to the hat of the Victor—in which manner it was handed down from one successful Captain to another. About thirty years since, this barbarous custom was superseded by a 'Hunt'—a *Mayor* being annually elected, and the Bell graces his rod of office."

This bell, which was shaped like a pear, was of small size, weighing under two ounces. Apparently Wreay was not the only place where such a bell was competed for. One was offered at Pocklington Grammar School. "The weight of it," says Andrews, "is one ounce and eight pennyweights Troy. It is not quite two inches in height, and its circumference round the bottom is seven and a quarter inches. At the top is a small band handle, and at the bottom is a slit one and a half inches in length. Round the side is engraved in cursive writing as follows: 'Tho Ellison Moderator 1666 Scholae Liberae Grammaticalis de Pocklinton. Johanes Clarke Moderator 1660 Scolae Liberae Gramaticalis de Pocklinton'."*

A similar trophy was in existence at Bromfield, Cumberland. At this school, says the Rev. J. Boucher, the winner of most battles was awarded a small silver bell as a prize. This trophy was "suspended to the button of the victor's hat and worn for three successive Sundays."

If cockfighting in schools had its supporters, notably in the persons of the schoolmasters themselves, it had its detractors too. Early in the sixteenth century the Statutes of the Manchester Free Grammar School, indicated the wish to put down the practice. One of these Statutes,

* William Andrews (ed. by), *Historic Byways and Highways of Old England*, London, 1900, p. 233.

say the authors of *Lancashire Folk-Lore*, provided that "he [the schoolmaster] shall teach freely and indifferently (not carelessly, but impartially) every child and scholar coming to the same school, without any money or other reward taking therefor, as cock-penny, victor-penny, &c." While another decreed: "The scholars of the same school shall use no cockfights, nor other unlawful games, and riding about for victors, &c., which be to the great let (hindrance) of virtue, and to charge and cost of the scholars, and of their friends."* According to Maitland, Dr. John Colet, chaplain to Henry the Eighth, on the establishment of St. Paul's School in 1509 ordained "that the scholars use no cockfighting nor Riding about of Victor nor Disputing at St. Bartholomew's; which are but foolish babbling and loss of time."†
No doubt, too, many of the parents and guardians of the boys were opposed to the practice. Hugh Miller says: "To my dislike of the annual cockfight my uncles must have contributed. They were loud in their denunciations of the enormity; and on one occasion, when a neighbour was unlucky enough to remark, in extenuation, that the practice had been handed down to us by pious and excellent men, who seemed to see nothing wrong in it, I saw the habitual respect for the old divines give way, for at least a moment. Uncle Sandy hesitated under apparent excitement; but, quick and fiery as lightning, Uncle James came to his rescue. 'Yes, excellent men!' said my uncle, 'but the excellent men of a rude and barbarous age; and, in some parts of their character, tinged by its barbarity. For the cockfight which these excellent men have bequeathed to us, they ought to have been sent to Bridewell for a week, and fed upon bread and water.' Uncle James was, no doubt, over hasty, and felt so a minute after; but the practice of fixing the foundations of ethics on a '*They themselves did it,*' much after the manner in which the Schoolmen fixed the foundations of their nonsensical philosophy on a '*He himself said it,*' is a practice which, though not yet exploded in even very pure Churches, is always provoking, and not quite free from peril to the worthies, whether dead or alive, in whose precedents the moral right is made to rest. In the class of minds represented among the people by that of Uncle James, for instance, it would be much easier

---

* John Harland and T. T. Wilkinson, *Lancashire Folk-Lore*, p. 221.
† William Maitland, *History and Survey of London*, 1756.

to bring down even the old divines than to bring up cockfighting."*

In some parts of the country, contemporaneous with the annual interest in cockfighting displayed in the schools, the sport was taken up by adults, and as the years went by, it appealed to an increasingly large proportion of the male population of Britain. To a certain extent this may and probably was a direct result of the practice of cockfighting in schools. Those who as boys were keenly interested continued to display an equal enthusiasm on leaving school.

The rise to popularity was rapid. By the time Elizabeth I came to the throne, cocking had become so firmly established and achieved such widespread popularity that it was already receiving the attention of the Puritans. From thence onwards for over two hundred years it reigned as Britain's premier sport. Philip Stubbes, who was bitterly opposed to cockfighting, in his famous work *Anatomy of Abuses*, stated that contests between fighting-cocks were drawn to the attention of the public by the display of flags and banners on the buildings which housed the cockpits, and on such occasions people flocked there. From the accounts of historians, and the amount of space devoted to the sport in the newspapers of the day, one may well conclude that cocking in the sixteenth, seventeenth, eighteenth, and early nineteenth centuries (in fact right up to the time when it was prohibited by law) occupied a place, as regards popularity, on a par with that held by football or racing today. Stow, writing in 1603, in his *Survey of London*, asserts that "Cocks of the game were yet cherished by diverse men for their pleasure, much money being laid on their heads when they fight in pits, whereof some be costly made for this purpose."

There are indications that towards the closing years of the seventeenth century an interest in cockfighting ranked as one of the hallmarks of an English gentleman. Writes Strutt: "A character in the Cornish Comedy, written by George Powell, and acted at Dorset Garden in 1696, says, 'What is a gentleman without his recreations? With these we endeavour to pass away that time which would otherwise lie heavily upon our hands. Hawks, hounds, setting-dogs, and cocks, with their appurtenances, are the true marks of a country gentleman.' This character is supposed to be a young heir just come to his estate. 'My cocks,' says he, 'are true

---

* Hugh Miller, *My Schools and Schoolmasters, or The Story of My Education*, 1860, pp. 50-51.

cocks of the game—I make a match of cockfighting, and then a hundred or two pounds are soon won, for I never fight a battle under'."*

Malcolm, the historian, refers to this most barbarous amusement of cockfighting being prevalent early in the eighteenth century, as indicated by the advertisements of that time, thus: "At the Royal Cockpit on the south side of St. James's Park, on Tuesday the 11th of this instant February [1700] will begin a very great Cock-match; and will continue all the week; wherein most of the considerablest Cockers of England are concerned. There will be a battle down upon the Pit every day precisely at three o'clock, in order to have done by daylight. Monday the 9th instant March will begin a great match of Cockfighting betwixt the Gentlemen of the City of Westminster and the Gentlemen of the City of London for six guineas a battle, and one hundred guineas the odd battle, and the match continues all the week, in Red-Lion fields. In the following April another match commenced, to continue for a week, at four guineas a battle, and forty guineas the odd battle, between the Gentlemen of London, and those of Warwickshire, at the new Cockpit behind Gray's-Inn-Walks."†

In this connexion there is the evidence of a letter from Sir Henry Savill. The letter is dated May 5, 1546 and in it Sir Henry invites his cousin Plompton to stay with him "and se all our good coxs fight, if it plese you, and se the maner of our cocking. Ther will be Lanckeshire of one parte, and Derbeshire of another parte, and Hallomshire of the third parte. I perceive your cocking varieth from ours, for ye lay but the battell; and if our battell be but £10 to £5, thear wilbe £10 to one laye, or the battell be ended."‡

In all parts of Britain this popularity continued to grow. It was not restricted to any one class of the populace. The wideness of its appeal is apparent from the observations of the famous diarist, Samuel Pepys. An entry dated 21st December 1663 reads: "To Shoe Lane to see a Cockfighting at a new pit there, a spot I was never at in my life: but Lord! to see the strange variety of people, from Parliament-man (by

---

* Joseph Strutt, *The Sports and Pastimes of the People of England;* Tegg and Co., London, 1855, p. xxxiv.

† James Peller Malcolm, *Anecdotes of the Manners and Customs of London During the Eighteenth Century,* second edition, 1810. Vol. II, p. 15.

‡ *Plumpton Correspondence,* Edited by Thomas Stapleton, from Sir Edward Plumpton's *Book of Letters,* Camden Society, London, 1839, p. 250.

name Wildes, that was Deputy Governor of the Tower when Robinson was Lord Mayor) to the poorest 'prentices, bakers, brewers, butchers, draymen, and what not; and all these fellows one with another cursing and betting. I soon had enough of it. It is strange to see how people of the poor rank, that look as if they had not bread to put in their mouths, shall bet three or four pounds at a time, and lose it, and yet bet as much the next battle, so that one of them will lose 10£ or 20£ at a meeting."

But although Pepys, in 1663, "soon had enough of it," there would appear to be ground for the belief that the lure of the "sport of Kings" was sufficient to overcome any feelings of dislike and disapprobation, for under date April 6, 1668, we read: "I to the new Cocke-pitt by the King's gate, and there saw the manner of it, and the mixed rabble of people that come thither, and saw two battles of cocks, wherein is no great sport, but only to consider how these creatures, without any provocation, do fight and kill one another, and aim only at one another's heads."

An English historian testifies to the popularity of the sport in the eighteenth century thus: "Cockfighting up to the end of the last century was a very general amusement, and an occasion for gambling. It entered into the occupations of the old and young. Schools had their cockfights. Travellers agreed with coachmen that they were to wait a night if there was a cockfight in any town through which they passed. A battle between two cocks had five guineas staked upon it. Fifty guineas, about the year 1760, depended upon the main or odd battle. This made the decision of a 'long main' at cockfighting an important matter. . . . . Matches were sometimes so arranged as to last the week. When country gentlemen had sat long at table, and the conversation had turned upon the relative merits of their several birds, a cockfight often resulted, as the birds in question were brought for the purpose into the dining-room.

"If apprentices on their parts agreed that they should not be obliged to eat salmon more than twice a week, masters, regarding their interests, stipulated that apprentices should not keep fighting-cocks or hunting-dogs till they had served seven of their ten years' apprenticeship.

"A carriage has been constructed to contain some cocks of a Cornish breed, which brought the valiant birds to London, drawn by post-horses, for a great match. The expense was £500."*

One of the most potent reasons for the appeal of cockfighting to the upper and middle classes, as well as to the lower orders, was the support accorded to it by royalty. When the eighth Henry had a cockpit built in the palace of Whitehall, the sport was lifted out of obscurity at one swoop. It is true there appears to be no evidence that Henry was sufficiently enamoured to grace the fights with his portly presence, but the very fact that he recognised its importance and its claims was enough. James the First, however, went one better. Not only did he recognise cocking as a national sport; he appointed a special official, known as a "cockmaster", to supervise the breeding, rearing and training of fighting-cocks destined to appear in the royal arena; he visited the pit himself and was in fact an enthusiastic spectator at least once and often twice a week. Indeed so well known and so widely recognised were these hebdomadal attendances of the king, that when, in 1617, he visited Lincoln, a cockfight was specifically arranged for his amusement. Other English kings who were patrons of the sport were Charles the Second, William the Third, and George the Fourth. Among foreign royal enthusiasts was King Christian VII of Denmark, who visited, in October 1768, the Newmarket cockpit.

Following the lead thus given by a succession of English kings, the aristocracy, too, took a keen interest in cockfighting, and at the leading cockpits of London and provincial towns many notable and well known members of society were always to be seen. The bulk of these, as of members of the poorer classes, were there purely as spectators and betters; but always were there a few members of the English nobility who were owners or breeders of fighting-cocks. Some indication of the popularity of the sport among the leisured and aristocratic classes is given by the fact that tenants of these land-owners were called upon each year to "walk" a specific number of cocks belonging to their landlords. Some of the leading naval men were enthusiastic cockers, and few ships-of-war sailed without a number of fighting-cocks on board. Among the keenest devotees of his day was Admiral Boscawen.

* George Roberts, *The Social History of the People of the Southern Counties of England in Past Centuries*, 1856, p. 421.

THE CELEBRATED GILLIVER SPURRING A FIGHTING-COCK

From an oil painting, bearing monogram D.B.C., formerly in the
National Gallery of British Sports and Pastimes

A TANDEM COCKING CART, WITH SPACE IN THE BOOT FOR
CARRYING COCKS TO A MAIN

From an aquatint by C. B. Newhouse, 1833

Apropos of the practice of ships-of-war carrying Gamecocks, the following account, quoted by Henry Alken, of an incident which occurred during a naval battle in which Lord Howe's fleet was engaged on June 1st 1794, seems worth reproduction here: ". . . . a gamecock on board one of the ships chanced to have his house beaten to pieces by a shot, or some falling rigging, which accident set him at liberty; the feathered hero, now perched on the stump of the mainmast, which had been carried away, continued crowing and clapping his wings during the remainder of the engagement, enjoying, to all appearance, the thundering horrors of the scene."*

The author of *Silk and Scarlet* testifies to this well-nigh universal popularity during the nineteenth century in the following revealing passage.

"The old families in Cheshire and the neighbouring counties were as proud of their breed of Black-Reds or Birchen-Duckwings, as ever Mr. Garforth was of his 'Marcia' or Mr. Pierse of his 'Tuberose'; and Potter and Gilliver (who fed for Mr. Leigh of Lyme) took rank in the public mind with Robson and Croft. The feeling had struck deep root for years. It had penetrated almost within the sombre walls of York, and quiet burgesses remembered how Mellish and Sir Francis Boynton had fought main after main at Botham Bar. There was a dim story, too, that Colonel Thornton had matched his best hawk against a Gamecock, at Preston or Knutsford, for a thousand guineas a side. Be that curious wager more or less, ten guineas a battle and two hundred the main was the usual standard. At race meetings they often fought one 'in-go' by candle-light, amid a perfect Babel of bets; and in the Royal Westminster Pit of yore, no mains were ever fought by day. To such a height had this Roger Ascham passion grown, that although the bye-battles were only honoured with common calico, the Derby main bag, with its rich lace, and its needle-embroidered coat of arms, was alone worth the five shillings admission to see."†

---

* Henry Alken, *The National Sports of Great Britain*, London, 1821
† H. H. Dixon, *Silk and Scarlet*, London, 1859. p. 94.

Perhaps the most noted aristocratic figure who ever owned his own strain of fighting-cocks was the twelfth Earl of Derby. The name of Lord Derby has ever been associated with British sport, particularly racing, for it was this same nobleman who achieved fame as a breeder of race-horses, as founder of the Jockey Club and the race which bears his name. But keenly enthusiastic though he was respecting the "turf", he was an even greater devotee of the "sod", as the sport of cockfighting was sometimes termed. An obituary notice published in *The Sporting Magazine* (December 1834) gives the following information respecting the Earl, who died on October 21st 1834, in his eighty-third year: " . . . . he was without question the most celebrated cocker of either ancient or modern days, and in this light we may say never had his equal, and during his life fought more mains, and very generally successfully, than any person ever known. His birds, to which he was extremely partial, were by judicious breeding brought to the finest possible perfection; and nothing inspired the noble Lord with more pleasure and gratification than the English Gamecock; indeed, many favourites have at times gained admittance to his presence even in the splendid drawing-room at Knowsley. The first feeder that the Earl of Derby employed, which is now a very long time ago, was Busley: he was succeeded by Potter the elder, at whose death his son, the present Potter, attained the post, which he has held to the present time."

The twelfth Earl's ancestors, too, had been interested in the breeding of fighting-Game, and it was from his grandfather that was handed down the strain of fighting-cocks that was later to become known throughout the marches of Britain as the Knowsley strain. These birds were white-legged Black-breasted Reds, and their fame was to remain undisputed for very nearly three centuries. Ferguson, writing in 1854, says of them: "The Knowsley strain of Black-breasted Reds, belonging to the late Lord Derby were, and still are, considered the finest and most select in the country. The pedigree has been carefully preserved, and the various admixtures with Lord Sefton's, and other distinguished strains registered for its preservation and further judicious admixture. This nobleman dearly loved witnessing the display of those distinguishing characteristics of the breed, exhibited in their dauntless prowess and resolute courage—their noble contour and aristocratic deportment

—together with their rapid but graceful actions, skilled fly, and powerful drive—their elegant posture and watchful eye. He possessed breeders, special feeders, and knowing setters-to, for the purpose of supporting this most exciting pastime."*

In the breeding of poultry for exhibition, provided the foundation stock is of the requisite degree of quality, the one who rears a thousand head, has, when it comes to selecting specimens to grace the show bench, a big advantage over one who rears a hundred or even five hundred. It is exactly the same when it comes to the question of breeding fighting-cocks. And without in any way wishing to disparage the merits of the Knowsley strain, here the Earl of Derby had, if contemporary accounts are anything to go by, a very considerable advantage. It is said that each year no fewer than three thousand birds were reared. The figure was a big one, and afforded the noble lord a field of selection that must have been denied to the majority of, if not all, his rivals. Little wonder that, with such an old-established and long-pedigreed strain of fighting-cocks as the Knowsley Black-breasted Reds, and with such a wide field of selection, Lord Derby was well-nigh invincible. During his long life he never wavered in his devotion to the Game Fowl, and was always to be seen not only at the Preston cockpit, the cost of which came from his own purse, but at all the leading venues throughout the country. The story goes that a few hours before his end came at the age of 82, a fight was staged for his amusement in the bedroom where he lay dying.

Among other members of the aristocracy whose names are indelibly associated with cocking were the Duke of Northumberland, the Earl of Mexborough, Lord Vere, the Duke of Hamilton, the Earl of Sefton, Lord Chesterfield, the Earl of Berkeley, Lord Clive, Lord Lonsdale, Sir Henry Houghton, and Sir H. Vivian.

The birds owned by these famous cockers were heavily backed by the spectators. In this connexion a story is told of the feeder of Sir Thomas Jermin, who owned a famous strain of fighting-Game. Sir Thomas, who was fond of a practical joke, sent his man to the cockpit in Shoe Lane, with a cock prepared for battle, and one hundred pounds in cash. His instructions were that he should get someone to enter the bird in Sir Thomas's name, and then lay the one hundred pounds against

* G. Ferguson, *Illustrated Series of Rare and Prize Poultry*, 1854.

it. This particular bird, far from being a pedigree fighting-cock of Sir Thomas's strain, was an ordinary dunghill-cock, and to the consternation of the spectators soon showed a clean pair of heels. The man returned to Sir Thomas with a couple of hundred pounds in place of the hundred he set out with.

A noted cocker, and a contemporary of Lord Derby, was Dr. Bellyse of Audlem. He, too, owned a famous strain of Brown-Red fighting-cocks, and was a breeder on a large scale. The Doctor was something of a personality, as is apparent from the following description culled from the pages of *Silk and Scarlet*.

"A blue dress-coat with gilt buttons, light-coloured kerseys and gaiters, a buff waistcoat, and a pig-tail, just peeping from beneath a conical low-crowned hat, completed his attire; while a golden greyhound, the gift of his friend Lord Combermere, lent a tasteful finish to his snowy frill. Never in his life had he seen either Derby or St. Leger, but his eyelids knew no rest in the long night of suspense which followed them. He was a walking polyglot on race-horse pedigrees, from the Godolphin Arabian to Memnon. The Grafton blood in the south, and Mr. Garforth's in the north, were both especially dear to him; but he would invariably toast General Minna, when he won, and troll forth with double emphasis, on that evening, all his lodge lays of 'A Free and accepted Mason', or his famous matrimonial ballad—

'We scold and fight, and both repent
That ding-dong went the bell.'

Pre-eminent and assiduous as he was in his profession, his patients had to show a clean bill of health during the Chester race week, or give up all hope of having him. The Stationers' Almanack was not truer to the year than his yellow gig with his fourteen-one Brown Tommy to the Hop Pole Yard at Chester, on that Saturday afternoon. On the Monday he sallied forth to the Hotel Row, and received a hearty annual welcome from all the lovers of 'the Turf and the Sod', to whom, from his quiet worth, and his wonderful memory and information on every point, he had become so endeared. Years wrought no change in the dress or figure of this old Cheshire worthy, or quenched his love for either science. The cockpit began at eleven, and the in-go ended soon after one;

and then before a Grand Stand arose, he was always to be seen stationed on Tommy, in the middle of the Roodee, to watch what horses were doing all round, and armed with a gigantic umbrella. He held the belief that there were 'always so many fools on a race-course', and hence he kept it to shoot out in self-defence, in the faces of the young blades as they galloped recklessly across him from the cords to the river rails."*

It must be remembered that in those days cockfights and races were held during the same periods, and the patrons of the one sport were, as a rule, patrons of the other. The truth of this is apparent from the following announcements, relating to the year 1768: "At Chester at the time of the Races a main of cocks was fought between Mr. Ogden and Mr. Waynne;" again "At Preston, during the Races, a main of cocks was fought between Mr. Dickinson and Lord Strange;" and again, in 1770, at Barnet Races "Cocking at the Green Man, as usual."

This practice of holding cockfights and horseraces contemporaneously became more and more popular. Towards the close of the eighteenth and during the early decades of the nineteenth centuries rarely did cockfighting fail to add to the attractions of a Race-week. The pages of *The Sporting Magazine* provide abundant evidence of this. Here are a few extracts:

(June 1830). "A main of cocks was fought during the Chester Races, between Lord Molyneux (Potter, feeder), and H. B. Houghton, Esq. (Woodcock, feeder), for 20 sovs. each main battle, 10 sovs. each bye battle, and 500 sovs. the main; thirty-eight in the main, and eight byes."

(July 1830) "During the Manchester Race-week a main was fought at the Pit in Salford, between the Earl of Derby (Potter, feeder) and H. B. Houghton, Esq. (Woodcock, feeder), for 10 guineas a battle, and 200 guineas the main; forty mains, five byes.

A main of cocks was fought during Newton Races, between Thos. Legh, Esq. (Philips, feeder) and Col. Yates (Gilliver, feeder), for 10 guineas a battle and 200 guineas the main: thirty-one main battles, and ten byes."

* H. H. Dixon (The Druid), *Silk and Scarlet*, 1859, pp. 91-92.

(August 1830) "A main of cocks was fought during the Races at Preston, between the Earl of Derby (Potter, feeder), and Col. Yates (Gilliver, feeder), for 10 sovs. a battle, and 100 the main: twenty-seven mains, five byes."

(September 1830) "*Rochdale*—During the Races a main of cocks was fought between James Dearden, Esq. (Fletcher, feeder), and G. O. Smith, Esq. (Merryweather, feeder), for 5 sovs. a battle, and 100 the main."

(June 1831) "A main of cocks was fought during the Chester Race-week, between Lord Derby and H. B. Houghton, Esq., for 20 sovs. each main battle, 10 sovs. each bye battle, and 500 sovs. the main."

(June 1832) "During the Chester Races a main of cocks was fought between the Earl of Derby (Potter, feeder) and Mr. Houghton (Woodcock, feeder), for 20 sovs. a battle, 10 sovs. a bye, and 500 sovs. the main. After various vicissitudes it ended in a tie."

(July 1832) "During York Races a long main of cocks was fought in the Royal Pit, between the Gentlemen of the West-Riding of Yorkshire (Weightman, feeder), and the Gentlemen of Northumberland (Bagnal, feeder).

During Manchester Races a main of cocks was fought at the Pit in Salford, between the Earl of Derby (Potter, feeder) and H. B. Houghton, Esq. (Woodcock, feeder), for 10 guineas a battle, and 200 guineas the main: twenty-nine mains, eight byes.

At Newton Races a main of cocks was fought between T. Legh, Esq. (Kendrick, feeder) and Gen. Yates (Hines, feeder) for 10 guineas a battle, and 200 guineas the main: twenty-four mains, eleven byes."

(June 1833) "A main of cocks was fought during Chester Races, between the Earl of Derby and H. B. Houghton, Esq., for 25 sovs. each battle, 10 each bye, and 500 the main: forty in the main, and eight byes.

A main was fought in the Liverpool Race-week between Capt. Hawkins (Hines, feeder) and Dr. Bellyse (Davies, feeder), for 10 sovs. a battle and 200 the main.

A main was fought on the 7th of May at Halnager, Sussex, between the Gentlemen of Chichester (Shaw, feeder) and the Gentlemen of Bishop's Weltham (Austin, feeder), for 4£ a battle and 20£ the main; which was a hollow thing in favour of Shaw, who won eight mains and one bye, while his competitor only won a single main and no bye."

(July 1833) "During Manchester Race-week a main was fought at the Pit in Salford, between the Earl of Derby (Potter, feeder) and H. B. Houghton, Esq. (Woodcock, feeder), for 10 guineas a battle and 200 the main.

A main was fought in Newton Race-week between General Yates (Hines, feeder) and T. Legh, Esq. (Hendrick, feeder), for 10 guineas a battle and 200 the main, which was decided in favour of the General.

A main was fought in Buxton Race-week between General Yates (Bradley, feeder) and G. Walker Esq. (Aldred, feeder), for 10 sovs. a battle and 200 sovs. the main : twenty-four mains, nineteen byes."

(August 1833) "A main of cocks was fought during the Liverpool Races in the Cockpit at the Racecourse, between the Earl of Derby (Potter, feeder) and Gen. Yates (Hines, feeder), for 10 guineas a battle and 500 guineas the main : twenty-three mains, seven byes."

(June 1834) "During Chester Races a main was fought between the Earl of Derby (Potter, feeder) and H. B. Houghton Esq. (Woodcock, feeder), for 20 sovs. a main battle, 20 sovs. a bye battle and 500 sovs. a-side for the grand main : thirty-four mains, nine byes.

A main was fought at Liverpool during the Race-week between Dr. Bellyse (Davies, feeder) and Capt. Hawkins (Hines, feeder), for 10 sovs. a battle and 200 sovs. the main : twenty-five mains and eight byes."

(July 1834) "During the Liverpool Races, a main of cocks was fought between the Earl of Derby (Potter, feeder) and General Yates (Hines, feeder) for 10 guineas a battle and 500 guineas the main: twenty main battles and five byes."

At the height of its popularity, cockfighting was even more widely acclaimed and attracted greater attention than did racing. It is noteworthy that Lord Derby, for one, certainly gave it a good deal more attention. Apropos of this popularity, Sir Walter Gilbey has this to say: "The relative importance attached to racing and cocking is shown by an incident which occurred at Chester in 1834. It was represented to the Executive of the race meeting that the battles in the pit were likely to be well fought and prolonged, and that the main would not be over at the hour fixed to begin racing. The Clerk of the Course made no demur to postponement of the first race till three o'clock."*

But to return to the redoubtable Dr. Bellyse. We learn that: "He spoke, too, out of the fulness of his strange experience, as he had the privilege of all the walks on the Combermere, Shavington, Adderley, Doddington, Peckforton, Beeston, Oulton, and divers other estates in Cheshire, Shropshire, and Wales. In some seasons he sent out a thousand chickens, of which barely one-third would be reared, or fit to produce at an important main." From which it will be seen that the Doctor left nothing to chance. Continues the chronicler:

"After dinner, on the Saturday of his arrival at Chester, he gave an audience to his feeder, to sound him as to the condition of his cocks, and learn his opinion of the forthcoming main; and not infrequently that functionary would arrive with a couple of bags slung over his shoulder, and the pets of his fancy remonstrating inside. During the week, he would over and over again slip away from those who wanted to talk to him about weights, and watch his Brown-Red champions busy in their pens, scratching at a fresh-cut sod, or a spadeful of the purest gravel, fresh from the bottom of the Dee. Any feeder who did not furnish these stimulants, at least every third day, would have held his place on a very frail tenure. He would have a hundred cocks taken up from

* Sir Walter Gilbey, *Sport in the Olden Time*, 1912.

their walks for Chester, in order that his feeder might select the best, and put them in training from the Thursday week to the Monday, when the smaller cocks led off in the five days' main."

There can be small room for doubt that this old medico, apart from the experience and knowledge of his feeder which were there for him to draw upon, was himself something of an expert when it came to the problems of mating and the art of breeding. For, writes Dixon: "He inaugurated his career on the sod with the original White Piles, which carried such a wonderful spur, that the 'Cheshire drop', which would occasionally come out in a long battle, when the odds were twenty to one, was considered as fatal as the 'Chifney rush'. These were the cocks which the Cholmondeleys, the Egertons, the Warburtons, the Cottons, and the Raylances fought all the great country mains; sometimes against each other, but more frequently against the Mexborough and Meynell families. The Doctor, however, convinced himself that their constitutions would not stand the discipline of modern feeders, and at last, by judicious crossing, made his brown and black-reds carry as good a spur, and bear the most punishing preparation to boot. They were chiefly bred from his old 'cut-combed-hen', whose descendants were crossed with his brown 'crow alleys', two of Gilliver's black-reds, and the Westgarth cock. Six pullets to one hen, and the eggs as closely bred in as he could get them, were two of his leading tenets; the greater part of his chickens were also hatched in April and May, and he used the same stud-birds for about three seasons."*

Naturally enough, breeders of fighting-cocks set a high value on their stock birds and also on the eggs for hatching produced by them. It is related that on one occasion Dr. Bellyse was offered fifty pounds for a sitting hen of his famous strain. He accepted the offer and then and there lifted the bird from the nest and with his foot squashed the eggs on which she was sitting. A remonstrance from the buyer to the effect that surely the eggs were included in the bargain, brought the retort that if this had been the case the price would have been not fifty pounds but a thousand!

The "feeders", as they were called, who had the fighting-cocks in their charge, and were responsible for getting and keeping them in the pink

* H. H. Dixon, op. cit., pp. 93-94.

of condition, handling them in the cockpit, and tending their wounds, in many cases achieved considerable fame. Handling the birds during the actual fight, known as "setting", called for great skill, and the well-known experts charged big fees for their services, often as much as 30 guineas for a big main. Originally, the "feeder" invariably handled the birds in the cockpit, but in the eighteenth century the professions of "feeder" and "setter" were often separate, though there were still those sufficiently skilled in both capacities to perform the dual role. Sometimes a woman acted as "feeder".

Lord Derby had several "feeders" in succession, all famous in their day. The first was Busley; then there was Richardson; to be followed by Paul Potter and finally Paul's son, to whom the Earl bequeathed his birds and cocking equipment. There were the two Gillivers, Joe and William; there was John Brough, known the world over as a judge of exhibition Game as well as a breeder of fighting-cocks; there was equally famous Charles Faultless; there was the Cornishman, John Harris, who came of a long line of cockers, his father, grandfather and great-grandfather all being keen devotees of the "sport of kings", and there were others, many others.

Of the aforementioned Joseph Gilliver (one time handler of the Royal cocks for George the Third and George the Fourth), who was proclaimed by the *Sporting Magazine* (November 1834) to be "the most celebrated cock-feeder England ever produced", Blaine gives these particulars: "The first main, we are told, which Gilliver ever fought in public was at Coleshill in Warwickshire, and the last was at Preston in Lancashire, in 1830. During his life he fed principally for Lord Mexborough, Mr. Featherstone, Mr. White, General Yates, Mr. Sitwell, and others too numerous to mention. His chief opponent was Potter, who was feeder for that veteran sportsman, the Earl of Derby, whose attachment for the 'sod' continued unwearied, and who was seen enjoying to the very last his favourite amusement with all the zest of a younger man. The largest sum ever fought for in England, was a main of only seven battles for 1000 guineas a battle, and 5000 guineas the main.*

---

* Although Blaine was not alone in attributing to Gilliver the distinction of winning the largest stakes ever contested for in Britain, the accuracy of this statement seems to be, to say the least, questionable. According to John Harris, the heaviest stake ever fought for within these islands, was at Burton, when John Weightman, with his famous "Park House Reds", vanquished the Lancashire champions.—G.R.S.

This was fought at Lincoln, and won by Gilliver, who was fortunate enough to gain five out of seven battles. At Lichfield, Chester, Manchester, Newton, Oxford, and Preston, he has fought great mains and generally with success. The last few years of his life were spent in a neat cottage in his native town, which he built himself from the produce of his ability in the profession to which he was devoted, and in which he was unrivalled. He died in 1833, in his seventy-fourth year."*

In the early decades of the nineteenth century it was customary to give names to fighting-cocks, especially the more famous ones. J. Fairfax-Blakeborough, in his extremely interesting book, *County Life and Sport*, says: "I have before me a number of old bills containing the 'entries' for mains at Newcastle, Durham, Ferryhill and other northern places at which cocking flourished. They give the name, colour and owner of each bird."† Among the many names cited are: "'I Will Show You How,' 'North Country Lad,' 'Little Thought Of,' 'First on the Road,' and 'Wallop Away.'"‡

Although the sport of cockfighting seems to have permeated every part of England and Wales, at one time certain districts were recognised centres. In the north of England, in particular, it achieved great popularity. Referring to the beginning of the nineteenth century, in Pierce Egan's *Book of Sports*, we read: "Cocking, at the present period, is kept up with great spirit at Newcastle, and the recent meeting of Cockers at the above place, in point of extent, exceeds everything of the kind ever known in this Country. .... It is also calculated that at the termination of the races, which will finish the Cocking for the present season, upwards of 1,000 cocks will have met their deaths. Newcastle may therefore challenge all the world for Cocking." Indeed, not only did patrons of the sport foregather regularly at the Newcastle cockpits, but here were fought some of the biggest battles of all time. In describing one such famous contest, Nolan has this to say: "Upwards of 200 cocks were fought, and the fighting generally good, particularly the cocks of Baglin-hill and Lockey, which all won great majorities."§

---

* D. P. Blaine, *An Encyclopaedia of Rural Sports*, 1852, p. 1211.
† J. Fairfax-Blakeborough, *Country Life and Sport*, Philip Allan & Co., London, 1926, p. 76.
‡ Ibid, p. 79.
§ J. J. Nolan, *Ornamental, Aquatic and Domestic Fowl and Game Birds*, Dublin, 1850, p. 35.

Liverpool was at one time a centre of the sport. At a place known formerly as Devil's Acre many cockpits were to be found, and in them numerous battles were staged. Says the Liverpool *Evening Express* (May 22, 1953): "These cockpits were the resort of all the low ruffians of the neighbourhood. In consequence of the fights and disturbances which continually took place, the 'Watch' had no other alternative but to suppress cockfighting in this district. Later, the promoters moved to Love-lane, which was another 'hot spot', for this type of sport."

"There are people still living with memories of cockfighting in and near Liverpool, and of gamekeepers who kept birds in their yards," we read in an earlier issue of the Liverpool *Evening Express* (March 7, 1952), and according to this same journal: "At one time it was a seasonal event among followers of the early Grand National, and an old cockpit existed near the site of the original racecourse at Maghull." The county of Cheshire, too, was the scene of great battles. "Lord Sefton, Mr. Price of Brynpys, Captain White, and Mr. Bold Haughton, all fought at Chester."* Incidentally, Gilliver was one of the relatively few professionals handlers who salted away what for those days represented a considerable fortune as a result of his cockfighting activities.

Birmingham was another great centre for the sport. The cockpits in Smallbrook Street and in Coleshill Street, in the early decades of the nineteenth century, resounded to the crowing of battling roosters. Langford instances several advertisements appearing in the Birmingham newspapers of that time. Here is one such:

"May 15, 1809—A Main of Cocks will be fought at the new Pit in Smallbrook-street, Birmingham, on Thursday, the 25th of May, and the two following days, between the Gentlemen of Warwickshire and the Gentlemen of Worcestershire; to weigh 51 Cocks each for five Guineas a Battle and one Hundred Guineas the Main. A pair of Shakes to fight for twenty Guineas on Saturday. Twist, for Warwickshire; Willets, for Worcestershire. A Pair of Cocks will be on the Sod precisely at Twelve o'clock."†

* H. H. Dixon (The Druid), *Silk and Scarlet*, London, 1859, p. 95.
† John Alfred Langford, *A Century of Birmingham Life*, 1868. Vol. I. p. 271.

Another announcement reads:

> "New Cock Pit, Coleshill Street, Birmingham. March 31, 1817—A Main of Cocks to be fought, at the above Pit, on Easter Monday, and the three following Days, between the Gentlemen of Warwickshire and the Gentlemen of Staffordshire, for one Hundred Guineas the Main, and two Guineas each Battle. Feeders: Gilliver, for Warwickshire; Partridge, for Staffordshire."*

A county within the marches of which cockfighting achieved great popularity was Suffolk. Many mains were contested at the town of Bury St. Edmunds. It was here that, on one occasion, unforgettable in cockfighting lore, a champion fighter of his day, bred and owned by George Wilson, was carried triumphantly, in a decorated cage, through the streets. At the head of the procession was a banner bearing a picture, painted by a local artist, of the bird, and these lines:

> "O noble Iipsey, such a Cocke are thou,
> As Burie Towne, did nere contain till now
> Wherefore to praise thy worth and spread thy fame,
> We make this showe in honour of thy name."

Bristol was the scene of many contests. According to a writer in the *Western Daily Press* (September 19, 1953): "A particular resort was the Ostrich Inn on the side of Durdham Down, where Down House now stands." In 1778, says this authority, a great fight was staged there, at which there was "a full attendance of West Country squires anxious to follow the vicious encounters of the 52 birds entered for the three hundred and fifty guineas in prizes."

It would appear that cockfighting did not become popular in Scotland until the closing years of the seventeenth century. It is said that the Duke of York was responsible for its introduction in the year 1683. But when the sport was at last introduced, it became popular to some tune. Rogers, in his interesting and valuable work, *Scotland Social and Domestic*, says: "A cockpit under the auspices of His Royal Highness was established at Leith. To this cockpit the public were admitted at

---

* Ibid. Vol. I. p. 404.

charges varying from tenpence to fourpence. The sport attained such popularity that, on the 16th February, 1704, the Town Council of Edinburgh interfered to prevent it becoming an impediment to business. Later in the century, it was largely patronized by the aristocracy. Every land-owner kept a number of Gamecocks."

The Grassmarket in Edinburgh was the scene of many cockfights. Forsyth, who mentions this, remarks that this cockpit was chiefly supported by racing-men, gamblers and visitors to Edinburgh. He says: "Persons engaged in business, however, or of sober manners, and a respectable character, are ashamed to appear in it, and could not do so without reproach."*

Nothing perhaps provides more cogent evidence of the hold which cockfighting secured on the British public and the universality of its appeal than the attitude of the clergy towards the sport. They did not denounce it, they tolerated it; nay, they did more, they encouraged it. In all parts of the country the cockpits were in full blast on the Sabbath day. More and further, cockfights were held in the churchyards; and on occasion, in the churches themselves. And to cap the lot, when a fight was staged between two cities or towns the church-bells of the victor sounded their peal of triumph.

In the parish register of the Yorkshire town of Hemingborough, under date February 2, 1661, appears an entry of a cockfight held in the church.†

The Worshipful Chancellor Ferguson, author of an article on Cockfighting in *Transactions of the Cumberland and Westmorland Antiquarian & Archaeological Society* says: ". . . . the writer's father used to tell how, as a boy, he had heard in church at Burgh-on-Sands the preacher's voice drowned by the vociferations of the 'gentlemen of the sod', as the cockers are called, crying the odds: to do them justice they generally waited to begin, until the preacher was finished, but if he was on any occasion extra long-winded, their patience fell short, and they commenced." This same authority quotes an excerpt from *The Guardian* (October 1, 1884) respecting cockfights which used to be held after the service, in a cockpit near the church of Crasswall, in Herefordshire.

* R. Forsyth, *The Beauties of Scotland*, Edinburgh, 1805. Vol. I. p. 87.
† Sir Walter Gilbey, *Sport in the Olden Time*, 1912.

An extract, for which I am indebted to the same source, from Walker's *History of Penrith* (second edition, p. 80) reads : "The cockpit was on the south of the churchyard, near the old Catholic Chapel. It was properly fitted up, and every way convenient for the purpose. On one occasion, when the clergyman was reading the burial service, his voice was totally drowned by loud cheers from the pit, in token of the victory of a favourite cock."

It is significant that at an endowed grammar school at Alston, Cumberland, the prize which was competed for in connexion with cockfights held there at Easter was a prayer book.

In his interesting book of reminiscences, the Hon. Grantley F. Berkeley tells the following amusing story : "The last sporting adventure at which I met Jack Musters, was at a main of cocks fought by my brothers and myself against the late Sir George Dashwood, at Cranford. Never shall I forget the intense amusement of my friend when I pointed out to him a rather tall, dingy figure, in black coat and waistcoat, kerseymeres, and brown top-boots, all looking as if they had seen much wear and tear, or had never been brushed nor blackened. The elderly gentleman was very busy taking his gamecocks out of their bags, which he had sent to fight on our side. Musters was intently watching him, and when the first cock was taken out of his bag, he asked—'What the devil is that parcel tied to one of the legs of the bird ?' 'The battle-money of the individual who wears it at his foot,' I replied ; 'my revered friend always stands his own battle-money in preference to standing any share of our main, and generally by so doing loses, for his birds are not so good as ours.' 'Your revered friend,' he remarked, eyeing me with that well-known clear glance of bantering inquiry, so good-natured, so funny, and yet so keen and handsome in its expressions ; 'What do you call him *your* revered friend for ?' 'Because he is a highly respectable and beneficed clergyman.' Musters burst into such a fit of laughter that he set twenty-one cocks crowing and flapping their wings in the excitement of the sudden noise he made."*

Cockers of past ages, like all sportsmen, and indeed the majority of human beings in all walks of life, were superstitious, and doubtless the

---

* The Hon. Grantley F. Berkeley, *My Life and Recollections*, Hurst and Blackett, London, 1866. Vol. III, pp. 32-33.

present-day devotees of the sport, in all parts of the world, are superstitious too. Prominent among these magical beliefs was the notion that a Gamecock hatched by a magpie would prove to be unbeatable in the cockpit, as such a bird was thought to be demoniacally possessed and to fight under the protective agency of the devil. Thus many cockers made a practice of searching untiringly for opportunities to have their Game Fowl eggs hatched by magpies. Sir Walter Gilbey, who mentions this particular superstition in his interesting book, refers also to the belief that if dust from the communion table is collected and a little sprinkled in the cockpit, any evil influence will be warded off, and victory will surely go to the better bird, by which, as the author rightly says, "we may safely infer, was meant the bird owned by him who sprinkled the dust."* A Gamecock fed on consecrated bread was believed to be endowed with extraordinary fighting powers, hence it was common for cockers to be among the most regular communicants.†

Before closing this chapter it seems well to make some mention of the effect which cockfighting has had on the English language. We have seen that fighting-cocks were fed on the finest food procurable, irrespective of its cost, and it was from this practice that arose the phrase "living like a fighting cock." Naturally, many phrases connected with a display of any lack of courage have arisen from the sport, thus "to turn tail," meaning to run away or avoid battle, from the habit of the cock who wished to avoid fighting turning his tail towards the other. "To show the white feather," meaning to give every appearance of being afraid, similarly arose from the belief, whether well-founded or not is beside the point, of cockers that birds with a white feather in their plumage were poor fighters. From this belief, too, arose the modern practice of attaching a white feather to the hat or clothing of a young man who did not voluntarily join up for active service in time of war. Similarly "to show a clean pair of heels" indicated a runaway cock which shirked fighting, as today it refers to a man who prefers to clear off rather than face the music. In an opposite sense the phrase "to die game" is another relic of cockfighting days, due to the well-known propensity of the Gamecock fighting to the death, however outmatched or in

---

* Sir Walter Gilbey, Bart., *Sport in the Olden Time*, 1912.
† Georgina F. Jackson, *Shropshire Folklore*, 1883.

whatever desperate straits he might be. "He's a game old cock," has a similar implication, and a similar derivation. Another well-known provincialism, "He's getten his spurs on," implies that a person is willing and prepared to fight. Somewhat similar is the term "well-heeled", which in cockfighting days meant the bird possessed a good pair of natural spurs, or had been provided with keen and well-fitting metal spurs. In modern phraseology the term means ready for meeting all comers and situations that may arise in the struggle of life, and often implies that one is provided with plenty of money. In much the same significance, the American slang term "heeled" means armed. "Pitted against", the meaning of which is obvious, is another relic of cockfighting days.

The modern usage of "battle royal" in reference to a general fight is derived from the employment of the term in connexion with a battle in which a number of cocks were turned loose in the pit to fight indiscriminately. The champion bird of the day was called "cock of the walk", a term used at the present time to describe a person who struts about emanating self-assurance, and who considers himself superior to his fellows. "Cocky" is used in much the same way.

Cockstride is defined by Thomas Wright, the lexicographer, as "a short space", and owes its origin to the fact that the stride of a cock is but a small one. Cocksure is given by the same authority as meaning "quite certain", while cock-eyed means squinting.

It is interesting to note that, according to the following extract from the *Lincoln Mercury* (July 11, 1952), one town at least owes its name to the result of a cockfight. Thus:

"Stamford, Connecticut, U.S.A., with which town we have so many links these days, derived its name as the result of a cockfight! This surprising piece of information is given by the Rector of St. John's at our Stamford (The Rev. J. W. Parker), in his Parish Magazine. The original settlers of the American Stamford borrowed the Indian name Rippowam for their new home. It was not until the year following their settlement (1641) that they petitioned the general court of New Haven to change the name to Stamford. There is an interesting legend about how the name Stamford was chosen. It seems that the citizens of the new town were divided in their choice between Ayrshire and Stamford, so some of the sporting element decided on an unusual way to make the decision. Two fighting-cocks were obtained and the debated names were bestowed, one on each bird. A cockpit was built in front of the town meeting-house and a battle was fought to the finish. Stamford was victorious."

CHAPTER X

HISTORICAL ASPECTS OF COCKFIGHTING IN THE UNITED STATES OF AMERICA

It may be taken as certain that cocking has existed in that part of North America now forming the United States, since the early days when the first Europeans settled there. "It is highly probable," says Finsterbusch, "that the most prominent early cockers were Irish and that the greatest percentage of cocks fought along the Atlantic coast States were also Irish."* It is evident some Spanish Game fowls found their way into America, but predominantly they were English and Irish. The various breeds were crossed, and an American type gradually evolved. And then, sometime in the 1880's, a famous American breeder of Gamecocks, to wit, Dr. Clarke of Indianapolis, imported the Aseel fowl, which he crossed with his existent strains.

From a study of the annals of American cocking many famous figures emerge, some of whom are spoken of even today whenever and wherever cockers congregate. In the third, fourth and fifth decades of the nineteenth century, there was Uncle Billy Rodger; there was Uncle Pete, a negro who owned the biggest gambling joint in New York City; there was Cornelius Van Sickles, who fought for big stakes (the minimum being one hundred dollars); there was Patrick Duff, the Brooklyn breeder, whose fighting-cocks were considered to be invincible. A peculiarity of this particular strain of Gamecocks, known far and wide as the "Connecticut Strawberries", was their unusual size: they ranged from 5 lbs. 4 ozs. to 6 lbs. 10 ozs. One particular specimen, which was matched against all comers, was almost continually in the pit for three successive years, during which time he was never beaten. He weighed 6 lbs. 8 ozs., and because of a congenital deformity, was known as "The Hump". It was this identical bird which, in 1847, won for Johnny Crapeau, a New York gambler, the sum of one thousand dollars, despite

* C. A. Finsterbusch, *Cock Fighting All Over the World*, Grit & Steel, Gaffney, S.C., U.S.A., 1929, p. 347.

the fact that unknown to Crapeau, "The Hump's" metal spurs were fixed upside down in an effort to cheat him of victory. In this most famous of all his battles, "The Hump" was badly crippled in the opening stages, but despite this, he surprised everybody present, including his backers, by beating his opponent. Yet another famous cocker was Nigger Jackson, whose strain of fighting-cocks, like the "Connecticut Strawberries" of Patrick Duff, were reputed to be unbeatable.*

In those early days of American cockfighting, the pit was circular, or octagonal. In either case the sides were padded; and if the pit was octagonal, the corners were filled in. These sides were from 16 to 24 inches high and the diameter of the pit 16 or 18 feet. The floor was covered with carpet. The centre of the pit was indicated as nearly as possible with a circular white chalk mark. At a distance of one foot from this central spot another mark was made; on the opposite side and at the same distance from the centre was another mark. These two marks showed where the opposing cocks were to be placed at the commencement of the fight.

The rules of the cockpit were strict and clear. There were to be two judges, one chosen by each handler or pitter; and a referee, chosen by the judges. The referee's decision was to be final in the event of the judges being in disagreement. Neither the pitter nor any other person was allowed to handle the cock he was in charge of after once placing him in the pit, unless able to count ten, slowly and distinctly, before either cock went into battle, or should the bird he was in charge of get his spur fast in the carpet, in the web of the pit, or in his own body or plumage. In the event of a cock becoming fast in any of these ways the handler had the right to withdraw the spur; but should the spur be fast in his adversary, the right to draw it out, in this case, rested with the pitter of the pierced bird. Each cock was to be placed standing on his feet, on the marked spot near the centre of the pit, facing his antagonist. No unfair means of inciting the cock to fight, such as pushing him towards his opponent, or pinching him, was allowed; neither was any cleansing of the bird's feet, or of his eyes permitted during the course of the fight. In the event of a cock being on his back, the handler of this bird could get him on his legs again, so long as he did not lift the bird

---

* For much of this information respecting the cockers of America I am indebted to that interesting little book *The Cockers Guide*, By an Expert, published by Richard K. Fox, N.Y., 1888.

from the floor in so doing. The count was of the utmost importance, as the cock which refused to fight was said to be counted out and lost the battle. When both cocks refused to fight until counted out a fresh cock was brought into the pit, and the pitters tossed as to whose cock should tackle the newcomer first. If this fresh cock fought and the other again refused, the battle went to the fighter; should both refuse, the result was a draw. In the event of one cock dying before the count out was completed, he lost the battle even were he the last to show fight: the only exception to this was when his antagonist ran away.

Few changes of any consequence have been made in these rules through the years, and the American cockfight of today is run much along these lines. There are stipulations as to the length of the steel spurs, which were apparently absent from the early regulations. The usual length is $1\frac{1}{4}$ or $1\frac{1}{2}$ inches. Also the fighting-cocks must have untrimmed hackles; indeed the only trimming allowed is in relation to the long feathers in the tail, the wing feathers, and the fluff around the vent. The count, which is undertaken by the referee, consists of three tens and one twenty.

The law in relation to cockfighting in the United States of America is not so clearly defined as it is in England. For instance, in several States, the possession of cocks for the purpose of fighting is in itself illegal; in others the spectators at a cockfight whether or not they are owners of the contesting birds, are liable to arrest and prosecution; while in a few instances the birds may be seized by the police. Of all the States, however, California takes the most rigorous measures against the sport, for not only does it have all the aforementioned penalties, but in addition the possession of artificial spurs is illegal, and dubbing is prohibited. On the other hand, the law in some States does little to prevent the holding of contests. Thus in Kansas cockfighting is permitted on any weekday; in Alabama it is legal so long as it is held in conditions of strict privacy; in Kentucky any prohibition applies only to such fights as are "for profit". In many States, however, there are no specific laws against cockfighting, and any proceedings must be taken on the grounds of cruelty. It has been contended that birds are not animals, and in order to avoid any possibility of legal quibbles on this score, certain States, notably Maryland and Vermont, have clarified the position by stating that the term "animal" includes every form of living creature except man. Apparently the one State in which cockfights may be held without the slightest efforts at concealment or any risk of interference by the law is Florida.

Despite its illegality in nearly every part of the Union, cockfighting still flourishes. For in many of the States where the sport, on the ground of cruelty, comes under legal prohibition, the law does not appear to be enforced, the authorities often deliberately turning shut-eyes on its violation.

As a result of these variations in the law and its application or enforcement, today in several parts of the United States cockfights are often held openly and members of the public (including, on occasion, women and children) are admitted. Sometimes these fights are advertised in the Press. I have seen advertisements of mains to be held in the States of Arkansas, Florida, Kentucky, Louisiana, Mississippi, Ohio, Oklahoma, Tennessee and Texas. In fact, generally speaking, there is not that element of secrecy* in connexion with American cockfighting that is so pronounced a feature of the British brand. And, in addition, artificial spurs are advertised and sold without the slightest suggestion of secrecy or illegality.

Apropos of this remarkable state of affairs, an editorial in *The National Humane Review* (November, 1952) states: "There is hardly a sizeable community in the whole of the United States in which cockfights are not being conducted more or less regularly. And where this condition exists it is very often the fact that local law-enforcement authorities know about it—or don't want to know about it. Cockfights are always fairly widely publicized. They have to be to attract the necessary crowd of 'fanciers' and spectators. They are staged over and over at the same pits. They often are announced weeks and months in advance in national magazines. Any law-enforcement officer who wants to prevent the cockfights will have little difficulty in locating most of them." Further, from the same magazine, we learn that: "Tens of thousands of birds are maimed, mangled, and killed in agony every year in illegal pits. The sport's devotees boast openly of corrupting public officials. In commercial terms, it is at least a $10,000,000-a-year business."

* The main restriction as regards publicity in connexion with these American contests would appear to relate to the publication of photographs of the fights. Rarely is a member of the public who is present at a fight granted permission to take such photographs.

The illegality of cockfighting in the United States is nothing new. Over fifty years ago the law prohibited the sport in a number of States. Clifton R. Wooldridge, the famous Chicago detective, in his book of reminiscences, refers to the difficulty which the police experienced in locating the venues of the fights which were frequently held in Chicago. He mentions one occasion where on January 9, 1897, the police received information respecting a cockfight which was to be held on Wabash Avenue. Eventually Wooldridge discovered that the fight was to be staged in a barn behind a six-story house. Disguising himself as a bum, the detective purchased two roosters at a poultry store, placed them in sacks and carried them with him to the barn, where after some difficulty, he secured entry. On the sixth floor of the building were "a large assembly of men, a canvas pit, and lamps with reflectors on the walls around the room. The windows were covered with blankets, and there was a bar in one corner, stocked with liquors and cigars. Everything was ship-shape, ready for the fight." The account goes on to tell how Wooldridge on "the pretence of going for some more birds," managed to leave the building and telephone the police station and arrange for the place to be raided, with the result that twenty-five men were arrested and seventeen fighting-cocks seized.*

Not unnaturally, despite all the care that is taken in those States where the law against cockfighting is strictly enforced, occasionally the police succeed in catching the culprits. For instance, on April 19, 1953, twelve men were fined ten dollars each, as a result of a raid carried out by State troopers. The fights were staged in a barn on a farm at Catlettsburg, Kentucky.† Again, in the State of Virginia, on July 4, 1953, at a farm near Hoadly, the spectators at a cockfight were taken by surprise when three deputies and sixteen State police appeared on the scene. Of the 73 persons present, 17 were arrested and charged with betting. According to a report published in the *Washington Post* (July 5, 1953) from which these details are taken, Sheriff Turner D. Wheeling "said the raid was carried out after two of his undercover-men had made bets from $5 to $25 with the persons who were arrested."

* For a full account of this incident see Clifton R. Wooldridge's book, *Hands Up : In the World of Crime or 12 years a Detective*, Charles C. Thompson Co., Chicago, 1906, pp. 267-269.
† Report in *New York Herald Tribune*, April 20, 1953.

CHAPTER XI

COCKFIGHTING IN OTHER COUNTRIES

THE Aseel or Indian Fowl is the oldest domesticated breed in the world, and in its pure and original form one of if not the greatest of all fighters. The male Aseel is the fighting-cock par excellence of India, and was used for this purpose, according to the ancient sacred books of India, long before the birth of Christ. It is powerfully built, it has a solid muscular body set up on strong legs, carrying punishing natural spurs. The comb is naturally small, and so are the wattles. The breed was imported into, bred, shown and used for fighting in England. The Indian Game exhibited today at British shows must not be confused with the type which, in India, had so high a reputation as a fighter, nor with the type originally imported and bred by English fanciers. The present-day exhibition Indian Game would come off badly in battle with any bird other than one of similar type and breed.

Not by any means all the fighting-cocks of the Hindus were of the Aseel breed however. There was a good deal of crossing with other breeds, and many birds which were described as Aseels were a long way from being typical specimens. In fact the term Aseel was used with a good deal of looseness even by the natives themselves, and it came to be customary to refer to any cock which was reputed to be a fighter or destined to appear in a cockpit, as being an Aseel.

In those days when cockfighting flourished in India, Hindu rajahs and princes, most of whom owned large numbers of fighting-cocks, watched the battles with the keenest interest. The stakes were high, making even those of the time when the sport was at its peak of popularity in England, seem pitiably small in comparison. One thousand pounds was considered a very ordinary stake by these plutocrats, and the tale goes that it was no unusual thing for ten times this sum to enrich the owner of the cock which won a single battle. The city of Lucknow was the venue for the greatest fights.

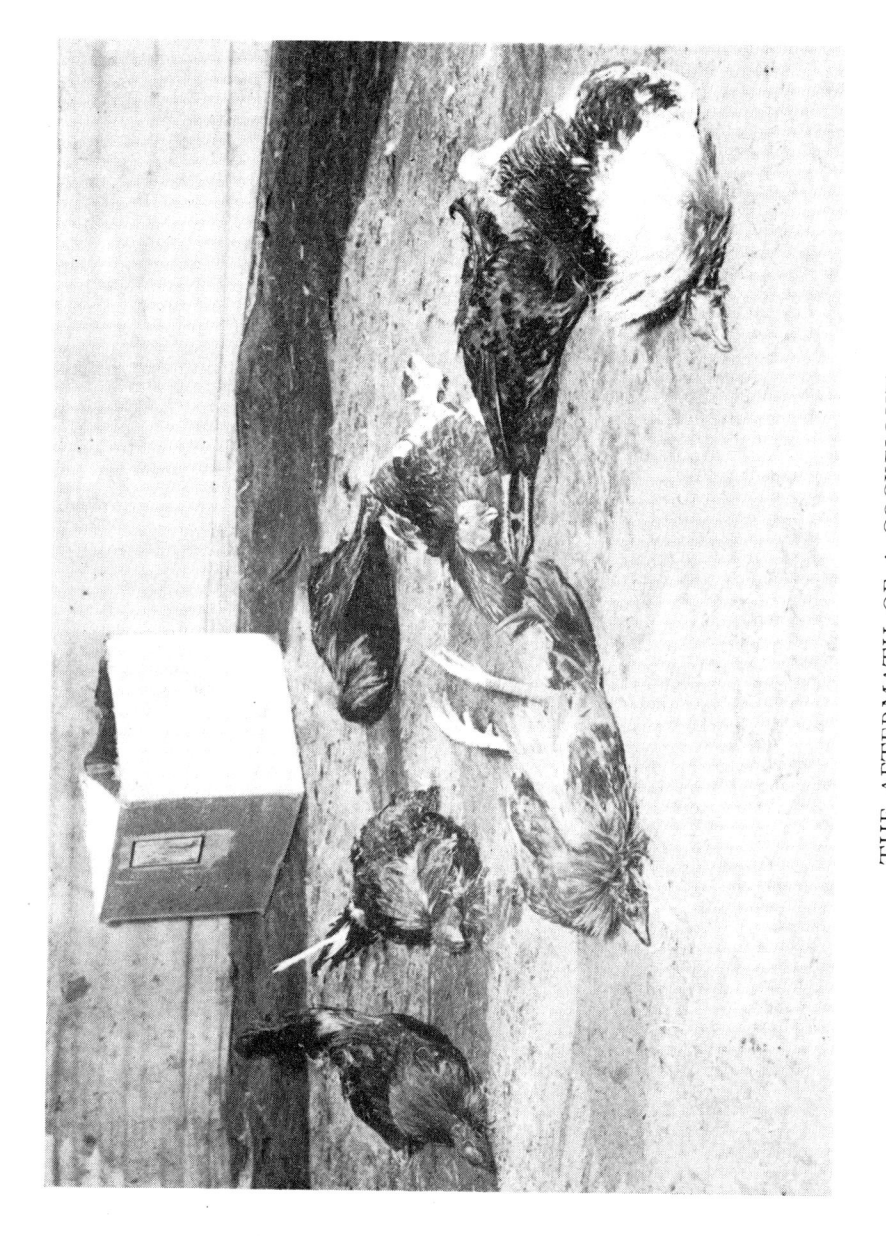

THE AFTERMATH OF A COCKFIGHT

These birds were found outside a pit after a raid by humane officers in the U.S.A.

WATCHING A COCKFIGHT IN HAITI

Long before any specimens of the Aseel were imported, news of the fame of the breed as a fighter reached England. This news, naturally and inevitably, aroused much comment, speculation, and consternation, for many persons had become firmly convinced that the fighting-cocks of England were invincible. Among those who heard of the prowess of the Aseel was Colonel Mordaunt, a well-known breeder of Old English Game. He decided to put these statements to the test, and accordingly hied him to India with a selected team of fighters. In the May of 1786, at Lucknow, Indian and English Game cocks met in battle, and to the colonel's great chagrin and surprise, his birds were defeated. It may be said, however, that the Indian cocks, fighting on their native soil and under conditions to which they were accustomed, undoubtedly had everything in their favour. Moreover, as every poultry exhibitor knows, no birds are at their best after travelling so considerable a distance and for so long a time, especially by sea.

In most Indian cockpits the birds usually fought with natural spurs, which had been shortened and sharpened. By this means prolonged battles were possible, and these appealed to the Hindu cockers far more than did the quickly decided contests. The birds were specially trained to this end. The most prolonged combats of all were known as "tape-fights", owing to the fact that strips of tape were wrapped over and around the spurs. The champions, selected for their strength and powers of endurance, could take and give a terrific amount of punishment. Few there were who could not manage a whole day's fight. More formidable and tougher specimens fought two-day battles; and, on occasion, the fight lasted into the third or fourth day. Today cockfighting is no longer the sport of millionaires; to the contrary it is the sport of the lower classes. Contests are staged in the open, often in the streets of large towns. The fighting-cocks are put through a long course of training and fed on a special diet.

According to Edgar Thurston, in some parts of India, cockfighting is a very serious affair, and great pains are taken to make each combat as prolonged as possible. The owner of a winning bird makes every effort to conserve the fighting powers of the bird and to ensure, where death does not intervene, that he will again be able to enter the pit. For instance, during the brief periods of rest given the combatants during a prolonged fight, the birds' heads are bathed and water poured into their mouths two or three times, while any feathers or blood that may have got into the mouth or are clinging to the beak are removed. In the fights witnessed by Mr. Thurston, at Chennapatna in Mysore, we are told that no artificial spurs were used, the natural spurs being sharpened until the points were of steel-like sharpness. On the other hand, among the Bants and other classes in South Canara, says the same authority, steel spurs of curved design were used.*

In China, too, cockfighting goes back to the days of antiquity, though, as in most countries, it was a long time before the practice ranked as being, in any sense, an organised sport. It would appear, however, that from comparatively early days quails as well as Game fowls were used for fighting. Writing in 1806, Barrow mentions this: "One of their most favourite sports is cockfighting, and this cruel and unmanly *amusement*, as they are pleased to consider it, is fully as eagerly pursued by the upper classes in China as, to their shame and disgrace be it spoken, it continues to be by those in a similar situation in some parts of Europe. The training of quails† for the same cruel purpose of butchering each other, furnishes abundance of employment for the idle and dissipated."‡ Fighting quails was a practice to which the Canton bargemen were much addicted, according to another observer, thus:

"There are other sports and gambling practices, common to most civilized nations, which are to be added to those already noticed; they include cockfighting, a favourite amusement of the Mandarins, and which was probably imported from the country of the Malays; quail and cricket fighting—all equally cruel and unmanly. Training is a profession which gives occupation to numbers, and the interest taken in these unworthy sports is so universal and exciting, that the gamester alone would credit their true history. The birds are furnished with steel spurs, as our Gamecocks in the pit, and the contest, therefore, seldom fails to prove fatal to one or both. The victor is put up for sale, or raffle, and the

---

* Edgar Thurston, *Ethnographic Notes in Southern India*, Printed by the Superintendent, Government Press, Madras, 1906.

† Quails rank as being second only to Gamecocks for pugnacity. Quail-fighting was not only practised for centuries in China, it was common among the ancient Greeks and Romans.

‡ John Barrow, *Travels in China*, 1806, p. 159.

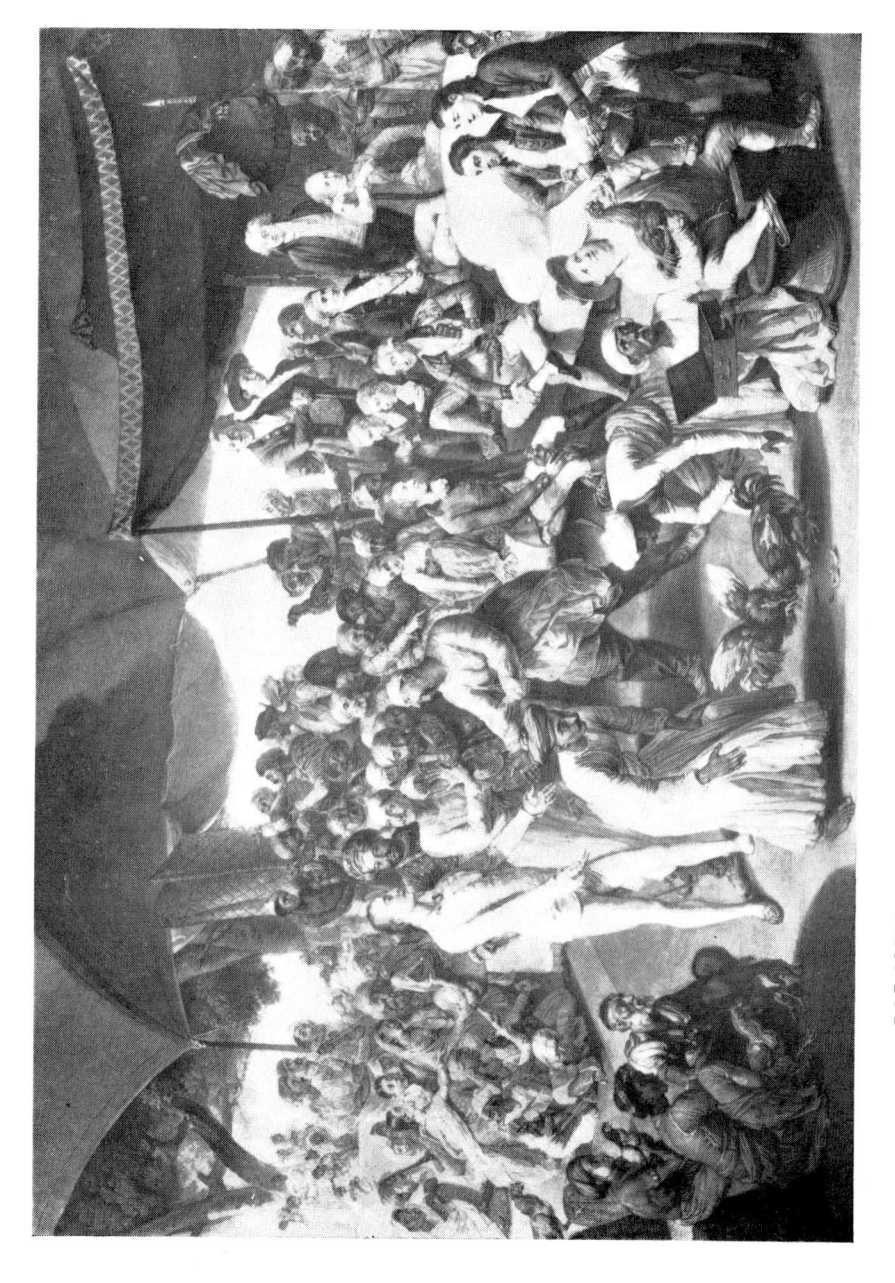

COLONEL MORDAUNT'S COCK MATCH AT LUCKNOW, 1786

From the painting by Johann Zoffany, R.A.

SPECTATORS AT A COCKFIGHT IN CO. DONEGAL 30 YEARS AGO. MATCHES ARE OFTEN HELD AT ISOLATED SPOTS ON THE BORDER TO FRUSTRATE POLICE ACTIVITY

CANTON BARGEMEN, FIGHTING QUAILS
From G. N. Wright, *China: In a Series of Views*, 1843

eagerness to become his master is demonstrated by the enormous sums staked, or paid down, for him."*

Cockfighting in the Philippine Islands is widespread. There is scarcely for the finding a town or even a village where it does not flourish. And all classes are addicted to it. According to an article on cockfighting in *The Encyclopedia Americana*, every peasant is the owner of a fighting-cock. And so great a value does he place upon the bird that "wherever he goes he takes it with him;" moreover, it is said that in the event of his habitation being threatened by fire his first thought would be of his Gamecock, which he would rescue "rather than his wife or child." Further, says the writer of the article; "The sport is there practised in a very cruel form, and many are ruined by excessive betting."†

In nineteenth-century Malacca cockfighting was tolerated by the authorities, and proved a profitable undertaking to the owners of the many cockpits in operation there. An observer on the spot, writing in 1853, remarked: "The cocks, which at the present day present specimens of the finest class, are trained much in the same way as in Europe, but are armed, in the place of a spur, with a broad flat blade, resembling their own favourite weapon—the kris; with which they were enabled to inflict frightful wounds, without being of so deadly a nature as with the more pointed instrument in use in our country; the battle was thus more doubtful and bloody, and of much longer duration."‡

Cockfighting has long been practised in Celebes. A wealth of information on the subject is given by Kaudern,§ who says: "The Orang Bugis as well as Orang Macassar most carefully attend their Gamecocks, even more than to their horses. A Gamecock is kept in a basket some time before a fight. Every night he has his bath and his shampoo to harden his muscles. On the day of the fight the comb as well as the wattles are trimmed down."‖ A Gamecock's value is dependent upon his pedigree, and also upon whether or not he has been born in a sacred place. Kaudern

---

* Rev. G. N. Wright, *China, in a Series of Views, Displaying the Scenery, Architecture and Social Habits of that Ancient Empire*, London, 1843. Vol. II. pp. 65-66.

† *The Encyclopedia Americana*, American Corporation, New York, 1937.

‡ Colonel Arthur Cunynghame, *An Aide-de-Camp's Recollections of Service in China*; Bentley, London, 1853, p. 46.

§ Walter Kaudern, *Ethnographical Studies in Celebes*, Vol. IV., Martinus Nijhoff, The Hague, Holland, 1929.

‖ It seems strange that the cutting down of the comb and wattles should be left until the actual day of battle. The most inexperienced of cockers should know better than this.—G.R.S.

says that, according to Matthes (an authority on the subject), "a fine Gamecock from Mecca could not be paid for with any gold in the world." Much importance is attached to the scales on the bird's legs, which are supposed to indicate "strength and courage." A metal spur is usually attached to the cock's left foot. Kaudern writes: "Matthes describes various methods of placing the spur. It is generally fastened underneath the foot, but it may also be attached on top of it either on the inside or the outside. If a big cock is to fight a small one, the spur of the former is placed inside his leg at the height of his heel, or the big cock sometimes will fight without a steel spur."*

One of the most peculiar features in connexion with cockfighting in Celebes is the use of a strange device known as the *parasila*. It comes into play only when one of the combatants is dead or badly-wounded and apparently beaten. At this stage, says Kaudern, "the victor is relieved of his spur and brought to his fallen adversary to peck at him, the more furiously the better. This properly done, the cock is declared the winner of the fight. Should the victorious cock refuse to peck at his adversary, the owner of this cock should be asked if he is willing to place the head of his cock in the so-called *parasila*. If not he has lost the game." This *parasila* is a wooden affair of simple construction. "Into one of the ends of a rectangular board, another and narrower board is set at right angles, having its top end bifurcated and joined with a thin lath. According to Matthes the head of the vanquished cock is placed in the fork for the victor to peck at. If the victor does peck, the owner of the worsted cock will lose his stake as well as his bird. Should the winner refuse to peck, the game is drawn or *pari*, and the owner of the defeated cock only has to give the left leg of his cock to the manager, unless he does not prefer to pay him the sum of five *doewit*. The game also is considered *pari* if the victorious cock, immediately after having administered the death-blow to his adversary, should happen to crow. In every day cockfights people are not so particular as this. A cock who has killed his adversary is declared the winner even if he should refuse to peck at his fallen antagonist, or crow immediately after having brought him down. . . . . If both cocks should fall, badly wounded, or both run away, the game is *pari*. In case of *pari* one of the cocks is awarded to the

* Kaudern, *Ethnographical Studies in Celebes*, op. cit., p. 340.

umpire and the other to the manager, but the owners may keep their cocks if they are willing to pay the sum of thirty *doewit* to the officials in question."*

Cockfighting has flourished in Borneo for many generations, and there never has been, nor is there now anything illegal about its practice. It is apparently not only a sport in which the commercial aspect enters, but it is invariably a feature of the festivities of the country. According to the writer of an article in the *West Australian*, while the native cockers of the interior of North Borneo use artificial spurs, the Mohammedans who inhabit the coast believe in naked-heel fighting. A peculiar feature of these North Bornean cockfights is described in the aforementioned article: "Each side has the right to stop the fight three times during its course and at any stage. This break is termed a 'purut' (corresponding to the end of a boxing round) and occupies an interval of no fixed duration, but it gives the owners an opportunity to revive their birds by fanning them, staunching the wounds, and washing off the congealed blood adhering to eyes and comb. After the third 'purut' the fight must proceed without further interruption until one or other of the cocks surrenders by turning tail."†

It was the publication of a picture of the 17-year-old Duke of Kent watching a cockfight in progress in the market-place of the Bornean village of Keta Belub that aroused a protest from the League Against Cruel Sports. The Society issued the following statement: "The League Against Cruel Sports deplores the attendance of the Duke of Kent at a cockfight in Borneo—a cruel sport which has for years been illegal in Britain." Apropos of this, it has been stated that as cockfighting is a popular sport in Borneo, the fact that one was taking place at the time when the Duke was present, was probably "quite incidental, and presumably he only watched it out of courtesy to the country's customs." According to the London correspondent of the *Johannesburg Star* (Oct. 30, 1952) "The League Against Cruel Sports, however, thinks the excuse of 'when in Rome . . .' does not suffice in this case. 'It does not matter what Tom, Dick or Harry do in Borneo', an official of the league told me, 'but Royalty are different—they are ambassadors and

* Kaudern, op. cit., pp. 341-2.
† *West Australian*, Perth, Oct. 25, 1952.

we expect them to refrain from any sport which is illegal in their own country'. An official of the Royal Society for the Prevention of Cruelty to Animals told me that while they could not remain indifferent to the fact that the Duke was present at a cockfight, his Society did not intend to make a formal protest. 'We recognise the difficulties of members of Royalty who go abroad'."

In Mexico there were keen cockfighters in those long-distant days when the sport was introduced by the Spaniards. No less enthusiastic are the present-day inhabitants of the republic. Contests are staged between naked-heel fighters as well as birds wearing artificial spurs. The deadly slasher is the type of metal spur most favoured today, each cock being furnished with one weapon only. Nevin O. Winter, in his interesting book on Mexico, refers to the prevalence of fighting-cocks, which travellers encounter "tied by the leg to a stake with a few feet of string," and further mentions that: "Itinerant cockfighters who travel across the country carrying their birds in hollow straw tubes are popular fellows."*

Cocking has been practised in most of the Central and South American republics for centuries. Of the lot, Peru has the distinction of having the longest historical association with the sport. In fact most of the other South American States, at any rate, procured their foundation breeding stock from Peru. In Pierce Egan's *Book of Sports*, we read: "At Lima the diversion of cockfighting is followed with great avidity, where it was not under any regulation till 1762; the duties of society were not only neglected by many individuals, but there were continual disputes among the amateurs. At length the little square of St. Catherine, near the walls of the city, was fixed upon for this amusement only. It is observed that the brook running here, and the gardens which almost surround this spot, the goodness of air, etc., render the situation most delightful. The building in which the sport is carried on forms a kind of amphitheatre; the seats naturally ascend, leaving nine open spaces between them for the spectators, who stand. On the outside of the amphitheatre is a very commodious staircase which leads to the upper galleries, twenty-nine in number, not including that of the judge, which is distinguished by its decorations and its magnitude. Here this

* Nevin O. Winter, *Mexico and Her People of To-day*, Cassell & Co., London, 1913.

amusement is permitted not only two days in the week, but on Saint's day and on Sundays; the seats in the corridors are let at different prices, but the spectators who stand in the nine open spaces between the area and the galleries are admitted gratis. Notwithstanding the crowd is often immense, no disorder occurs, and the judge who decrees the prizes has always a guard with him to enforce his authority."

The above description will give some slight idea of the measure of popularity cockfighting held in Peru some one hundred years ago. In this country, however, cockfighting is permitted and regulated by the State.

From a century-old travel book are gatherable some revealing references to cockfighting in Central America. The contests which the author describes were staged in the yard of an empty house, and attracted a large gathering, "all Mestitzoes or White men." Presumably the female spectators were whites too, though this detail is not specifically mentioned. Each cock that was destined to do battle was tied by one leg to some part of the yard wall. After much fussing about on the part of the owners of the birds, with a view to matching for size and weight, a couple of combatants were selected, and long needle-sharp metal spurs affixed to their legs. A space was cleared, the birds put on the ground, immediately upon which, with hackles ruffled, and to the accompaniment of much noise and heated vociferation from the male spectators, they were at each other with beak and spur. In a matter of minutes one combatant, with protruding tongue and blood-oozing mouth, was in the throes of death. As regards the female element among the spectators, the narrator writes: "I owe it to the ladies to say, that in the city they never are present at such scenes. Here they went for no other reason that I could see than because they were away from home, and it was part of the fete. We must make allowances for an education and state of society every way different from our own. They were not wanting in sensibility or refinement; and though they did not turn away in disgust, they seemed to take no interest in the fight, and were not disposed to wait for a second."*

In Cuba, too, cocking was extremely popular, especially on Sundays.

---

* John Lloyd Stephens, *Incidents of Travel in Central America, Chiapas and Yucatan*; revised by Frederick Catherwood, Arthur Hall, Virtue & Co., London, 1854, pp. 159-160.

Samuel Hazard gives a most interesting account of a visit to a Cuban cockpit some eighty years ago. The building in which the fights were staged could accommodate about a thousand spectators. He was especially struck with the smallness of the fighting-cocks. Apparently, although artificial spurs were known and used there, naked-heel fighting was also practised. In Mr. Hazard's own words: "There are various modes of fighting: *Al cotejo*—that is, in measuring, at sight, the size of spurs of both chickens. *Al peso*—or by weight, and seeing if the spurs are equal. *Tapados*—where they settle the match without seeing the chickens, or, in fact 'go it blind'. *De cuchilla*—where they put on the artificial spurs, in order to make the fight sharper, quicker, and more fatal. *Al pico*—where they fight without any spurs." Usually, however, the birds were matched for weight, their spurs trimmed to increase their sharpness, and superfluous feathers clipped away. Hazard goes on to describe the "shouting, bawling, vociferating, and motioning to each other in the making of their bets, until the place is a very Babel." Men of all ranks and stations in life jostle each other as they shout their bets. Eventually however the scene of confusion and disorder clarifies itself, the spectators take their seats, the fighting-cocks are placed in the pit, the battle begins. Excitement mounts, screams and yells punctuate the blows in the process of this sanguinary combat. "At last," writes Hazard, "the combatants are both seriously hurt, and perhaps blinded, by the blood and dust; and then there is a lull in the fighting, while the backers doctor up their birds, wiping the blood from their heads, blow through a quill a little alum to heal their eyes, or spirt a mouthful of *aguardiente* over their heads; the audience, meanwhile, keeping up the racket until the chickens commence at it again, with just the same fury, clawing, nipping and dodging, until one or the other is either dead or so disabled he can no longer fight, when the play is up, and a roaring cheer breaks from the lucky betters."[*]

For a long time cockfighting was suppressed in Puerto Rico, but recently it again became legal, and now ranks high among the sports of the country. The fights draw hundreds of spectators, and both stakes and bets often run into big figures.

Although cockfighting has been practised at one time or another in

[*] Samuel Hazard, *Cuba with Pen and Pencil*, Sampson Low, Marston, Low & Searle, 1873, p. 194.

A COCKFIGHT IN THE AUSTRIAN TYROL

COCKFIGHTING IN THE EAST INDIES
From *The Graphic*, 1892

most of the countries comprising the continent of Europe, as distinguished from the United Kingdom, it is in France that the sport has continued to retain its popularity for the longest period of time. Some authorities are of opinion that it was introduced by the Phoenicians, others are certain that the responsibility rested with the ancient Gauls, but however this may be, there is evidence of its popularity in the France of antiquity. It would appear, however, that the greatest developments in French cocking occurred after the British government had prohibited the holding of cockfights throughout Great Britain, for the most celebrated figure in the history of French cockfighting was not born until 1850. This was Henri Cliquennous. In adolescence and in manhood, Henri devoted a good deal of his energies to the breeding and judging of the Game Fowl. His knowledge and skill resulted in great improvements, not only in the birds placed on the show bench, but also in those which found their way into the cockpit. The French Gamecock was soon to be known as one of the largest, most powerful, and most courageous fighting-cocks in the world.

At that time, steel spurs made along the lines of those used in England, were favoured. They were $1\frac{3}{4}$ inches in length and only very slightly curved. In the first clash with specimens of Old English Game, taken across the channel by Atkinson, the French champions came off second best, and no doubt Henri Cliquennous was a very disappointed man. But there were other and greater disappointments in store. Towards the close of the nineteenth century, the celebrated American breeder, Dr. Clarke, sent over a number of Gamecocks, which after they had become accustomed to the French climate and environmental conditions, were pitted against the French fighters. The American birds had, however, a big advantage. They were armed with the long, strong, curved spurs in vogue at that time in the States. Using their deadly weapons with lethal effect, they made quick work of the best fighting-cocks the French were able to bring against them. Dr. Clarke scored a notable triumph.

Cliquennous and his fellow cockers had learned a valuable lesson. They were not slow to act on it. Forthwith they discarded the short-bladed English type of spur and adopted the long curved American. The result was a turning of the tables. Henceforth the French fighting-cocks, owing to their greater size and strength, had the advantage. It was the turn of the English cocks to suffer annihilation.

The coming of the twentieth century did not see the end of the sport in France. In the *Daily Express* there is a descriptive account of cockfighting in Calais, not at the private rendezvous where birds fought for stakes sometimes reaching £100, but in "a covered courtyard behind a café, where half a crown was a big bet." According to this report, some 200 persons paid to watch the contests and among them were women and children. The fighting-cocks were big barnyarders, armed with steel spurs. The battles varied in duration from 15 seconds to 13 minutes, the longest. "At the end of the 13-minute fight both birds, torn, bleeding, barely breathing, were apparently dying. The crowd shouted insults, then roared applause as one slowly lifted himself, pecked at his opponent's eye, leaped in the air and struck one steel spur clean through the other bird's head."*

Today cockfighting retains a good deal of its popularity in France, where it is legal. Until comparatively recently it was legal in Belgium too. Before the war there was a Belgian society, boasting a membership of over 100,000, known as the "National Federation of Cockfighters." Today, owing to its illegality, the sport is carried on surreptitiously. In point of fact, the Gamecock figures more in the breeding pen than in the cockpit, as pedigree birds of both sexes are saleable in France at most remunerative prices.

Majorca is the scene of many cockfights, for here again there is nothing illegal in connexion with the sport. Far from it. The fights are advertised ; the police attend them as spectators. Naked-heel fighting is the vogue.

---

* *Daily Express*, March 14, 1939.

CHAPTER XII

THE WAR ON COCKFIGHTING

During the centuries when cockfighting ranked as the most popular of British sports the authorities from time to time took steps to regulate and to curb the sport rather than to stop it altogether. Indeed, apart from the short-lived prohibitory measure of 1654, and the restrictive Act of 1835, cockfighting continued to exist and to enjoy great popularity until the passing of the Cruelty to Animals Act of 1849.

It is noteworthy, however, that all *early* measures enacted, or steps taken by the authorities, against cockfighting were not *concerned with the birds*, but with the persons to be found in the cockpits, whether actively participating in the sport or being spectators. In other words the question of cruelty or barbarity was not considered at all. The government on the one hand and the local authorities on the other were not motivated by feelings of humanity; the reason for their interference was a very different one.

Cockfighting, bearbaiting, horseracing, and other diversions of the public, were often the scenes of disorder and, on occasion, of rioting. At the cockpits, men of all classes were present, passions rose high and blows were frequently exchanged when there were disputes as to the issue of a battle. Cheating and "welshing" occurred in connexion with nearly every contest. Misson, a French observer, refers to this in the following passage: "Cockfighting is one of the great English diversions; they build Amphitheatres for this Purpose and Persons of Quality sometimes appear at them. Great Wagers are laid; but I'm told that a man may be damnably bubbled if he is not very sharp."*

Apart from the possibilities and indeed the likelihood of these unruly gatherings ending in riotous behaviour, the wasting of time that could

---

* *M. Misson's Memoirs and Observations on his Travels over England*, translated by Mr. Ozell. London, 1719, p. 39.

be given to cultivating the art of defence was officially frowned upon. According to Maitland, in the year 1365, King Edward the Third addressed a letter to the Sheriffs of London ordering that cockfighting and certain other amusements should be forbidden as they occupied hours of leisure which could be better employed in practising the art of shooting. From this it is apparent that even in those early days the government had mastered the art of exercising, in indirect and insidious ways, control over the lives of the citizenry.

Moreover, the government in those days took a very serious view of the possibilities which cockpits, bowling alleys, and other such public gathering places presented for traitors, rebels and other trouble-makers to meet and hatch their plots in comparative security. The much-trumpeted humanitarianism ascribed to the Cromwellian Act of 1654, which prohibited cockfighting, was actually inexistent. Cromwell was concerned not with the prevention of cruelty but with the prevention of rebellion. The Statute of 1654 was not a humanitarian act; it was a political measure.

The passing of Cromwell saw the end of the prohibitory Statute. Cockfighting flourished once again. Indeed, so popular was the sport with all sections of society, that at a time when those individuals who had any thought for the feelings or sufferings of birds and animals were remarkably few, it was unlikely that actual prohibition would, by any other than a totalitarian government motivated by feelings for its own safety, be contemplated.

Something had to be done to preserve order, however. The quarrelling, fighting and often downright rioting, which were such common incidents in connexion with sports of every kind, had to be curtailed. To this end a law was passed in the reign of Charles the Second forbidding betting at the public cockpits, the penalty being the forfeiture of double the amount won. Local authorities forbade the holding of cockfights at public houses, the penalty in this case being the loss of the licences.

Many of those attending cockfights and in some cases the owners of the fighting-birds were of the lowest possible type, the scum of the cities. It is such a man who is the subject of the following verses by Lemoine:

"A saucy rolling blade am I,
   I keep a Donkee Dick;
Thro' London streets my wares I cry,
   Up *peck* and *booze* to pick.

In Black-boy alley I've a *ken*,
   A *tyke* and *fighting-cock*;
A saucy tip-slang, *moon-eyed hen*,
   Who oft *mills doll* at *Block*.

I'm known by all the deep ones well,
   About Saltpetre Bank;
And always ready, *prigs* can tell,
   To *gig* a Smithfield *hank*.

I'll race my Jack, or bait a bull,
   Or fight my *doodle-doo*;
I'll *flash* a *quid* with any cull
   And *fly* a *pigeon blue*.

I'll back my *ginger* to make a hit,
   My fine, my true *Game Cock*;
The *Swells* can't *do* me in the pit,
   I'm *down* to ev'ry *lock!*

I'm up to all your knowing *rigs*,
   Ye biddies queer and flash;
I'm company for *scamps* and *prigs*,
   Sometimes for men of cash.

My Moll oft' tips the knowing *dive*,
   When *Sea-crabs* gang the stroll;
Unless she did, how could we thrive,
   And in warm *flannel* roll?

I shew more conscience in my whack,
   Than Fox, with all his skill;
While he takes Houses on his back,
   I but my pockets fill.

Sometimes those guilty of riotous behaviour were prosecuted. In the Staffordshire town of Wednesbury, where cockfighting was not only widely practised but also notorious for its rowdiness, things reached such a stage in the middle of the eighteenth century that the prescribed punishment for causing rioting was a dose of the cat-o'-nine-tails. Some popular verses, which we are told were chanted by the Wednesbury cockers, give an idea of the conditions prevailing at that particular time.

> "At Wednesbury there was a cocking,
>   A match between Newton and Skrogging;
> The colliers and nailers left work,
>   And all to Spittles' went jogging
> To see this noble sport.
>   Many noted men there resorted,
> And though they'd but little money,
>   Yet that they freely sported.
>   Raddle tum rum tum ra,
>   Fol de rol la lal la,
>   Raddle tum rum tum ra
>   Fol de rol la lal la.
>
> There was Jeff'ry and Boburn from Hampton,
>   And Dusty, from Bilstone, was there,
> Frumity he came from Darlaston,
>   He was as rude as a bear:
> And there was old Will from Walsal,
>   And Smacker from West Bromwich came;
> Blind Dobbin, he came from Rowley,
>   And staggering he went home.
>   Raddle tum, &c.
>
> Ruff Mory came limping along,
>   As though he'd some cripple been mocking,
> To join the blackguard throng
>   That met at Wednesbury cocking;
> He borrow'd a trifle of Doll,
>   To back old Tavener's grey,

He laid fourpence halfpenny to fourpence,
  Lost, and went broken away.
    Raddle tum, &c.

But soon he returned to the pit,
  For he borrowed a trifle more money,
And ventur'd another bet
  Along with blubber-mouth Coney;
When Coney demanded the money,
  As was usual upon such occasions,
He cried, 'B — — st you, if you don't hold your rattle,
  I'll pay thee as Paul paid the Ephesians.'
    Raddle tum, &c.

The morning's sport being over,
  Old Spittle a dinner proclaimed
That each man should dine for a groat,
  If he grumbled he ought to be damn'd;
For there was plenty of beef,
  But Spittle he swore by his troth,
The devil a man should dine,
  Till he'd eaten his noggin of broth.
    Raddle tum, &c.

The beef it was old and tough,
  Of a bull that was baited to death;
Bunny Hide got a lump in his throat,
  That had like to have stopped his breath:
The company fell in confusion
  To see poor Bunny Hide choke;
They took him into the kitchen,
  And held his head over the smoke.
    Raddle tum, &c.

They held him so close to the fire,
  That he frizzled just like a beefsteak,
Then threw him down on the floor,
  And had like to have broken his neck;

> One gave him a kick in the stomach,
>   Another a thump on the brow;
> His wife cried, 'Throw him in the stable,
>   And he'll be better just now.'
>   Raddle tum, &c.
>
> Then soon they returned to the pit,
>   And the fighting went on again;
> Six battles were won on each side,
>   The next was to decide the main,
> For these were two famous cocks
>   As ever that country bred,
> Skrogging's a duck-wing black
>   And Newton's a s– – – – – wing red
>   Raddle tum, &c.

And so on: in crude verse the fight is described, and the quarrel between the owners of the competing birds, each of whom accuses the other of cheating, is depicted. Each, too, has his supporters, and a fight of another kind develops, in which, says the poet:

> Ruff Mory bit off a man's nose,
>   It's a wonder no one was slain,
> They trampled both cocks to death,
>   And so they made a draw main.
>   Raddle tum, &c.
>
> The cockpit was near to the church,
>   An ornament to the town,
> On one side an old coal-pit,
>   The other was well goss'd round;
> Peter Hadley peep'd through the goss,
>   In order to see them fight;
> Spittle jobb'd his eye out with a fork,
>   And cried, 'B – – st thee, it served thee right.'
>   Raddle tum, &c.

> Some people may think this is strange,
>   Who Wednesbury never knew,
> But those who have ever been there
>   Won't have the least doubt but it's true;
> For they are all savage by nature,
>   And guilty of deeds the most shocking,
> Jack Baker whacked his own father,
>   And so ended Wednesbury cocking.
>   Raddle tum, &c.

Through the centuries there did, on occasion, arise protests against cockfighting on grounds other than those which actuated the authorities in their efforts to curb or control the sport. Protests were made that cockfighting was cruel and sinful. That these protests were largely unheeded and futile was due to the lack of humanitarianism on the one hand, and the fact that they reached very few members of the public on the other. The huge majority could neither read nor write.

Looking at the matter from another angle, Dr. Johnson was full of condemnation for the sport. He said: "Cocking and bearbaiting may raise the spirit of a company just as drinking does, but they will never improve the conversation of those who take part in them."

There has been much controversy as regards the reaction of Lord Byron, and the lines

> "It has a strange quick jar upon the ear,
>   That cocking———"

have repeatedly been quoted as evidence of his disapproval. In this connexion, however, the opinion of encyclopaedist Blaine is of interest and value:

> "In early life we were on terms of intimacy with Mrs. Massinberg, of 16 Piccadilly, as the numbers then ran: she was a relative of Lord Byron, and whenever he left college on a visit to London he used to domesticate at her residence, and there we also on several occasions met him, and enjoyed his conversation, which, as might be supposed, led him to remark on the scenes he met with in London; and as our

pursuits among animals were well known to him, and much interested his inquiries, so there were none at that time prevalent that his capacious mind did not mention, and make inquiries about. But while we own we never heard him eulogise cocking, we can conscientiously aver we never heard him utter a word against it, although we have a faint remembrance of being told by him that he had on a previous day visited a cockpit, and that he inquired of us, also whether we had seen the same. Beyond this we affect to know nothing of Lord Byron's sentiments on cocking; but it may be supposed from his promptitude at that time in 'speaking his mind', that had he then conceived any disapprobation of the sport of cocking, he would have stated it. If it were not that every sentiment known to be entertained by this truly eminent writer is a matter of record with the public, we should not have introduced this seemingly irrelevant matter unto any minor consideration."*

Perhaps the first serious attack was launched by Philip Stubbes in his *Anatomy of Abuse*, published in 1583. The main point of this attack was concerned with the fact that cockfighting and other sports were practised on Sundays. Others denounced the cockpit and its supporters on the grounds of brutality. Richard King writes: "Cockfighting, of all games, is surely one of the most barbarous, and a scandal to the practitioners who follow it, both high and low; for, notwithstanding its antiquity as a diversion in England, it is now become a disgrace to humanity; and surely none but the most notorious gamblers can be elated therewith, or give a sanction to barbarity that even shudders the Indian to hear of. At these scenes of cruelty the greatest depredations are committed by the attendants thereon, the most prophane and wicked expressions made use of, the most horrid and blasphemous oaths and curses denounced against Fortune for the loss of an odd battle, with a jargon of disconsonant tongues as hard to be understood, and in as great confusion, as that at Babel, composes the group, among whom are to be found my Lord in dispute with a butcher, and his Grace with a farrier, all hail fellow well met. From these, and other meetings of the like nature, let me dissuade my readers, where nothing is to be

---

* Delabere P. Blaine, *An Encyclopaedia of Rural Sports*, 1852, p. 1210.

A MID-AIR BATTLE BETWEEN TWO COCKS IN PAKISTAN

COCKS FIGHTING IN PAKISTAN

obtained but at the expense of humanity, and to the discredit of Christianity."*

It was, however, Edmund Ellis, who, writing in the seventeenth century, not only himself attacked cockfighting as a sinful and barbaric practice, but also collected together a number of denunciatory outbursts from others. Ellis says:

"Though it be my opinion, that the sport of Cockfighting is absolutely sinful, yet I would not have thee think, as the vulgar will be ready to say, that I esteem as unregenerate all those who are of a contrary judgment. I do not so little consider that of the Apostle, 'In many things we offend all': and certainly, the immediate cause of our offences, the perverseness of the will, always proceeds from the understanding, or judgment perverted, in apprehending anything the wrong way, by which it is inclined to accept, or refuse the object, or thing proposed. But though I do not conceive that the ignorance of the impiety of this sport is altogether inconsistent with a regenerate state, or the habit of true godliness, in some degree; yet I am not afraid to make known to the world, that I cannot imagine how any man, whilst he is actually like unto God, the Father of mercies, can possibly delight and recreate himself, in seeing his fellow-creatures (which are infinitely less inferior to us, than we to our, and their Creator) so subtle and active to wound and destroy each other. Having this opinion of the sport of Cockfights, and seeing it so frequently used in the country where I live; no man, that I can hear of, opposing it as absolutely sinful, I could not retain the confidence I have, that I am, indeed, a faithful servant of the great God in the Gospel of his Son, and a true lover of the souls of men, if I should not venture to oppose it myself; though I am not ignorant, that, endeavouring to destroy this common opinion, that this sport is not meet for Christians, I must necessarily expect to be counted a foolhardy and imprudent fellow. Methinks I hear many men saying unto me, appearing in public upon this occasion, as Eliab (1 Sam. XVII. 28) said to his brother David, 'I know thy pride and the naughtiness of thine heart.' This indeed would somewhat disturb me, if I did not consider that omniscience is one of the attributes of the God whom I serve.

* Richard King, *The Frauds of London Detected*, 1770, pp. 29-30.

"Thinking with myself, what means I should use to effect this design, to convince the world, that the temper and disposition of any man's soul, whilst he actually delights in such a sport, must necessarily be offensive to God ; at last I considered (though it be my opinion) that for any man, who has attained to a competent degree of the art of expression, to publish those notions which he has gathered from his own experience of such Christian truths, as are, in some sort, generally believed, in his own words, is a work most acceptable to the God of truth : for, certainly, those notions of spiritual things which fix themselves, and reside in the head only of the generality of those 'who are called Christians', are usually guided unto the heart by such expressions of the same things, as come from the hearts of others. Yet, I say, at last I considered, that truths of this nature, which are like to find so much opposition, will hardly be received by any, who now oppose them, unless they be brought in, as it were, with drum and trumpet ; I mean, by the hands of some famous and excellent writers : and therefore I would not, at present, write of this subject, any more than only to speak my opinion ; but have rather chosen to shew the world, what some eminent divines have written of it, which I conceive was never yet read and considered by any of those who delight in such sports, and profess to walk as Christ walked. And here, in the name of a Christian, I call to my aid (in endeavouring to evince this, that such a temper, as may actually consist with a delight in such sports, must needs be unchristian) all those who are of the same opinion ; and, withal, are conscious to themselves, that God has given them an art of persuasion, an ability of conveying their own thoughts into the breasts of others, not only of those who are simply void of them, but of those also who oppugn and resist them. Such men I entreat upon all occasions to manifest their dislike of such sports, and their reasons for it.

"If these papers shall chance to be seen by the worthy and renowned author of *The Whole Duty of Man*, I shall humbly entreat him, as one who serves with him under Christ, the Captain of our salvation, to afford me some aid in this combat with the world ; if he be of the same judgment, as, by his works, I presume he is. I doubt not, but the small thoughts and fancies, which those who delight in this sport, are apt to conceive in favour of it, which arise in their minds, like mists and dark vapours, to obscure the reason of anything they can ordinarily hear spoken against it, would suddenly vanish, like a morning cloud, when the sun appears, if it should be opposed by so noble a person; whose style, like a diamond, is bright and solid; whose excellent rhetoric, and beauty of expression, does not, like weaker beauty, consist chiefly in colour and complexion (in words which are so apt to take, as they say), but in symmetry and exact proportion. And I hope, the amiable subject of his beauteous expressions will, in time, by the help of God's Spirit, draw into itself the love of many, who, as yet, are lovers of the world. If the thoughts I have expressed of this sport be not suitable to his, I desire to be better informed by him. For, I must profess, at present, it scandals me extremely to see Christians, those who profess to have their bosoms a nest for the Heavenly Dove, to be companions of the Lamb of God, to recreate themselves in blood, though it be of the meanest creatures; and to me no man's reason seems more strong, or expression more clear, than what I find in the writings of this excellent person. So that, whatever he shall be pleased to write on this subject, it will either make me see myself in an error, or lead me on further in the way of truth; if my opinion be true indeed, which, as yet, I have no reason to doubt, but that so many speak against it. All that I have to say farther is this, that, if I did not as much despise the shame, as I am thought to desire the praise of the world, I would rather lose the hand I write with, than employ my pen upon such an occasion: but I fear not the terms of fool or madman. It was said of my Saviour 'He hath a devil'. My Lord was reviled, shall I be applauded? What greater comfort can a Christian have than in thinking how like he is to 'the Lord of glory', not only in what he did, but even also in what he suffered?

" 'The baiting of the bear, and cockfights, are no meet recreations. The baiting of the bull hath its use, and therefore it is commanded by civil authority; and so have not these. And the antipathy, and cruelty, which one beast showeth to another, is the fruit of our rebellion against God; and should rather move us to mourn, than to rejoice'. These are the words of the most learned and godly Mr. Perkins, in that famous treatise of the *Cases of Conscience*, printed in quarto, A.D. 1632, p. 346.

"That man of God, Mr. Bolton, was of the same mind with Mr. Perkins, concerning such sports: 'Consider', says he (in his excellent treatise entitled, *General Directions for a Comfortable Walking with God* (p. 156), 'that rule which divines give about recreations. We must not make God's judgments and punishments, either upon man or beast, the matter or object of them. Now, the best divines hold that enmity among themselves was a fruit of our rebellion against God, and more general judgment inflicted upon the creature after the fall: which misery coming upon them by our means, should rather break our hearts, and make them bleed, than minister matter of glorying in our shame, and vexing those very vexations which our impiety hath put upon them. Alas, sinful man! what a heart hast thou, that canst take delight in the cruel tormenting of a dumb creature? Is it not too much for thee to behold, with dry eyes, that which only thy sin hath impressed upon it; but that thou must barbarously also press its oppressions, and make thyself merry with the bleeding miseries of that poor harmless thing, which, in its kind, is much more, and far better serviceable to the Creator than thyself? Yet I deny not, but that there may be another lawful use of this antipathy, for the destroying of hurtful, and the enjoying of useful creatures; so that it be without any taint or aspersion of cruelty on our parts, or needless tormenting of the silly beasts'."

"Mr. Dod and Mr. Cleaver (scorned by none but those whose revilings are praises), in their exposition of these words of Solomon (Prov. XII. 10): 'A righteous man regardeth the life of his beast', having spoken against the hard usage of labouring beasts, as horses, etc. conclude thus: 'And yet, in another sort, more extremity than this is used against other sorts of creatures, and that is, when men make a sport of making them miserable; when it is a pleasure to put them to pain; when it is a pastime to behold their torment and tearing. This proceedeth not of a tender heart, this is not the work of righteousness; this delight will leave no comfort behind it. Have our sins in Adam brought such calamities upon them, and shall we add unto them by cruelty in our own persons? Have our corruptions been a cause of that fierceness that is in many of them one against another, and shall we solace ourselves in seeing them execute it? ... The souls of those, that are truly pious, are exceeding mild and gentle, not only towards relations, but strangers also. And this lenity, or softness of heart, they extend even to irrational creatures : therefore, the wise man saith 'A righteous man regardeth the life of his beast'. (Prov. XII. 10)."

"To all those who affect this sport [Cockfighting]: Having shewn you what these men thought of the sport you affect, I shall entreat you, if you believe so to be a matter of eternal concernment, to consider seriously what here you have read. If you are not convinced at present that these learned and godly men were in the right, yet I doubt not but you will be in time, if you more fully consider the matter without prejudice : at least, if you are regenerate persons. For, I conceive, by the instinct of the new creature, a man may often perceive that to be a sin, whose sinfulness is not capable of any express or verbal demonstration, *viz.* apprehending it so to be, merely through a sense of the antipathy it has to that in him, which he knows is born of God. Whether or no this be but a fanatic notion ; and whether or no the printing of these papers, and such like actions of mine, be indeed so foolish, and imprudent, as the world judges them to be, I will appeal only (for my own satisfaction) to the only wise God. Yet I shall not deny to render an account of any of my actions, in which I do, and must usually thwart the example of the generality of men, good or bad, to any man, whose authority obliges him, in any respect, to demand it of me, as my lawful superior, or conscience, as my fellow-Christian."*

I have given the foregoing copious extracts from Mr. Ellis's famous pamphlet because they show, probably as nothing else does or can, the approach to cockfighting displayed by the godly and supposedly humane men of those days. It is quite evident that few of these men dared to attack the sport at all, and that the majority of those who professed to be subscribers to and upholders of the Christian faith, saw nothing in cockfighting that was in any way contrary to their religious principles. Note the exact words of this writer Ellis : "No man that I can hear of opposing it [cockfighting] as absolutely sinful" ; and again, as a denouncer of the sport, "I must necessarily expect to be counted a foolhardy and imprudent fellow." Then, after the display of a farrago

---

* *The Opinions of Mr. Perkins and Mr. Bolton, and others, Concerning the Sport of Cockfighting. Published formerly in their Works, and now set forth to shew, that it is not a Recreation meet for Christians, though so commonly used by those who own that Name.* By Edmund Ellis, Master of Arts, and some time Fellow of Balliol College in Oxford, 1660.

of excuses, apologies, and justifications in the shape of the quoted opinions of others, he says: "whether or no the printing of these papers, and such like actions of mine, be indeed so foolish, and imprudent, as the world judges them to be, I will appeal only (for my own satisfaction) to the only wise God." Truly, these statements are as revealing as they are extraordinary; they form a strange commentary on the humanitarianism, or, rather, the lack of it, displayed by seventeenth-century theologians and metaphysicians. It is further particularly noteworthy (later I shall have more to say on this point) that in the quotation from the much praised compassionate writings of Mr. Perkins, no strictures were given in regard to bullbaiting, which it was conceded "hath its use." Nor was the wrath of God called down upon other barbarous so-called sports of the period.

And so very nearly another two centuries had to go to glory before cockfighting was declared illegal in Britain. In 1824, Christ's Hospital, which owned the building in St. James's Park where the Cockpit Royal was housed, refused to renew the lease on the ground of the cruelty of cockfighting. This was a definite step against the sport. And then some ten years later came government action. In an Act of 1835 (5 & 6 Will. IV. C.59) cockfighting, bullbaiting and badger-drawing became misdemeanours.

CHAPTER XIII

THE CASE FOR AND AGAINST COCKFIGHTING

Since the days of Gervase Markham, who, unashamedly said of cockfighting: "there is no pleasure more Noble, Delightsome or void of Cozenage and deceit than this pleasure of Cocking is"; and who, deigning not to make any excuse or justification for the publication of a practical work on a sport which, again to use his own words, "many of the best Wisdomes of our Nation have been pleased to participate with the delights therein"; most cocking enthusiasts have paraded the advantages of the sport to the nation.

The courage of the Gamecock has always been something to marvel at and to admire. Since the days when, as the historians have it, Themistocles was so greatly impressed by the indomitable bravery displayed by the fighting-cocks of the Persians, that he made his never-dying and oft-quoted remarks to his soldiers, no one has been able to deny this courage. And through the centuries, writers have repeatedly commented upon it, and spoken of the influence which the sport of cockfighting has had in developing the bravery of individuals and of nations. Thus, in a letter published in the *Times* (June 18, 1875) Admiral Rous said:

"Pomponius Mela, the historian, asserted that the Roman Empire did not begin to decline until cockfighting had fallen into disrepute among its Governors. He proves that Severus was not able to conquer Britain until he had rendered his principal officers passionately emulous of glory by exhibiting a main of cocks every day before them. The soothsayers warned Mark Antony to take heed of Caesar, because his cocks were always beaten by him. The great Gustavus told the King of Denmark he had no cause to fear the Imperialists since they had given up cocking, and were devoted to drinking and dancing. Christian, King of Denmark, said: 'Were I to lead an army against the great Infidel of

Constantinople I would choose none but cockers for my commanders, and none but lovers of the sport for soldiers'."

In addition to the promotion of bravery, it was contended by the supporters of the sport, that other estimable qualities were engendered and developed by the witnessing of cockfighting. As the poet puts it:

> "   And some more Martial are,
> But Cocking fits a man for Peace, or War;
> It makes Men bold and forward for the Field,
> And learns them there rather to die than yield.
> Cocking does also Constancy create,
> And arms a Man to Wrestle with his Fate;
> Be it more happy, or severe, his Mind,
> Is still the same to a brave end inclin'd."

And again:

> "The lureing Falkner flies over the Downs,
> And Tom the Huntsman with his deep-mouth'd Hounds,
> Joler, & Smooker made the Woods to ring
> Whilst Poacher with his Light-foot in a String,
> Goes silent on, beating each Hedge and Bush,
> With a design to snap poor frightful Puss:
> And next Jockey comes prancing o'er the Plain,
> Guiding his Courser with an Artful Rein;
> And off the Scoreful speed he scours away,
> And whips, and spurs in hopes to gain the Day.
> Whilst th' wanton swains they Dance, and piping sit,
> As if in amrous airs were only wit.
> Next these Gamesters at Cards and Dice we place,
> The Rook, the Silver Fool, and Sattin Ass,
> That play the Knave, and Cogg a Dye to make
> Themselves a gainer by the ill got stake,
> These are all sports that little profit bring;
> But noble Cocking is the Game I sing,
> Worthy of the greatest Captain, greatest King."

ADMIRAL ROUS WATCHING A COCKFIGHT AT MALACCA, 1875

THE TRIMMED COCK
By Francis Sartorius

OLD TRODGON
By R. Hodgson

And yet again:

> "This Pastime I above the rest prefer,
> In that it fits a Man for Peace or War.
> Cocking breeds Courage, where before was none,
> And makes men Stout and die that us'd to run,
> Cocking breeds cunning too, makes men contrive,
> And put them in a way to live and thrive:
> And if the pious Indians say true,
> It makes men witty, Good, and Godly too.
> Who then would Hunt and Hawk their time away
> Or at the Cards, or Dice sit down to play:
> When they by Powerful Cocking, this may do,
> Gain Courage, Wit, and Wealth, and Heaven too."

It was this reputation for the promotion of courage which was paraded as the justification for the cockfights which were for centuries held in the schools of England and Scotland. The poet Cleveland says:

> "Heaven-born-boys that in Cocking delight,
> Are ever true-hearted and constant in Fight."

Howlett, one of the earliest writers on the Game Fowl, himself adopted the poetic form to express his admiration for the fighting-cock.

> "Of all the numerous Feathered Flock
> Which Jove created, the brave Fighting-Cock
> Contains within his truly generous Breast,
> By much, a Nobler Courage than the Rest.
> When first he spies the Bloody trampled Pit,
> He claps his Wings, and Crows for Joy to see't.
> And when set down, he proudly struts along,
> Careless, and unconcerned at the great Throng;
> Who shouting clap their Hands to see him go
> So eagerly to meet his threatening Foe;
> Whose lofty Crimson Front, when first he spies,

> He like the Bazilick thro' his swol'n eyes
> Darts Flames of Fury, Death, Revenge, and Spight,
> And thus enrag'd begins the Bloody Fight.
> Then on they fall and like two Dragons meet,
> Rending the Air both with their Wings and Feet.
> Untill at length grown mad, they cease to Ward,
> And desperately closing scorn their Guard.
> Then, like to Thunder, fall their dreadful Stroaks,
> And as that slives the strong and mighty Oaks,
> So their fierce whirling Blows sharply rush thro'
> The tender Flesh, and slive the Bones in two.
> Whilst from their gaping Wounds there streams a flood
> Which like a Deluge drowns the Pit with Blood:
> The wounded Warriors reeling to and fro',
> At length grow faint, and stagger at each blow.
> But bravely still maintain the doubtful fight,
> Altho' the one wants Limbs, the other Sight;
> 'Till faithless Fortune with a fatal Frown,
> Sends giddy Chance to pull the destin'd down.
> Whilst cruel Death in Crimson Colours meets
> The mangled Carcass, and in Purple sheets,
> Presents him strait before the Victor dead;
> Who views him stretcht upon his Bloody Bed,
> And hears the Crowd with Shouts Ring his last Peal,
> Which mournful Eccho Chimes his dying Knell.
> And Praises pierce the skies from the vast Throng,
> Who shout the Victor as he Rides along."*

Undeniable is the reality of the bravery displayed by the Gamecock. Anyone who has seen one of these birds fight will bear witness to it. In rare instances only will the bird give in. Even to the point of exhaustion does he carry on the struggle.

So much for the reputed virtues of cockfighting as a means of sustaining and developing courage and other qualities in the onlookers. The arguments in support of this view are, as I think the most en-

---

* R. H., *The Royal Pastime of Cock-fighting*, London, 1709.

thusiastic cockers must admit, a little strained, and it is significant that, in recent years, when presenting the case in favour of the sport, this particular point has not been stressed with the vigour and constancy noticeable in the days when cockfighting was legal and fashionable.

Although in arguing the case for cockfighting, enthusiasts have either abandoned or soft-pedalled the courage-arousing aspect, they have displayed other points in its favour of a more cogent character. They have, for instance, pointed out that the Gamecock is by nature a fighter. It would appear that the greatest delight in life, so far as a Gamecock is concerned, is to fight. This much seems to be incontrovertible. At any rate no one has ever been able to produce a shred of evidence in contradiction of the statement. Cockers have further pointed out, again with absolute truth, that a Gamecock fights on his own initiative only: he cannot be *forced* to fight. And anyone who knows anything about poultry will and must support this statement to the hilt. For neither the rival and opposing male bird, nor any onlooker, whether owner, backer or mere spectator, can induce a cock to fight if he does not want to. It is here that cockfighting must, to the impartial observer, appear much less cruel than any sport where the animal, in a state of fear, panic, or distress, must flee for its life. When the Gamecock prances toward his opponent he is not actuated by fear or panic or distress; on the contrary, he hurls himself into the battle with glee. How different is the case of the fox with a pack of hounds chasing it!

It is because of this addiction to fighting that again and again have apologists for and devotees of cockfighting pointed out that there can be little or no cruelty in a sport in which *all* the participants take pleasure. It is largely because of this that it has been said that "Cockfighting is the most humane, perhaps the only humane sport there is."*

Apropos of the fighting instinct which is so strongly developed in the Gamecock, Blaine says: "This disposition to pugnacity is inherent in them, so as to make the task of rearing them anything but pleasant; for it shows itself at very early periods of their growth, and blinds very many of them. This aptitude is so great, that it appears almost equal in the half-breds also, which prevents this race from being much

* Capt. L. Fitz-Barnard, *Fighting Sports*, Odhams Press, London. n.d., p. 12.

cultivated. However, this irresistible attachment to fighting among themselves has certainly furnished the cockpit amateurs with their best defence against the tax of cruelty, and the more this natural pugnacious predilection is taken notice of, the more it will appear that if these birds are kept, they must be allowed to fight. It is, in fact, an irresistible passion; deprive them of it, and misery assails them. There are innumerable philanthropic admirers of animals abroad in the world, but there are but few who have had the hardihood to openly and personally attack those who flagrantly commit unnecessary cruelty on animals. One of the oldest among us of this class was Mr. John Lawrence, lately deceased at an age, as we believe, nearly if not quite ninety years. This gentleman has all his life proved a staunch advocate for humane treatment towards animals, and a determined enemy of cruelty towards them in any shape. What does he say on this subject in his treatise on *Rearing Domestic Poultry*: 'Philanthropists are in the habit of declaiming much against the practice of cockpit battles; but, on reflection, the cruelty of that sport will be found among the least wherein the feelings of animals are concerned, since fighting in the Gamecock is a natural and irresistible passion, and can never take place against his will; and since those engaged in regular combat upon the arena would do so voluntarily and with equal ardour did they meet in the desert'. Our own opinion of cocking coincides very much with that of Mr. Lawrence. We neither encourage it, nor do we rail at it to show our sensibility; were the birds forced to the task, we should think much worse of it than we do; but when we find this pugnacious disposition implanted by Nature, we cannot readily fancy ourselves wiser than this universal mother."*

In this connexion it is noteworthy there are *opponents* of cockfighting who cannot deny the power of this argument. Consider, for instance, the remarks of William Henry Scott: " Cockfighting is pronounced in a breath—horrible! Weighed, however, in the balance of reason and fact, it is attended with the least cruelty of all our Diversions, not even my favourite *Horse-racing* excepted. I shall be very expeditious with my proof—*The Gamecock is kept in a state of happiness and comfort, until the day of battle; he cannot then be forced, but in fighting is actuated*

---

* Delabere P. Blaine, *An Encyclopaedia of Rural Sports*, 1852, p. 1213.

by his natural instinct—is, in fact, gratified ; and if he fall by his adversary's weapon, he is the sooner out of the sense of Pain. Let not the reader, however, mistake me for an advocate of cockfighting, for which in truth, I have no kind of relish, and probably, should feel almost as wearied and out of place, at the Cockpit Royal, as at sitting to hear a long-winded puritanical sermon."*

The cockfighters, however, in a burst of enthusiastic support verging on fanaticism, do overlook *one* point. They fail to perceive or to admit that the sport, *as practised*, tends to arouse a form of unconscious cruelty on the part of the participating champions. The birds are placed in circumstances where their urge to fight is likely to be *aroused* and *intensified* ; more and further, any disposition to give in is countered by consistent encouragement to continue the battle. True enough, it is impossible to *make* a cock fight ; but it is not impossible to *reduce his inclination to desist from fighting*. In addition, nobody possessing the slightest love for birds and animals, can uphold the barbarities of the "Welsh Main" and the "Battle Royal," where fighting occurs in circumstances and to a degree that could never be duplicated or equalled in nature and outside a cockpit.

Then there is the question of the use of artificial spurs. This practice has been condemned as cruel in the extreme, and the early denouncers of the sport stressed the barbarity of the sharp-pointed, death-dealing silver or steel spur. The cockers countered this with a statement that in actuality the use of the metal spur was not in any way cruel, but on the contrary greatly reduced the suffering of the combatants. Here again the cockfighting fraternity presented an argument of much force, and one which, as was apparent to anyone with practical knowledge of poultry and particularly of the Game Fowl, was brimming with truth. Any two Gamecocks, or indeed any male specimens of other pugnacious breeds, will fight long and bloodily without the help of artificial spurs. They will, often enough, fight to the death. The natural spur of a strong mature cock is a powerful weapon indeed. In naked-heel battles the struggle is usually a prolonged one, involving much damage and suffering, with the possibility of the infliction of deadly, poisonous and slow-

* William Henry Scott, *British Field Sports*, Sherwood, Neely and Jones, London, 1818, p. 564.

healing wounds. On the other hand, with the use of artificial spurs, the battle is short; death, if it comes, is swift; the wounds suffered are clean and healable.

The same argument cannot be brought forward in favour of all the forms of preparation to which the fighting-cock is submitted before he enters the pit. Mention has already been made of the trimming process, part of which consists of removing some of the wing feathers. The old cocking books deal at some length with this practice, and in so doing emphasise (perhaps unconsciously) a potential element of barbarity which would appear to be a consequence of this mode of preparing for battle. Let me quote a typical passage: ". . . . then take his wings, extending them forth by the first feather, clip the rest slopewise, with *sharp points*, that in his rising he may *endanger the eyes of his adversary* (my italics); then with a sharp knife, scrape smooth and sharpen his beak."*

Dubbing, or the removal of the bird's comb and wattles, in preparation for fighting, is, by many persons, considered to be a cruel practice, and has from time to time been brought forward as a major count against the sport. Indeed, this contention has been upheld at least once in an English court of law. According to *The Law Journal* (September 12, 1952) "cutting the combs of cocks was held to be an offence under the Cruelty to Animals Act 1849 s.2 in *Murphy* v. *Manning* (1877—2 Ex. D. 307) where Kelly, C.B., remarked appropriately: 'Is there any purpose or reason which can legalize or justify an act of such extreme barbarity? To my mind the object, as shown by the whole of the evidence, is that the animals may be used for cockfighting. . . . Taking off the combs makes them more fit for fighting. It is cruelty, and an abuse and ill-treatment—the very words in the Act'."†

The rise to perfection of the Game Fowl was undoubtedly coincident and contemporaneous with the development of cockfighting. Apropos of this, Tegetmeier, writing in the middle of the nineteenth century, voiced what must represent the consensus of authoritative opinion,

---

* T. Fairfax, *The Complete Sportsman; or Country Gentleman's Recreation*, 1764, p. 10.

† There are circumstances which have no relation whatever to cockfighting in which dubbing is advisable in the interest of the bird itself (see page 35).

when he said: "There cannot be a doubt that the superiority of the Game Fowls bred in England has been entirely due to the practice of cockfighting which was extensively indulged in by all classes of society until the comparatively recent legal enactments, rendering its practice punishable with heavy pecuniary penalties. The practice of cockfighting may be regarded as one which carries out, under man's supervision, the principle of action which has been so ably described by Darwin as 'the struggle for life.' Those cocks which have proved the strongest, most active and courageous, and have stricken down their antagonists in the pit, have been preserved by man as the progenitors of their kind, this process of 'selection' has been carried on for a long series of generations, and the ultimate result has been that the English Game fowl is unequalled in the elegance of form, and is universally regarded as the highest possible type of gallinaceous beauty."*

Not to be wondered at therefore was the contention of many breeders that the risk of the famous Old English Game degenerating, should cockfighting be abandoned, was a very considerable one. Ferguson, himself opposed to the sport, puts the case well: "But however urgent might be the claims of humanity and refinement for the prevention of the opportunities of indulging in this cruel sport, it becomes equally patent, if its provisions were sufficiently stringent to entirely outroot it, this breed, the glory of the British poultry keeper, and the most beautiful and noble of fowls, would soon degenerate into mere nominal value, and the emblem of courage would be plucked from British soil to flourish elsewhere. Without an occasional trial of quality no certainty can be established, since admixture is equally necessary, and admixture with that which has received uncertain mingling is equally contingent. Were the race horse not permitted to run, equally deteriorating to the breed would be the effect, seeing propagators unable to discover blemish would be compelled to match indiscriminately. The Game Fowl among poultry is analogous to the Arabian among horses, the high-bred Shorthorn among cattle, and the Greyhound among the canine race."†

---

* W. B. Tegetmeier, *The Poultry Book*, 1867.
† G. Ferguson, *Illustrated Series of Rare and Prize Poultry*, 1854.

Now to some degree this warning given by Ferguson proved true in those years immediately following the prohibition of cockfighting. There was a gradual but nonetheless plainly discernible change in the characteristics of the breed; notably a tendency towards increased length of leg, shorter breast, more elongated head, and less abundant feather. Moreover, in many cases, the male bird lacked staying power and virility; while the female was less robust in constitution than were her ancestors.

Faced with the prospect of these changes becoming more or less permanent features of the breed and in consequence the possibility of serious deterioration, a number of breeders formed a society the main object of which was the perpetuation of that type of bird which, in the past, had won for the Old English Game Fowl world-wide fame as a fighting-cock *par excellence*. The efforts to this end were successful, and through the many decades that have since gone to glory, this primary objective was kept well in mind. The result is that today the ideal male, as delineated in the Old English Game Club's standard of perfection (see Appendix I), is practically a replica of the Old English Game fighting-cock of a century-and-a-half ago. I am told by a well-known breeder that if there *is* any slight variation it lies in a tendency for the present-day exhibition specimen to be rather bigger than the typical fighting-cock of old; but the Club by its policy of discouraging excessive weight in either sex, will doubtless manage to keep even this tendency within bounds.

Apropos of the risk of degeneration there is much to be said for the method of preserving the characteristics of the typical fighting-Game recently adopted by at least one society. According to the *Cumberland Evening Star* (January 5, 1953): "Illegal since Victorian times, cockfighting is dead in the Lake District, but the birds are still bred for admiration and curiosity, and were a feature at the seventh annual open show of the Cumberland Bantam Club, held in Brigham Memorial Hall, near Cockermouth on Saturday. There was even a class for the likeliest fighting-cock, and this was won by an aggressive-looking and beautiful bird shown by Mr. J. D. Barwise of Hensingham, near Whitehaven."

The opponents of cockfighting based their case on the cruelty which they averred, despite every argument to the contrary, was inherent in the sport. The birds were encouraged to fight by every conceivable method the ingenuity of man could devise. While it was true that a battle between cocks armed only with the weapons nature had given them could be a bloody and prolonged combat, the provision of spurs increased greatly its deadliness and the possibilities of fearful wounds being given and received.

A tribute to the matchless courage of the Gamecock and a depiction of the cruelty inherent in cockfighting is presented in a poem published in the *Gentleman's Magazine*. Here it is:

> "Where Dudston's walks* with vary'd beauty shone,
> And some are pleas'd with bowling, some with wine,
> Behold a gen'rous train of Cocks repair,
> To vie for glory in the toils of war;
> Each hero burns to conquer or to die:
> What mighty hearts in little bosoms lie!
> Come, Hogarth, thou whose art can best declare,
> What forms, what features human passions wear,
> Come, with a painter's philosophic sight,
> Survey the circling judges of the fight.
> Touch'd with the sport of death, while ev'ry heart
> Springs to the changing face, exert thy art;
> Mix with the smiles of Cruelty at pain
> Whate'er looks anxious in the lust of gain;
> And say, can ought that's gen'rous, just or kind,
> Beneath this aspect, lurk within the mind?
> Is lust of blood or treasure vice in all,
> Abhorr'd alike on whomsoe'er it fall?
> Are mighty states, and gamblers still the same?
> And war itself a cock-fight, and a game?
> Are sieges, battles, triumphs, little things;
> And armies only the gamecocks of kings?
> Which fight, in Freedom's cause, still blindly bold,
> *Bye-battles* only, and the *main* for *gold*?

---

* A gentleman's seat, about a mile from Birmingham, fitted up for the reception of Company, in imitation of Vauxhall Gardens.

The crested bird, whose voice awakes the morn,
Whose plumage streaks of radiant gold adorn,
Proud of his birth, on fair Salopia's plain,
Stalks round, and scowls defiance and disdain.
Not fiercer looks the proud Helvetians wear,
Tho' thunder slumbers in the arms they bear :
Nor Thracia's fiercer sons, a warlike race !
Display more prowess, or more martial grace.
But, lo ! another comes, renown'd for might,
Renown'd for courage, and provokes the fight.
Yet what, alas ! avails his furious mien,
His ruddy neck, and breast of varied green ?
Soon thro' his brain the foe's bright weapon flies,
Eternal darkness shades his swimming eyes ;
Prostrate he falls, and quiv'ring spurns the ground,
While life indignant issues from the wound.
Unhappy hero, had thy humbler life
Deny'd thee fame by deeds of martial strife,
Still hadst thou crow'd, for future pleasures spar'd,
Th' exulting monarch of a farmer's yard.
Like fate, alas ! too soon th' illustrious prove,
The great by hatred fall, the fair by love ;
The wise, the good, can scarce preserve a name,
Expung'd by envy from the rolls of fame.
Peace and oblivion still thro' life secure,
In friendly glooms, the simple, homely poor,
And who would wish to bask in glory's ray,
To buy with peace the laurel or the bay ?
What tho' the wreath defy the lightning's fire,
The bard and hero in the storm expire.
Be rest and innocence my humbler lot,
Scarce known thro' life, and after death forgot."*

Edward Herbert, in the *London Magazine* (November 1822), states the case—based upon the diabolical, flinty, callous, cold-blooded barbarity

---

* *Gentleman's Magazine*, Vol. XVII, June 1747, p. 292.

displayed by its supporters—against the sport. After describing in detail his visit to the Royal Cockpit, he goes on to say:

"Such is cockfighting. I began like the bird, in bravery and spirit, but I have drooped in the contest, and find myself struck down and helpless at the last. In vain would I try to sustain its character, to hold it up as an ancient and noble sport; my pen refuses the office—its feather drags—and my very gorge rises at the cold-blooded cruelty of its abettors and lovers. To see the rich and beautiful bird towering in his strength, mantling in his comeliness—and in a moment to see him *bodkined*, and gnawed to death, in the presence of those who have pampered him up to an obstinate heroism and a stubborn savageness—is more than heart can bear! I saw the cocks go by me one minute, all life, and power, and beauty—I saw them pass the next—languid, discoloured, bleeding from the beak—dead. The gladiator scenes of Rome seemed to be wretchedly mocked here—and when all was over, what remained in the mind, but the dirty dregs of brutality and vice? . . . . . I have seen the *sport*! I have described it!*—and I shall certainly never again do either the one or the other. You know I am not by any means a squeamish person; but when I have come to reflect on the fighting and its consequences, all the glory of the contest has faded from me."

In this controversy respecting cockfighting many defenders of the practice have made much of the inconsistency of so many persons who denounce the sport while apparently seeing nothing wrong in fox-hunting, salmon-fishing, pigeon-shooting, the trapping of rabbits, and other practices. In this connexion the following passage from Ferguson's poultry manual merits attention: "He [Lord Derby] regarded it no more inhuman to place cock with cock than trained hounds with hare or fox; no further violation of good faith with the animal world to subject the noble character to a violent but valiant, rapid, and fearless decease for the value of sport, than hunting the tenants of the wood, and exposing them to that fatiguing, heart-distressing, and alarming condition consequent upon a protracted death, without regard to the

---

* For the description here referred to see page 58.

awful sensations of fear they endure, but merely with a view to the self-indulgence of pleasure. In the name of humanity, we ask our gentle hunting readers, what moral difference they perceive ? Not whether the former is equally humane with the latter, but rather whether the latter is not as much at variance with the dictates of humanity as the former ?"

Again in Tegetmeier's *Poultry Book* it is pointed out that without denying the "demoralizing and brutalizing spectacle" which the cockpit presents, the writer is of opinion "that there is something to be said for everything in this world, even for cockfighting." He goes on to say : "On the general principle of common sense, let me ask you, who are in the habit of eating veal that is half an hour in the process of slow killing, and of enjoying your hunted hare that has for fifty minutes been in an agony of mortal fear, until at last, exhausted and shrieking, with every fibre in its body quivering with intense excitement, and every air-cell in its lungs filled with blood and lymph, it sinks and receives a death-bite from hounds more merciful than their masters— are you, I ask, the man to rail against allowing two gallant and noble animals to follow an impulse that has been implanted in them for a wise purpose, that you are too short-sighted or wilfully obtuse to see ? The natural instinct of gregarious animals is to fight, so that the stronger males should destroy the weaker and perpetuate the noblest race ; all, consequently, are provided (by Nature—ay, there's the rub) with lethal weapons for this purpose. As I once heard asked, suppose you were to inquire of a Gamecock, whether he would rather have his cervical vertebrae dislocated by the hand of Betty the poultry maid, or take his chance of life in mortal combat with his gallant antagonist in the next farm-yard, can you doubt his answer ?"

This writer might have gone much further. He might, for instance, have asked whether any unprejudiced person could contend that the cruelty to the contesting cocks, whether or not the battle ends in the death of one of or both the contestants, can in any way be likened to the cruelty involved in the catching of rabbits and other animals in traps, the skinning alive of baby lambs to furnish furs for the adornment of fashionable women, the imprisonment for life, in tiny cages, of birds and animals ; the forcible cramming of poultry, *et al.* It may well be wondered whether there is any comparison at all, in the matter of humanity, between the slaughter of one cock by another in the heat of battle, and the cold-blooded killing of a pig, or an ox, by a licensed slaughterer. In the one case the bird goes to his unanticipated fate without fear and with glee; in the other, the animal goes to its sensed fate with horror and fear writ large on its face.

Now if there was nothing to be said against cockfighting other than the points already enumerated it might conceivably have been permitted to continue, though even then there is some doubt in the matter. But just as cockfighting is a sport which in some respects is unique, insomuch that it is difficult to sustain a charge of cruelty in respect of inciting or allowing the victims to do that which Nature intended them to and which apparently they take a delight in doing, there are other points to take into consideration. Apart from the aforementioned practice of placing male birds in circumstances where the urge to fight is likely to be aroused and intensified (see page 157), cockfighters are known to have been responsible for adopting methods which cause needless suffering to the birds not only during the actual fight but while they are training. There are tales of trainers who prod the birds with needles, who force them to run to the point of exhaustion; there are tales of fights in which, with the object of increasing the length of the battle, the combatants' spurs are encased in rubber. And there is the tale, oft repeated in cockfighting annals, of an occasion when, to prove the courage of his strain of Gamecocks, the owner, for a wager, sprinkled his bird's plumage with turpentine and set it alight. Undismayed by the fact that he was enveloped in fire, the cock battled on, eventually killing his opponent. Here are examples of cruelty and barbarism that cannot in any way be glossed over or excused.

In another respect cockfighting shares with the gladiatorial contests of ancient Rome a different form of barbarism. The outstanding evil of the sport is not concerned with the combatants; it is concerned with the spectators. And this would appear to be a point which enthusiastic cockers overlook or ignore. To call cockfighting cruel, in all but exceptional circumstances and apart from special forms, is perhaps not strictly correct. But it is brutal. It arouses and develops brutality in the onlookers. This is *the* evil of cockfighting. In an unforgettable poem George Crabbe draws attention to this barbarity, thus:

> "Here his poor bird th' inhuman Cocker brings,
> Arms his hard heel and clips his golden wings;
> With spicy food th' impatient spirit feeds,
> And shouts and curses as the battle bleeds.
> Struck through the brain, deprived of both his eyes,
> The vanquish'd bird must combat till he dies;
> Must faintly peck at his victorious foe,
> And reel and stagger at each feeble blow:
> When fallen, the savage grasps his dabbled plumes,
> His blood-stain'd arms, for other deaths assumes;
> And damns the craven-fowl, that lost his stake,
> And only bled and perish'd for his sake."*

It is difficult to imagine how any sane, humane, enlightened individual possessing one iota of ornithophilism or zoophilism can voluntarily and undisturbedly continue to watch two birds grievously wounding one another. One is astounded at the mentality of a person who can be a party to any so-called sport which allows, approves and applauds this deliberate and sustained mutual infliction of injuries, whether the parties concerned are birds, animals or men. "In almost every fight" says *The National Humane Review* (November, 1952, p. 11) "at least one cock is seriously mutilated or killed. In about half of the fights, more or less, *both* birds are maimed beyond further use if not killed. Eyes are gouged out, abdomens slit and slashed until the birds are anguished monstrosities, legs and wings are broken. But so long as a bird can and will keep facing toward the opposing cock he is left in the pit and cheered for his 'courage'."

If the reaction to such a fight is not that of being compelled to withdraw in horror, and to resolve never again to witness such a performance, there must be present some morbid fascination, an overriding financial interest, a type of fanaticism which blinds one to the brutality inherent

---

* From *The Parish Register* by the Rev. George Crabbe, in *The Poetical Works of the Rev. George Crabbe*, John Murray, 1834. Vol. II. p. 151.

in the sport, or a large measure of that apatheticism which is becoming an increasingly pronounced element in mankind's attitude toward disturbing and unpalatable facets of life.

At all events, the spectacle of one of these sanguinary battles is well calculated, in any gathering of spectators, to arouse emotions of the worst possible character. No one who is not prejudiced in favour of cockfighting can deny the truth of this. Unbiased observers have commented on the fact time and time again. Thus, writing of cockfighting in Cuba, Samuel Hazard has this to say: "Thus it keeps up; pair after pair are fought, amid the same scenes, the same noise and confusion; and, reader, if you want to see the workings of all the evil passion in the human face, just pay one visit to a cockfight, and I guarantee you'll not go again, but will come away intensely disgusted."*

Hogarth, Rowlandson, and other artists have depicted the atmosphere of the cockpit time after time. It is an atmosphere in which members of the public gloat over the bloody scene of carnage, showing a shudder-arousing pitch of excitement and delight when one or other of the battling birds suffers a mortal blow. It is the same sinister scene of tenseness, of stimulation as is exemplified in any spectacle in which life, whether of man or animal, is being risked, as in bullfighting, entering a lion's den, *et al.*

---

* Samuel Hazard, *Cuba with Pen and Pencil*, 1873, p. 195.

CHAPTER XIV

COCKFIGHTING AND THE LAW

IN 1835 an Act was passed making the practice of cockfighting, bull-baiting or badger-drawing a misdemeanour in certain circumstances. Under S.47 of the Metropolitan Police Act it became illegal to have a cockpit in the metropolitan area. Then in 1849 more stringent measures against the sport were taken in the Cruelty to Animals Act, cockfighting being specifically mentioned.

For some years after these Acts were passed enthusiastic cockers were inclined to defy the law. In the *Transactions of the Cumberland and Westmorland Antiquarian & Archaeological Society* (1888) we read: "A friend tells me that he saw a main fought at the Raffles, near Carlisle, in 1842, the setters being Dick and Davey. Another was fought at the Dandie Dinmont, in 1846, without much pretence of concealment, a coach and four taking the sportsmen out from Carlisle: another Dick, Dick the Daisy, was one of the setters on that occasion. Within the last ten years, a gentleman in Carlisle, now dead, kept his cocks in a sodded attic in his home, and fought them within the city; while in Newcastle, a well-known knight, alderman, and magistrate, who died in 1871, had a cockpit at the back of his house, where frequent fights took place, and one of My Lord the Queen's Justices, Baron – – – – –, was a frequent spectator."

Indeed, it was not until the activities of the cockers actually brought them into conflict with the law that public fights were brought to an end. In 1863 an appeal against a conviction was successfully made on the ground that a "place" for cockfighting mentioned in the Act did not include an old stone quarry, which had been the venue of the cockfight in question. In 1865 a case appeared in the courts in which a number of persons, including a descendant of the famous Gilliver, were fined for taking part in or attending a cockfight held at the Queen's Head Tavern in Great Windmill Street, London. In 1874, a fine of £5 was imposed

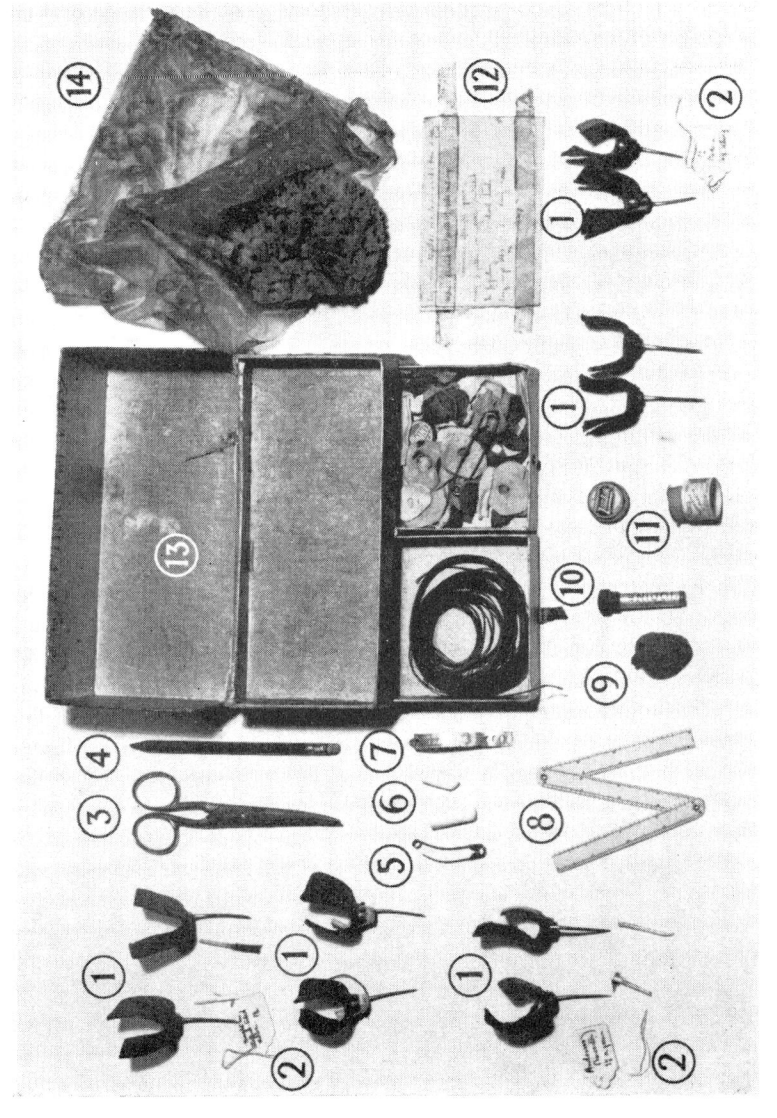

COCKFIGHTING IMPLEMENTS SEIZED NEAR CHESTER, 1956

In this case 36 persons were fined £615 and £540 costs. Sixty-two fighting cocks and the articles pictured above were exhibited in court:

1, Spurs. 2, Spur tags indicating counties. 3, Bloodstained scissors. 4, Pencil. 5, Safety pin. 6, Chalk. 7, Identification tag. 8, Foot rule. 9, Wooden ball presumed for spur tips. 10, Iodine tube. 11, Ointments. 12, List allocating spurs to different types of birds. 13, Box of spares. 14, Sponge in waterproof bag

EAGER SPECTATORS IN HAITI

on a man named Broadlik of the Bay Horse Inn, Newcastle-on-Tyne, for having a cockpit, known far and wide as the Gallogate Pit, on the premises.

Cockfighting continued to be practised surreptitiously in London long after the sport was made illegal. In Endell Street was a notorious rendezvous where many members of the aristocracy were regular visitors. It was run by Charles Faultless.

Jack Stobart, one of the most famous and successful cockfighters of his day, in conversation with Mr. J. Fairfax-Blakeborough, confessed that he had practised cockfighting long after it had become illegal in England. After recounting certain instances in which he had, by little more than a hairsbreadth, escaped falling into the hands of the police, he said: " 'I could fill a book wi' sike tales, but I was lucky nivvor to be caught, seeing the hundreds o' battles I've been at since 1860'."*

For years after the law stamped out public cockfights in England, they continued to exist across the border, for it was not until 1895 that an Act was passed making the sport illegal in Scotland. This Act amplified the provisions of the eleventh section of the Cruelty to Animals (Scotland) Act, by adding "or any Game or fighting-cock, or other domestic fowl or bird."

And so, towards the close of the nineteenth century, throughout Britain, all the cockpits had been closed and turned to other uses. Public cockfights were things of the past. This did not mean the end of cockfighting, however. In many parts of the country the sport continued surreptitiously. Private cockfights were numerous. They were numerous because the law was practically powerless to stop them. The loopholes were too many and too large. In order to prosecute it was necessary for the police to catch the offenders in the very act of attending a cockpit (whether of a temporary, improvised or permanent character) while a fight was actually in progress. To hear of a projected fight, to know the name of the parties who were promoting it, or even to appear on the scene in a matter of minutes after the fight had taken place, was not enough. Apropos of the difficulty experienced in the securing of evidence that would lead to conviction, it was stated in *The Times* (March 6, 1952) that: "R.S.P.C.A. inspectors knew that cocks were prepared

---

* J. Fairfax-Blakeborough, *Country Life and Sport*, Philip Allan & Co., London, 1926, p. 99.

for fighting and the owners were known, but it was not sufficient to see birds with their comb and wattles cut off, with their wing and tail feathers cut, or with the natural spurs on their legs cut off. Under the existing law a conviction could only be obtained if evidence was produced that a main had been held. Since these took place in remote countryside—mostly in the north of England—with an elaborate system of sentries and the people proposing to attend being told of the meeting place only at the last minute, it was difficult to see a fight in progress."

It must, too, be remembered that these fights were not held in cockpits as such: the indoor contests were staged in barns, lofts, cellars, and even in the drawing-rooms of country houses; the outdoor mains were fought in disused quarries, remote woods, or other lonely or unfrequented spots. The birds could be picked up and taken away at a moment's notice. Little wonder therefore that in such circumstances prosecutions were few and far between.

In his interesting autobiography, Sir John Dugdale Astley mentions journeying to the north of England to witness a cockfight in which his brother's birds took part. Sir John tells how he was met at Manchester "*by a party in the know,*" taken a long train journey, and, after following the directions given him, arrived at a country house. Here the floor of a shed was covered with pieces of green turf, the Gamecocks produced, and a number of battles fought. Then, says the narrator, "all of a sudden the birds were thrust into bags, and these were gently pushed into a large hole in the wall, and some straw piled over it; the turfs were carried away."* As a result of these measures, no evidence of the fight remained when the police, of whose coming the cockers had received warning from watching scouts, arrived on the scene. Sir John goes on to say: "I attended another main one day near a town in the Eastern counties, where everything was brought off nice and comfortable without any disturbance." There was an amusing side to this incident. It appeared that somehow or other the police had got wind of the projected affair and were on the alert. The cockers, however, were strategists. On the day set for the fight, an omnibus, with its windows rendered opaque by means of a coating of whitewash, was driven, apparently with great caution and secrecy, from the yard of the

---

* Sir John Dugdale Astley, *Fifty Years of My Life*, Hurst and Blackett, London, 1894. Vol. II. p. 235.

inn in which the birds were reputed to be secreted. The watching police, emerging from their hiding place, followed the conveyance at a good distance until, after travelling a matter of seven or eight miles, it pulled up in a farm yard; to their chagrin however it was an empty bus they had followed. Meanwhile another bus, devoid of camouflage, had driven openly into the country with the birds and the cockers.*

These stories illustrate the manner in which men of position and unimpeachable respectability looked upon a sport which the law held to be illegal. There have been many such cases. There have, too, been instances of lawgivers themselves attending fights. Tegetmeier gives the following case: "I afterwards heard that, though the head magistrate of the place, he was known to be very partial to cockfighting; and that he was once present at a main when the police burst in, and being too fat and pudgy to slope off with the rest, he got into the large chimney, standing with one foot on each hob of the grate. The police saw and knew the boots, but of course they did not look up the chimney, as they could have no suspicion that his worship's legs were in them."†

Then there is that oft-related story of a fight in the court itself: it was between two cocks brought into a Bishop Auckland court after a police raid, and was followed by the dismissal of the case. There is, too, a tale told of a well-known Yorkshire poultry fancier, who was also a magistrate, holding fights in a secluded spot on his country estate on Sunday mornings. And there is the amusing account, for which I am indebted to the *Daily Telegraph* (September 11, 1953), of the late Jamaican judge, Samuel Constantine Burke, famous breeder of Game Fowls, and enthusiastic devotee of the illegal sport of cockfighting, who, says a contributor to this newspaper: ". . . . often during a case would receive a whispered message from an usher. 'Court adjourned' would be the immediate order, protests by solicitors notwithstanding, and Burke would jump into a waiting car with cockerels and speed off to fight a main."

In all parts of Britain cockfighting goes on secretly. It is extremely difficult to secure reliable information about something which is sur-

* Ibid. p. 237.
† W. B. Tegetmeier, *The Poultry Book*, 1867.

rounded with so much secrecy; but apparently the counties of Westmorland, Cumberland, Yorkshire, Lancashire and Derbyshire are the main places where fighting-cocks are still bred and trained.

The sport is highly organised. There is big money in it, not only for the breeders and owners of the fighting-cocks but also for the promoters of the contests. In those rare instances where the police are able to secure sufficient evidence for successful prosecutions, it is not unusual for the fines to be paid by an organised body which, it is stated, has been in existence for centuries and is still active. "It is called," says a *Daily Mail* correspondent, "the Ancient Society of Cockfighters—has members in all parts of the country, and, according to one of them, has many distinguished names on its subscription lists."*

At these secretly-held contests the stakes are heavy, five hundred pounds being a not uncommon sum to win or lose as a result of the death of a fighting-cock. High admission prices are paid by those privileged to attend the fights, which are usually held on Sunday mornings.

The birds themselves are of considerable value: they are prized as fighters and also as breeders of fighters. They change hands among the cocking fraternity at prices ranging from £25 to £100 each. Many are sold for export to France, Belgium, Persia, the U.S.A. and other countries.

In the Welsh mountains cockfighting persisted long after it was prohibited by Act of Parliament. In these hills it was possible to defy the law, as it was comparatively easy for lookouts to warn the cockers long before the police, even on such occasions as they had got wind of the cockfights, could get anywhere near the venue. According to an article entitled "Cockfighting in Montgomeryshire", contributed by Mr. A. Stanley Davies to *The Montgomeryshire Society Year Book* (1950-51), one of the favoured spots was the Welsh Harp on the summit of the Long Mountain, and the contests were usually staged in a room at the back of the inn on Sunday mornings. Most of the supporters were miners, and when, at the end of the nineteenth century, lead mining was abandoned, cockfighting in this particular part of the country at any rate, came to an end with it.

* *Daily Mail*, Nov. 21, 1938.

Cockfighting is illegal in Ireland, but there is plenty of evidence that the sport continues surreptitiously, much the same safeguards being adopted as in England. According to the Dublin *Times Pictorial* (November 15, 1952): "Not so many sunrises ago a cockfighting venue was arranged for a spot within thirty miles from the town of Portaoise. At 5.15 a.m. some forty cars converged on a small field off a bye-road near the Hill o' Down. Nearly 200 people, including some women, walked through the dewy grass to the corner of the field. A man with a spade quickly marked out a small ring. From beneath their overcoats two others brought forth the contestants—two short-combed, white-hackled Gamecocks; the one representing the North and the other the South."

As recently as 1953 a case came before the court. According to *The Irish Times* (May 8, 1953): "A crowd of over eighty people at Craig's Moss, Cullybackey, Co. Antrim, quickly dispersed when they saw two policemen approaching. The police gave chase and, as a result, two men were charged at Ballymena Petty Sessions for causing, procuring and assisting in the fighting of Gamecocks." Each defendant was fined £3. This was one of the rare instances where the police managed to catch the culprits in the act. A month later, however, "somewhere in Meath," a contest was staged in which the birds of Munster defeated those of Ulster, winning "four out of the five mains that were fought." The fighting-cocks and their owners travelled to the meeting ground during the night, and says the *Cornish Evening Herald* (June 4, 1953), to which I am indebted for these particulars: "There was some very heavy betting on the outcome of the mains and the southerners returned home much the richer."

In most cases, so great is the degree of secrecy observed by all taking part in or concerned with these illegal contests, that no news of them ever reaches the ears either of the general public or the police. But in July of 1953 the Press referred to a series of cockfights which had been held at Derrytresk, near Coalisland, Co. Tyrone, where large crowds, including visitors from England and Scotland, at daybreak, witnessed the mains which were fought by champions of Armagh, Monaghan and Tyrone. Of this tournament, one of the most successful ever staged in Northern Ireland since cockfighting became illegal, says

The Irish Press (July 3, 1953): "In all, fourteen battles were fought. Large sums of money changed hands in side stakes, and the meeting ended in favour of Tyrone." It owed much of its success to the fact that the cockers had seized the opportunity presented by the depletion of the local police force in consequence of special duties concerned with the Royal visit to Belfast. Apropos of this, from Bermuda's newspaper, *The Royal Gazette* (August 17, 1953), I lift the following amusing note, which appears under the heading "Irish Cockfighting Fans Welcomed Royal Visit,"—"Belfast, Northern Ireland, (AP)—. . . . County Tyrone now holds the championship of Ireland. But Monaghan is looking for another Royal visit soon so it can have another crack at the title."

In Canada, cockfighting is prohibited, and anyone organizing, assisting at, or being present at a cockfight is liable to prosecution. On July 7, 1952, at London, Ontario, a total of 76 Gamecocks (10 of which were dead) were seized by the police and 84 persons (of whom five were women) present while a cockfight was actually in progress, were arrested. The 79 men, all of whom pleaded guilty, were each fined 200 dollars; but the charges against the women, who had attended with their husbands, were withdrawn. The Gamecocks, crowing lustily during the court proceedings, were ordered to be confiscated and destroyed.*

In March of 1953 a raid on a cockfight in Nova Scotia, resulted in the destruction of 23 fighting-cocks and a fine of $100. In June of the same year, 52 spectators were arrested by the police, when they raided a cockpit while a $2,000 fight was in progress near Brantford. *The Toronto Globe* (June 23, 1953), in reporting these facts, says: "At first it appeared that many Brant County farmers were listed among the 52 found at the pit, but since the raid it has become apparent that the cockfights were being staged by a ring that moves its weekly fights from one place to another all over Southwestern Ontario and attracts big-time gamblers." The total value of the birds seized was estimated to be more than $4,000, according to this report, which mentions that it was stated by an authority that "the price of good fighting-cocks ranges from $200 to $500 per bird."

---

* As it cannot surely be contended that the birds participating in the fight are themselves guilty of any crime, their destruction (which is customary in many countries where cockfighting is illegal) would appear to be not only unjustifiable, but to constitute a form of cruelty in itself. It should be comparatively easy, without condemning them to death, to prevent these birds taking part in any future fights.

A curious and at the same time an amusing interpretation of Argentine law is reported in the columns of the *Aberdeen Evening Express* (September 5, 1953), thus: "Forty-six people charged with violating anti-gambling laws by betting on cockfights, were freed in Buenos Aires today by the judge, who ruled that, since cockfighting itself was illegal, they could not be sentenced for betting on a sport that was not recognized."

As existing English law was powerless to prevent secret cockfights, early in 1952, Mr. Sidney H. Marshall, Conservative member for Sutton and Cheam, introduced a private member's bill designed to remedy omissions and defects in existing legislation relating to cockfighting. In its original form this Bill made it unlawful to possess "any domestic fowl prepared for use in fighting or of any instrument or appliance designed or adapted for use in connexion with the fighting of a domestic fowl." Obviously, the words "any domestic fowl prepared for use in fighting" were capable of a very wide interpretation, and might be the cause of grave injustices. The removal of the comb and wattles, which was one of the main steps taken in preparing a cock for battle, could and often was adopted for other purposes altogether. It was customary for breeders of Game Fowls intended purely for exhibition to remove the comb and wattles of all male specimens. The procedure was in the interests of the birds themselves and so far from its object being to prepare the birds for battle it was intended to render them less likely to injure themselves in the case of getting into a conflict with another male bird. Similarly breeders of other fowls of a pugnacious temperament, such as the Rhode Island Red; and of exceptionally large-combed birds liable to suffer from frost-bite, such as the Minorca or Leghorn; find it necessary to remove the comb and wattles. Again the injuries suffered in a fight may make the operation essential. Also the clipping of a fowl's wings might, conceivably, have nothing whatever to do with promoting its fighting powers; it might, on the contrary, be done with the sole object of preventing the bird flying into and fighting with the occupant of an adjoining pen; or trespassing in the beloved garden of a neighbour and thus causing hostilities of another kind.

Eventually, therefore, the Bill was amended so that "a domestic fowl should not be deemed to have been prepared for fighting only because its comb or wattle had been removed, or its wings or wing feathers had been cut or clipped." The clipping of the tail was however considered to be "unnecessary for any legitimate reason, and therefore a cockfighting bird could be distinguished by that, if in no other way."

The Bill was passed, and under the title of the Cockfighting Act, 1952, came into force on October 30, 1952. This Act provides that: "If any person has in his possession any instrument or appliance designed or adapted for use in connexion with the fighting of any domestic fowl, he shall, if the court be satisfied that he had it in his possession for the purpose of using it or permitting it to be used as aforesaid, be guilty of an offence under this section and shall be liable, on summary conviction, to imprisonment for a term not exceeding three months, or to a fine not exceeding twenty-five pounds, or to both such imprisonment and such fine." The court is empowered, where any person is convicted, to order "any instrument or appliance in respect of which the offence was committed to be destroyed or dealt with in such other manner as may be specified in the order." The Act does not apply to Northern Ireland.

Despite the additional powers given to the police by the 1952 Act it is doubtful if cockfighting will be eradicated. It will no doubt be curtailed to a greater extent than was possible in the past, but I have an idea that surreptitious fights will still be held. The main point in the Act lies in the power it gives to the police to take action against anyone in possession of "any instrument or appliance designed or adapted for use in connexion with the fighting of any domestic fowl"; but spurs, and these are the only important "instruments", are easily concealed or got rid of; moreover it must be remembered that spurs are not essential, and it is possible that the Act may cause a reversion to nakedheel fighting. Because of this possibility, it might have been advisable, in framing the Act, to make it compulsory for any Gamecock over a year old to have his spurs cut away and the stubs trimmed in the way that is customary with male birds used for breeding purposes. While a clause of this nature would not prevent cockfighting altogether, it would, in conjunction with the prohibition of spurs, have the effect of reducing it to negligible proportions and might lead to the virtual extinction of the sport.

APPENDICES

APPENDIX I

STANDARDS OF PERFECTION* FOR THE OLD ENGLISH GAME AS TODAY RECOGNISED BY THE CLUB DEVOTED TO THE BREED

POINTS APPLICABLE TO ALL VARIETIES

Head. Strong, bold, medium length.

Eyes. Large, bright and prominent; full of expression and alike in colour.

Beak. Strong at base and slightly curved.

Comb. Small, both in cock and hen, and serrated at its edge; single, erect and of fine texture.

Wattles. Fine texture and small.

Ear-lobes. To match the comb and wattles as nearly as possible.

Face. Of fine texture, to match the comb and wattles.

Neck. Long and very strong at junction with body.

Neck-Hackle. Wiry, long feathers, covering the shoulders.

Breast, Back and Body. Short back, broad across the shoulders, tapering well to the tail, with a full, broad, well-rounded chest, showing as little keel as possible. The keel or breast-bone to be straight and of medium depth, tapering well up behind, giving a very small and compact belly. The whole body with wings as seen from the top to appear flat and as near heater-shape as possible.

Wings. Full and round, inclining to meet under the tail, with strong prominent butts; feathers to be fairly broad and furnished with hard strong quills. The primaries not to be too long and to be nicely rounded at the ends, and to project past the body as little as possible.

---

* These Standards are reproduced here by kind permission of, and from the booklet issued by, the Old English Game Club (Honorary Secretary, Wm. Graham Reed, Esq., Low Cotehill Farm, Carlisle.)

Tail. In the cock, to be carried at a nice angle, neither too low nor too high, and to be straight. Wry and squirrel tails to be considered serious defects. Feathers to be broad and strong, with a pair of good curved sickles of fair length and well furnished with side-hangers. In the hen, well carried, fairly close, and of medium length.

Legs. Thighs short, thick and muscular, and set fairly well apart; shanks of medium length, with good round bone; not flat on shins. Inkneed or bow-legged state to be considered a serious fault.

Feet. Four toes on each foot; should be clean, even, long and spreading, the back toe standing well backward and flat on the ground.

Spur. Low on the leg.

Carriage. Bold, smart, the movement quick and graceful, proud and sprightly, as if ready for any emergency.

Handling. Flesh firm but corky, with plenty of muscle. This to be considered an important factor.

Plumage. Hard, glossy and firm.

Weight. Cocks: it is considered not desirable to breed cocks over 6½ lbs.

SCALE OF POINTS FOR JUDGING

Shape and Carriage	40
Handling and Condition	15
Head and Eye	10
Legs and Feet	15
Colour and Plumage	20
Total	100

POINTS OF COLOUR IN SPANGLE GAME COCK

Face. Bright red.
Eyes. Red, both to be alike.
Neck-Hackle and Saddle. Dark red, finely tipped with white.
Breast and Thighs. Black, finely and evenly tipped with white.

Back and Shoulders. Dark red, finely tipped with white.

Wings. Wing bow dark red, finely tipped with white, with a rich dark blue bar across, finely tipped with white; secondaries, deep bay intermixed with white, bay predominating; primaries, black intermixed with white.

Tail. Sickles and side hangers black, tipped with white; straight feathers black, intermixed with white.

Legs. White.

HEN

Face. Bright red.

Eyes. Red, both to be alike.

Neck-Hackle. Golden red, streaked with black, finely tipped with white.

Breast and Thighs. Dark salmon colour, finely and evenly tipped with white.

Back and Shoulders. Dark partridge-coloured feathers, finely and evenly tipped with white.

Wings. Secondaries, dark partridge intermixed with white, partridge predominating; primaries, dark intermixed with white. All other feathers dark partridge colour, finely and evenly tipped with white.

Tail. Black with partridge coverts, finely and evenly tipped with white.

Legs. White.

POINTS OF COLOUR IN BLACK-BREASTED RED GAME

COCK

Face. Bright red.

Eyes. Red, both to be alike.

Neck-Hackle and Saddle. Orange red, free from dark feathers.

Breast and Thighs. Black.

Back and Shoulders. Deep red.

Wings. Wing bow, deep red with a rich dark blue bar across; secondaries, bay colour on outer web; primaries, black.

Tail. Sound black, with lustrous green gloss.

Legs. White.

HEN (PARTRIDGE)

Face and Eyes. Same as cock.
Neck. Golden red and streaked with black.
Breast and Thighs. Shaded salmon colour.
Back and Wings. Partridge colour : to be as free from rust and shaftiness as possible.
Tail. Black with partridge coverts.
Legs. White, yellow, or willow.

POINTS OF COLOUR IN BRIGHT-RED GAME

COCK

Face. Bright red.
Eyes. Red, both to be alike.
Neck-Hackle and Saddle. Light golden red, free from streaks.
Breast and Thighs. Black.
Back and Shoulders. Bright red.
Wings. Wing bow, bright red ; in other respects similar to Black-red.
Tail. Similar to Black-red.
Legs. White.

HEN (WHEATEN)

Face and Eyes. Same as cock.
Neck-Hackle. Golden red, free from striping.
Breast and Thighs. Light wheaten.
Back and Wings. Wheaten, level on colour.
Tail. Black, with a shading of wheaten corresponding with body colour.
Legs. White.

HEN (CLAY)

Clay Hens. Similar to Wheaten, only darker or harder in colour.

POINTS OF COLOUR IN BROWN-RED GAME

COCK

Face. Gipsy or red.
Eyes. Dark, both to be alike.
Neck and Saddle. Lemon or orange, streaked with black.
Breast and Thighs. Black, laced with brown.
Back. Lemon or orange.
Wings. Shoulders and wing bow, lemon or orange, rest of wing black.
Tail. Black.
Legs. Dark.

HEN

Face. Gipsy or red.
Eyes. Dark, both to be alike.
Neck-Hackle. Lemon or orange, striped with black.
Breast and Thighs. Black, laced with brown.
Body. Black.
Tail. Black.
Legs. Dark.

POINTS OF COLOUR IN BLUE-RED GAME

BLUE-RED COCK

Face. Bright red.
Eyes. Red, both to be alike.
Neck-Hackle and Saddle. Orange or golden red.
Breast and Thighs. Blue, medium shade.
Back and Shoulders. Deep or bright red.
Wings. Wing bow, deep or bright red, with a rich dark blue bar across; secondaries, bay colour on the outer web; primaries, blue.
Tail. Blue.
Legs. Any self colour.

BLUE-RED HEN

Face. Bright red.
Eyes. Red, both to be alike.
Neck. Golden red, streaked with blue.
Breast and Thighs. Shaded salmon colour.
Back and Wings. Partridge colour, intermixed with blue.
Tail. To correspond with body colour.
Legs. Any self colour.

BLUE-TAILED WHEATEN HEN

Face. Bright red.
Eyes. Red, both to be alike.
Plumage. Similar in all respects to Wheaten, with the exception of wing primaries and tail shaded with blue.
Legs. White.

SELF-BLUE COCK AND HEN

Face. Bright red.
Eyes. Red, both to be alike.
Plumage. Blue, medium shade.
Legs. Any self colour.

POINTS OF COLOUR IN PILE GAME

COCK

Face. Bright red.
Eyes. Red, both to be alike.
Neck and Saddle. Orange or chestnut red.
Breast and Thighs. White.
Back and Shoulders. Deep red.
Wings. Wing bow, red with a white bar across; secondaries, bay colour on outer web; primaries, white.
Tail. White.
Legs. White or yellow.

HEN

Face. Bright red.
Eyes. Red, both to be alike.
Neck. Lemon.
Breast. Salmon colour, lighter towards thighs.
Back and Wings. White.
Tail. White.
Legs. White or yellow.

POINTS OF COLOUR IN DUCKWING GAME

GOLDEN-DUCKWING COCK

Face. Bright red.
Eyes. Red, both to be alike.
Hackle. Creamy white.
Saddle. Orange or rich yellow.
Breast and Thighs. Black.
Back and Shoulders. Orange or rich yellow.
Wings. Wing bow, orange or rich yellow ; wing bars, black ; secondaries, white on the outer web ; primaries, black.
Tail. Black.
Legs. Any self colour.

SILVER-DUCKWING COCK

Face. Bright red.
Eyes. Red, both to be alike.
Neck and Saddle. Silver white, free from dark streaks.
Breast and Thighs. Black.
Back and Shoulders. Silver white.
Wings. Wing bow, silver white ; wing bar, steel blue ; secondaries, white on outer web ; primaries, black.
Tail. Black.
Legs. Any self colour.

DUCKWING HEN

Face. Bright red.
Eyes. Red, both to be alike.
Neck. Silver, striped with black.
Breast and Thighs. Salmon colour.
Back and Wings. Steel-grey, free from rust and shaftiness.
Tail. Black. Coverts corresponding with body colour.
Legs. Any self colour.

POINTS OF COLOUR IN CRELE GAME

COCK

Face. Bright red.
Eyes. Red, both to be alike.
Neck and Saddle. Chequered orange colour.
Back and Shoulders. Deep chequered orange.
Wings. Wing bow, deep chequered orange, with a dark grey bar across; secondaries, bay colour on the outer web; primaries, dark grey.
Tail. Dark grey.
Legs. White preferred.

HEN

Face. Bright red.
Eyes. Red, both to be alike.
Neck. Lemon, chequered with grey.
Breast and Thighs. Chequered salmon colour.
Back and Wings. Chequered blue-grey.
Tail. To correspond with body colour.
Legs. White preferred.

POINTS OF COLOUR IN WHITE GAME

COCK AND HEN

Face. Bright red.
Eyes. Red, both to be alike.
Plumage. All over pure white.
Legs. White.

POINTS OF COLOUR IN BLACK GAME

COCK AND HEN

Face. Red or dark.
Eyes. Red or dark, both to be alike.
Plumage. All over glossy black.
Legs. Any self colour.

Among other varieties recognised are: Hennies, Muffs and Tassels in all colours; Furnesses, Crow Wings, and Birchen Greys.

The judges, as men of experience, will exercise their discretion in judging these varieties.

APPENDIX II

A GLOSSARY OF TECHNOLOGIC AND JARGONIC TERMS

BATTLE ROYAL. A species of cockfight in which any number of cocks are engaged, the one that remains on his feet longest being proclaimed the victor.

BLENKER. Same as *Blinker*, q.v.

BLINKER. A fighting-cock that is blinded or seriously injured in one eye.

BLOODY-HEELED. Descriptive of a fighting-cock with a deadly stroke of the spur.

BOXING GLOVES. A name sometimes given to *Muffs* or "*Hots*."

BREED. A specific type of fowl possessing certain well defined characteristics which distinguish it from other types.

COCK. A male fowl that is more than twelve months of age, in contradistinction to a cockerel, which is a male specimen under the age of twelve months.

COCK-BAG. A bag used in the transportation of a fighting-cock to the pit : it was usually made of linen, but the bag used by wealthy cockers was often made of silk or velvet.

COCKER. A person who directs or promotes cockfights. A breeder of Game Fowl for cockfighting. One who is a regular attender at cockfights or a supporter of cockfighting.

COCKEREL. A male fowl that is under the age of twelve months.

COCKFIGHT. A contest between two or more fighting-cocks.

COCKFIGHTER. A person who prepares cocks for fighting, who arranges or superintends cockfights, or who regularly attends such contests.

COCKFIGHTING. The sport in which battles between fighting-cocks are held.

Cocking. The sport of cockfighting.

Cock-Match. Same as *Cockfight*, q.v.

Cock Of The Game. A fighting-cock.

Cock-Penny. An annual contribution at one time made by a pupil at Shrovetide towards the cost of purchasing or training fighting-cocks for use in school cockfights. These contributions or fees were collected by the schoolmaster.

Cockpit. An arena or other enclosure in which cockfights are held.

Coverts. The small feathers which overlap and conceal the bottom parts of the main tail and wing feathers; often termed *Tail coverts* and *Wing coverts* respectively.

Devonshire Main. A type of cockfight in which birds were matched in pairs according to weight, starting with a pair of the minimum weight (usually four pounds), each of the next contestants weighing an additional ounce, and so on until the maximum weight (usually about five pounds) was reached.

Dub. To cut off a cock's comb and wattles.

Dubbed. The state of a male fowl which has had his comb and wattles amputated.

Dubbing. The act or process of cutting away the comb and wattles of a male fowl.

Ducker. A type of fighting-cock, so-named because of his manner of fighting.

Dunghill Fowl. A mongrel fowl or one of mixed or unknown breeding, usually not having pronounced pugnacious qualities. Hence, among cockers, the term is applied to any bird (other than a pure-bred Gamecock) that declines to fight. *To die dunghill*: to give up the struggle.

Feeder. One who rears and conditions Gamecocks for the pit.

Gablocks. An old term for artificial spurs.

Gaff. A steel or other form of artificial spur.

Gaffet. A cock's artificial spur (variant of *Gafflet*).

Gaffle. Same as *Gafflet*, q.v.

Gafflet. A cock's artificial spur (variant of *Gaffet*).

Gaft. Same as *Gaff*, q.v.

Gavelocks. Artificial spurs (variant of *Gablocks*).

HACKLE. That part of the plumage of a fowl comprising the long slender feathers covering the neck or saddle.

HACKLE-FEATHER. One of the long slender feathers forming the hackle.

HANDLER. One with expert knowledge of preparing cocks for battle and handling them during the actual fights. Formerly called a *setter* or *setter-to*.

HEATER-SHAPED. Triangular.

HEEL. A spur, artificial or natural. In a verbal sense, to affix an artificial spur to a cock's leg.

HEELED. Descriptive of a fighting-cock with his spurs strapped on ready for battle.

HEELER. A Gamecock which displays exceptional striking power or skill. A person who affixes the artificial spurs to a cock's legs before a fight.

HEN. A female fowl that is more than twelve months of age, in contradistinction to a pullet, which is a female specimen under the age of twelve months.

HEN-COCK. Same as *Henny*, q.v.

HEN-FEATHERED. Descriptive of a male fowl with plumage resembling that typical of the female specimen.

HENNY. A cock with the kind of plumage that is characteristic of the female specimen of its breed or variety. Used as an adjective to describe a male bird possessing plumage typical of the female specimen.

HOTS. Same as *Muffs*, q.v.

HOTTS. Alternative spelling of *Hots*, q.v.

INBREEDING. The act or process of continuously mating together closely related specimens of the same breed or variety, e.g. brother and sister. The term is usually restricted in its application to promiscuous matings of this character. (cf. *Linebreeding*).

LACED. A term used to describe a feather which is edged with some colour or shade of colour other than that forming the body of the feather.

LEATHERING. The act or process of fixing artificial spurs to the legs of a Gamecock by the use of narrow strips of leather or kid.

LINEBREEDING. The name given to a specific form of inbreeding where related specimens are mated together along definitely prescribed lines, as father and daughters, or mother and sons, in contradistinction to indiscriminate or promiscuous inbreeding (cf. *Inbreeding*).

LONG MAIN. See under *Main*.

LUNGED. Struck in the lung by a spur.

MAIN. A collective term for an odd number of battles between the matched cocks of two persons, the owner whose birds win the majority of the matches being the winner of the main. The term *Long main* was given to a main lasting four or more days; the term *Short main* to one of from one day to three days' duration.

MAT. The sheet of netting, carpet or other material with which the floor of the cockpit is covered.

MOLT. American spelling of *Moult*, q.v.

MOLTING. American spelling of *Moulting*, q.v.

MOULT. The period during which a fowl discards old and dons new plumage. In a verbal sense, to discard old and acquire new feathers.

MOULTING. The act or process by which a fowl of either sex loses old feathers and acquires new ones in their place: it occurs once a year, usually in the autumn.

MUFFLES. Same as *Muffs*, q.v.

MUFFS. Soft balls or pads of leather or other material for attaching to a fighting-cock's legs, over the spurs, to prevent his opponent receiving injuries during training.

NAKED-HEEL. The sharp-pointed bony spur that grows on the leg of a mature cock: it does not become long enough or sufficiently strong to rank as a weapon of offence until the bird reaches the age of two years.

NAKED-HEELED. Descriptive of a fighting-cock which is not fitted with artificial spurs.

NECK-HACKLE. See under *Hackle*.

OUTBREEDING. That form of breeding in which unrelated specimens of the same breed or variety are mated. The crossing of different strains. (cf. *Outcrossing*).

OUTCROSSING. The act or process of breeding from a male of one breed or variety and females of some other breed or variety (cf. *Outbreeding*).

PIN-FEATHER. A young and immature feather.

PIT. Abbreviated form of *Cockpit*, q.v.

PITCHFORK. A spur which is unusually long.

PITTER. An old and now disused term for a *handler* or *setter*.

PRIMARIES. The main flight feathers in the wing of a fowl: they are visible only when the wing is opened.

PULLET. A female fowl that is under the age of twelve months.

SADDLE. That part of the back of a cock or cockerel adjacent to the tail.

SADDLE-FEATHER. One of the long narrow feathers that hang down on each side of and adjacent to the tail of a cock or cockerel.

SADDLE-HACKLE. See under *Hackle*.

SECONDARIES. The feathers which form the visible portion of the wing when closed.

SETTER. Same as *Handler*, q.v.

SETTER-TO. An old and now disused synonym for *Setter*, q.v.

SHAKEBAG. A large Gamecock, usually one that could not be matched because of his abnormally large size.

SHANK. The section of a fowl's leg above the foot.

SHORT MAIN. See under *Main*.

SHURL. To trim or cut the feathers of a fighting-cock's neck-hackle.

SICKLE. A steel spur of curved formation.

SICKLE-FEATHER. One of the long slender feathers bearing a high sheen, which hang downwards on each side of a male bird's tail.

SIDE-HANGERS. Same as *Saddle-feathers*, q.v.

SLASHER. A steel spur of curved design and large size.

SPARRING. That part of a fighting-cock's training in which he practises fighting with another cock, both birds wearing muffs to prevent injuries.

SQUIRREL-TAIL. A term used to describe a tail which is carried vertically or so as to form an acute angle with the back. This condition is a defect and strongly hereditary.

STAG. A cocker's term for a male bird that is under twelve months of age.

STEEL. A metal spur.

STUB. The short bony projection remaining after the natural spur has been removed. It is to this remnant that an artificial spur is fixed.

TAIL-COVERTS. See under *Coverts*.

TRIMMED. Descriptive of a cock that has been prepared for battle by having his hackle, wings and tail clipped.

TURN-OUT. A name for a fighting-cock of large size. (This term was later superseded by *Shakebag*, q.v.).

VARIETY. A subdivision of a breed of fowls, thus the Black-red Game is a variety of the Old English Game.

WALK. A place, usually in the country, where a fighting-cock is able to have his liberty and yet not come in contact with other fowls. Also a separate enclosure in which a fighting-cock can take exercise.

WATTLE. A pendant piece of red flesh attached to the head of a fowl immediately below the beak. There is one on each side.

WELSH MAIN. In this type of cockfight, a number of cocks of the same weight were staged and fought in pairs, victory going to the winner of the final contest between the two survivors of the preceding battles.

WING-COVERTS. See under *Coverts*.

WRY TAIL. A tail which persistently hangs or leans towards one side: it is a serious defect in all fowls intended for breeding or exhibition.

APPENDIX III

BIBLIOGRAPHY

R. Ackermann, *The Microcosm of London; or, London in Miniature;* 3 vols; London, 1904.

Henry Alken, *The National Sports of Great Britain*; London, 1821.

William Andrews, *Bygone England*; Hutchinson & Co., London, 1892.

William Andrews (edited by), *Historic Byways and Highways of Old England*; William Andrews & Co., London, 1900.

William Andrews (edited by), *Legal Lore: Curiosities of Law and Lawyers;* William Andrews & Co., London, 1897.

John Ashton, *Social Life in the Reign of Queen Anne*; 2 vols., Chatto & Windus, London, 1882.

John Ashton, *Social England Under the Regency*; Chatto & Windus, London, 1899.

Sir John Dugdale Astley, *Fifty Years of my Life*; 2 vols., Hurst and Blackett, London, 1894.

Herbert Atkinson, *Cockfighting and the Game Fowl*; George Bayntun, Bath, 1938.

H. A. (Herbert Atkinson), *The Life and Letters of John Harris, The Cornish Cocker;* Privately printed, 1910.

John Barrow, *Travels in China*; London, 1806.

The Hon. Grantley F. Berkeley, *My Life and Recollections*; 4 vols. Hurst and Blackett, London, 1865.

Thomas Bewick, *A History of British Birds;* Bernard Quaritch, London, 1885.

Sir Richard Blackmore, *A Poem on a Cock Match*, London, 1709.

Delabere P. Blaine, *An Encyclopaedia of Rural Sports*, new edition, revised and corrected by "Harry Hieover", A. Graham, Esq., "Ephemera", etc. etc.; Longmans, Brown, Green, and Longmans, London, 1852.

Richard Blome, *The Gentleman's Recreation*; London, 1686.

William B. Boulton, *The Amusements of Old London*; 2 vols., Nimmo, London, 1901.

N. Carlisle, *A Concise Description of the Endowed Grammar Schools in England and Wales*; 2 vols., London, 1818.

R. Chambers (edited by), *The Books of Days, A Miscellany of Popular Antiquities*; 2 vols., Edinburgh, 1863.

The Cockers Guide, by an Expert; Richard K. Fox, New York, 1888.

Alex D. Cumming, *Old Times in Scotland: Life, Manners, and Customs*, with an introduction by Professor Cooper; Alexander Gardner, Paisley, 1910.

Colonel Arthur Cunynghame, *An Aide-de-Camp's Recollections of Service in China*; Richard Bentley, London, 1853.

Daniel Defoe, *Journey Through England*; London, 1724.

H. H. Dixon (The Druid), *Silk and Scarlet*; Rogerson & Tuxford, London, 1859.

Pierce Egan, *Book of Sports*; T. T. and J. Tegg, London, 1832.

Pierce Egan, *Life in London*; Hotten, London, n.d. (c. 1869).

Edmund Ellis, *The Opinions of Mr. Perkins and Mr. Bolton, and Others, Concerning the Sport of Cockfighting. Published formerly in their works, and now set forth to shew, that it is not a Recreation meet for Christians, though so commonly used by those who own that Name*; Oxford, 1660.

T. Fairfax, *The Complete Sportsman; or Country Gentleman's Recreation*; London, 1764.

J. Fairfax-Blakeborough, *Country Life and Sport*; Philip Allan & Co., London, 1926.

G. Ferguson, *Illustrated Series of Rare and Prize Poultry*; Culliford, London, 1854.

C. A. Finsterbusch, *Cock Fighting all over the World*; Gaffney, S. C., U.S.A., 1929.

Capt. L. Fitz-Barnard, *Fighting Sports*; Odhams Press, n.d.

R. Forsyth, *The Beauties of Scotland*; Edinburgh, 1805.

Sir Walter Gilbey, Bart., *Sport in the Olden Time*; Vinton & Co. London, 1912.

Frederick W. Hackwood, *Old English Sports*; Fisher Unwin, London, 1907.

John Harland and T. T. Wilkinson, *Lancashire Folk-lore*; John Heywood, Manchester, 1882.

Samuel Hazard, *Cuba with Pen and Pencil*; Sampson Low, Marston, Low & Searle, London, 1873.

Robert Howlett (R.H.), *The Royal Pastime of Cock-fighting*; 1709.

Walter Hutchinson (edited by), *Customs of the World*; Hutchinson & Co., London, n.d.

Georgina F. Jackson, *Shropshire Folklore*; edited by C. S. Burne, 1883.

Walter Kaudern, *Ethnological Studies in Celebes*; 6 vols., Martinus Nijhoff, The Hague, 1929.

Richard King, *The Frauds of London Detected*; London, 1770.

John Alfred Langford, *A Century of Birmingham Life, or a Chronicle of Local Events from 1741 to 1841*; 2 vols., E. C. Osborne, Birmingham and Simpkin Marshall & Co., London, 1868.

Sir Sidney Lee, *Bearbaiting, Bullbaiting and Cockfighting* in *Shakespeare's England, an Account of the Life and Manners of His Age*, (Vol. II); Clarendon Press, 1916.

S. H. Lewer (edited by), *Wright's Book of Poultry*; Cassell & Co., London.

William Machrie, *An Essay upon the Royal Recreation and Art of Cocking*; Edinburgh, 1705.

James Peller Malcolm, *Anecdotes of the Manners and Customs of London During the Eighteenth Century*, second edition; London, 1810.

James Peller Malcolm, *Anecdotes of the Manners and Customs of London from the Roman Invasion to the Year 1700*, second edition; 3 vols., London, 1811.

Gervase Markham, *Country Contentments, or, the Husbandman's Recreations*, eleventh edition; London, 1675.

Hugh Miller, *My Schools and Schoolmasters, or The Story of my Education*; Thomas Constable & Co., Edinburgh, 1860.

J. J. Nolan, *Ornamental, Aquatic and Domestic Fowl, and Game Birds; Their Importation, Breeding, Rearing, and General Management*; published by the Author, Dublin, 1850.

William Augustus Osbaldiston, *The British Sportsman*; London, 1792.

Rev. Samuel Pegge, *A Memoir on Cock-Fighting*, in *Archaeologia*, Vol. III, pp. 132-150; The Society of Antiquaries of London, 1786.

Rev. Charles Rogers, *Scotland Social and Domestic*; Grampian Club, London, 1869.

Arch Ruport (Muff), *The Art of Cockfighting. A Handbook for Beginners and Old Timers*; The Devin-Adair Co., New York, 1949.

Henry Ling Roth, *The Natives of Sarawak and British North Borneo*; 2 vols., Truslove & Hanson, London, 1896.

Harry R. Sargent, *Thoughts Upon Sport*; Photo-Prismatic Publishing Co., London, 1894.

Monsieur Cesar de Saussure, *A Foreign View of England in the Reign of George I & George II*, Translated and edited by Madame Van Muyden; John Murray, London, 1902.

William Henry Scott, *British Field Sports*; Sherwood, Neely and Jones, London, 1818.

Richard Seymour, *The Compleat Gamester*, sixth edition; London, 1739.

W. Sketchley, *The Cocker*; London, 1814.

The Sportsman's Dictionary: or, the Gentleman's Companion for Town and Country; London, 1778.

John Lloyd Stephens, *Incidents of Travel in Central America, Chiapas and Yucatan*; revised by Frederick Catherwood; Arthur Hall, Virtue & Co., London, 1854.

Joseph Strutt, *The Sports and Pastimes of the People of England*, new edition, with a copious index, by William Hone; William Tegg & Co., London, 1855.

William Connor Sydney, *England and the English in the Eighteenth Century*; John Grant, Edinburgh, c. 1891.

W. B. Tegetmeier, *The Poultry Book*; George Routledge and Sons, London, 1867.

William John Thoms, *Anecdotes and Traditions illustrative of Early English History and Literature*; London, 1839.

Edgar Thurston, *Ethnographic Notes in Southern India*; Printed by The Superintendent, Government Press, Madras, 1906.

John Timbs, *Romance of London: Strange Stories, Scenes and Remarkable Persons of the Great Town*; 3 vols., R. Bentley, London, 1865.

Transactions of the Cumberland and Westmorland Antiquarian & Archaeological Society, Vol. IX. ; T. Wilson, Kendal, 1888.

J. T. Tregellas, *Amusing Adventures of Josee Cock, the Perran Cockfighter* ; 2nd edition, Hotten, London, 1857.

Edward Walford, *Old & New London* ; Cassell & Company, London, 1897.

T. T. Wilkinson, see under John Harland.

George Wilson, *The Commendation of Cockes, and Cockfighting* ; London, 1607.

Rev. G. N. Wright, *China, in a Series of Views, Displaying the Scenery, Architecture and Social Habits, of that Ancient Empire* ; 2 vols., Fisher, Son & Co., London, 1843.

INDEX

Age of cocks for fighting, 38, 52
Agreements for cockfighting, 64
Alabama, 123
Alcohol important part of diet, 48
Alken, Henry, 103
America, Central and South, 55, 132
America, North, 121ff
Antiquity of cockfighting, 87ff
Argentina, 175
Aristophanes, 53
Arkansas, 124
Artificial spurs, 51ff, 92, 123, 130, 134, 135, 157
Aseel game, 121, 126
Ashton, John, 55n, 59n, 67
Astley, Sir John Dugdale, 170
Athenaeus, 87
Atkinson, Herbert, 53, 57, 60

Bantams, 25
Barnet, 107
Basketing, punishment of, 86
Battle Royal, 55n, 73, 157
Beastal, John, 46
Beastal's cordial, 32
Belgium, cockfighting in, 136
Bells, silver competition, 96ff
Bellyse, Dr., and Bellyse strain, 23, 106, 109, 110ff
Berkeley, Earl of, 105
Berkeley, Hon. Grantley F., 117
Betting, 138
Beverley Piles, 32
Bewick, Thomas, 17
Birchens, 20, 24, 103
Birmingham, 69, 70, 114, 115

Bishop Auckland, 171
Black-breasted Reds, 20, 21, 23, 24, 27, 46, 103, 104
Black Sumatras, 16, 28
Blackmore, Sir Richard, verses of, 81
Blaine, Delabere P., 112, 143, 155
Blood sports, 11
Borneo, 87
Boscawen, Admiral, 102
Bourne, Thomas, 41, 44
Boxing matches, 11
Boynton, Sir Francis, 24, 103
Brahma, 89
Brass spurs, 54
Bread for feeding, 41, 42
Breeding game, 29ff
Breeds of game, 16, 20
Bridgnorth, 70
Bristol, 115
Britain, introduction of cockfighting to, 92, 93
Brown-breasted Reds, 20, 25, 27, 110
Brutalisation of spectators, 11, 165
Buffon, 15
Bullock strain, 23
Bury St. Edmunds, 115
Buxton, 68, 109
Byron, Lord, 143

Calais, 136
California, 123
Cambridgeshire, 68
Canada, cockfighting in, 174
Candlelight, cockfighting by, 103
Care of gamecocks after battle, 48
Carlisle, 66, 168

INDEX

Case against cockfighting, 11, 157
Celebes, cockfighting in, 129
Centres, cockfighting, 113
Charles II, 53, 102, 138
Chesterfield, Lord, 105
Cheshire, 66, 68, 103, 106, 108, 109, 110, 113, 114
"Cheshire drop", 111
Cheshire Piles, 32
Chicago, 125
Chichester, 109
"Chifney rush", 111
China, cockfighting in, 128
Chislehurst, 57
Christ's Hospital, 150
Christian VII, 102
Churches and churchyards, cockfights held in, 116
Clergymen, cockfighting enthusiasts, 116ff
Cliquennous, Henri, 135
Clitheroe, 94
Clive, Lord, 105
Cochin, 89
Cockfight, description of, at Westminster, 74ff
Cockfight, description of, by Tegetmeier, 79ff
Cockfighting, Act of 1952, 176
Cockfighting rules, 61ff, 122
Cockpits, 57ff, 122
Colet, Dr. John, 98
Colour of legs, 23
Colour of plumage, 20, 23
"Connecticut Strawberries", 24, 121
Cornwall, 53, 57
Counties, cockfighting battles between, 66
Courage of gamefowl, 9, 18
Cromarty, 95
Cromwell, Oliver, 137
Cross-breeding, 23
"Crowing hens", 18
Cruelty, 5, 157, 165
Cruelty to Animals Act of 1849, 137, 168
Crystal Palace, 25
Cuba, cockfighting in, 133
Cumberland, 97, 117, 160, 168, 172
Curved spurs, 135

Defoe, Daniel, 78
Derby, Earl of, and Derby strain, 21, 23, 24, 38, 103, 104, 107, 108, 109, 110, 112, 163
Derbyshire, 172
Devonshire Main, 73
Diet, gamecocks', 41, 48
Dioscorides, 87
Districts noted for cockfighting, 113
Dixon, Thomas, 30
Downey strain, 23
Dubbing, 35, 158, 175
Duckwings, 24
Duff, Patrick, 24, 121
Dumfries, 96
Duns, 20, 23, 24
Durham, 113

Edgar, Rev. Dr., 94
Edinburgh, 116
Edward III, 138
Egan, Pierce, 45, 66, 113, 132
Ellis, Edmund, 145
Environment, effects of, 31, 127
Essex, 67, 68

Fairfax-Blakeborough, J., 28, 113, 169
Faultless, Charles, 24, 112, 169
Feeders, 111ff
Feeding, 41, 48
Female Game Fowl, 18
Ferguson, G., 16, 18, 21, 23, 92, 104, 159, 163
Ferguson, Worshipful Chancellor, 55, 116
Fighting, mode of, 40
Finstersbusch, C. A., 121
Fitzstephen, William, 93
Fixing of artificial spurs, 55
Flagellation, punishment for rioting, 140
Florida, 124
France, cockfighting in, 135

Game-hens, 19, 20
George III, 112

George IV, 102, 112
Gilbey, Sir Walter, 60, 66, 73, 116, 118
Gilliver (feeders), 103, 107, 112, 114, 115, 168
Gloucestershire, 67, 69
Gold spurs, 54
Grays, 24, 46
Greece, ancient, 53, 87
Gwenap Pit, 57
Gwyn, Nell, 53

HACKLE, trimming of, 47
Hamilton, Duke of, 105
Harris, John, 23, 53, 112
Heber, Reginald (cockfighting rules), 61, 85
"Hector", 25, 26
Heels, 38ff, 51ff
Hen-cocks, 24ff
Henry VIII, 58, 98, 101
Hens, emphasis on, for mating, 29
Herbert, Edward, 58, 74, 162
Herefordshire, 69, 116
Herodotus, 92
Hogarth, 11, 167
Holcombe, 57
Holford strain, 23
Hoods, 42
"Hots", 42, 43n
Houghton, Sir Henry, 105
Howe, Lord, 103
Howlett, Robert, 23, 65, 88, 153
Hoyle (cockfighting rules), 61
Huntingdonshire, 68

ILLEGALITY of cockfighting, 124, 150
Inbreeding, 30, 31
India, cockfighting in, 87, 126
Indian Game, 15, 52, 126
Indianapolis, 121
Inhibiting effect of artificial spurs, 56
Injured cocks, care of, 48, 50
Ireland, cockfighting in, 173
Iron spurs, 54
Isle of Wight, 67

JAMES I, 58, 102
Jermin, Sir Thomas, 105
Johnson, Dr. Samuel, 143

KANSAS, 123
Kendal, 94
Kent, 57, 68
Kent, Duke of, 131
Kentucky, 123, 124, 125
King, Richard, 144
Knowsley breed, 21, 23, 104 (*and see* Derby, Earl of)

LANCASHIRE, 172
Language enriched by cockfighting terms, 118
Last public cockfight in London, 59
Law relating to cockfighting, in Great Britain, 168ff; in United States 123
"Leathering", 55
Leghorns, 90, 175
Legs, colour of, 23
Leith, 115
Lichfield, 113
Lincolnshire, 68, 102, 113, 119
Linebreeding, 30
Liverpool, 60, 109, 110, 114
London, cockpits in, 58ff
Long mains, 72, 101
Lonsdale, Lord, 105
Loughborough, 32
Louisiana, 124
Lowther strain, 23
Lucknow, 126, 127

MACHRIE, William, 39, 42, 47
Mackintosh, Sir James, 96
Magistrates who were cockfighting devotees, 168, 171
Magpie, hatching by, 118
Mains, Devonshire, 73
Mains, long and short, 72
Mains, stakes for, 65ff
Mains, Welsh, 73

Majorca, cockfighting in, 136
Malacca, cockfighting in, 129
Malay game, 15, 20, 28
Manchester, 97, 107, 108, 109, 113
Manchet, 41
Markham, Gervase, 23, 29, 33, 37, 38, 41, 42, 43, 44, 48, 151
Marshall, Sidney H., M.P., 175
Maryland, 123
Matching, 62, 65
Mauchline, 94
Measures against cockfighting, 137ff
Melton Mowbray, cockpit at, 60
Metal spurs, 51ff
Mexborough, Earl of, 24, 105, 112
Mexico, cockfighting in, 55, 131
Miller, Hugh, 95, 98
Mississippi, 124
Modern breed, 16
Montgomeryshire, 172
Mordaunt, Colonel, 127
Muzzles, 43

NAKED-HEELS and naked-heel fighting, 38ff, 51ff, 134, 136, 157, 176
Name of town chosen by cockfight, 119
Names of fighting-cocks, 113
Nash (feeders), 26, 75ff
Newcastle-on-Tyne, 66, 68, 113, 168, 169
Newmarket, 65, 102
New York, 121
Nickel spurs, 53
Nolan, J. J., 113
North Borneo, 131
Northamptonshire, 68
Northumberland, 68
Northumberland, Duke of, 105
Nottinghamshire, 68
Nova Scotia, 174

OHIO, 124
Oklahoma, 124
Old English Game, 12, 20, 31, 90, 159, 179
Old stock, breeding from, 22
Oldest English metal spurs, 53

Open-air cockpits, 57
Opponent, selection of, 44
Opposition to cockfighting, 137ff
Origin of Game Fowl, 15
Origin of organised cockfighting, 89
Osbaldiston, W. A. (cockfighting rules), 63
Outbreeding, 30
Oxford, 113

PARASILA, 130
Pegge, Rev. Samuel, 89, 94
Penrith, 117
Pens, 40
Pepys, Samuel, 58, 100
Perching, 33
Perfection, standards of, in old English Game, 160, 179
Peru, cockfighting in, 132
Philippine Islands, 55, 129
Piles, 20, 23, 24, 32, 111
Pliny, 88
Plumage, colour of, 20
Pocklington, 97
Potter (feeder), 103, 104, 107
Preparation for battle, 40ff
Preston, 67, 103, 105, 107, 108, 112, 113
Private cockfights, 169
Puerto Rico, cockfighting in, 134
Pugnacity in poultry, 89
Punishment for welshing, 86

QUAILS, 92, 128

RACE-MEETINGS, cockfighting matches held during, 66ff, 103, 107ff
Rearing game, 29ff
Recipe for feeding, 41
Redruth, 57
Removal, deleterious effects of, 31, 32
Rhode Island Reds, 31, 51, 90, 175
Rochdale, 108
Roman remains in Britain, 53
Romans, ancient, 53, 88
Rome, 51

INDEX

Ross-shire, 94
Rous, Admiral, 151
Rowlandson, Thomas, 11, 167
Royal Pit, Westminster, 27, 58, 150
Rules, cockfighting, 61ff, 122

SABBATH cockfights, 116, 133, 144, 172
St. Paul's School, 98
Salford, 108, 109
Savill, Sir Henry, 100
Schools, cocking in, 93ff
Scotland, 94, 95, 96, 115
Scotland, Act making cockfighting illegal in, 169
Scott, William Henry, 156
Scouring, 43
Sebright bantams, 25
Secret cockfights, 125, 169ff
Sedbergh, 94
Sefton, Earl of, 104, 114
Selection of fighting-cocks, 37
Setters, 62, 72, 112
Severus, 91
Shakebags, 55n, 65
Short mains, 72
Shropshire, 32, 68, 69, 110
Shrove-Tuesday, day for cockfighting, 93, 96, 97
Silver Duckwings, 20
Silver spurs, 53, 54
Sinclair, Sir John, 94
Size of cocks, 37
Size of spurs, 52, 54
Sketchley, W., 21, 23, 32, 34, 37, 40, 46, 64
"Slasher" spur, 54
Somerset, 57
Spain, 52
Spangleds, 20
Sparring, 42
Spurs, artificial, 51ff, 92, 123, 130, 134, 135, 157
Spurs, brass, 54
Spurs, curved, 135
Spurs, gold, 54
Spurs, iron, 54

Spurs, natural, 38ff, 51, 127
Spurs, nickel, 53
Spurs, silver, 53, 54
Spurs, "slasher", 54
Spurs, steel, 53, 54, 123, 135
Staffordshire, 66, 67, 68, 70, 115, 140
Stakes, 65ff, 107ff, 112, 172
Stamford, 68, 119
Standards of perfection in Old English Game, 160, 179
Steel spurs, 53, 54, 123, 135
Stobart, Jack, 27, 169
Stourbridge, 69
Stow, 99
Strutt, Joseph, 99
Stubbes, Philip, 99, 144
Suffolk, 68, 115
Sumatra, cockfighting in, 87
Sumatra game, 28
Sunday cockfights, 116, 133, 144, 172
Surreptitious cockfights, 125, 169ff
Sussex, 67, 109
Sweating, 43, 44
Syrians, ancient, 87

TAPE-FIGHTS, 127
Tegetmeier, W. B., 24, 26, 27, 79, 159, 164, 171
Tellers, 62, 72
Telum, 53
Tennessee, 124
Texas, 124
Themistocles, 89, 91, 151
Timbs, John, 59, 60
Towns, cockfighting battles between, 66
Training for battle, 40ff
Travelling, deleterious effects of, 31, 32, 127
Tufton Street cockpit, Westminster, 58, 74

UNITED STATES, cockfighting in, 121ff
United States, fixing of spurs, 56
United States, sale of spurs in, 54
United States, town's name chosen by cockfight in, 119
Urine, use of, 42, 49

INDEX

Varieties of Game Fowl, 20
Vere, Lord, 21, 105
Vermont, 123
Virginia, 125
Vivian, Sir H., 105

Wakefield, 67
Wales, 57, 172
"Walks", 34
Walsall, 69
Warwickshire, 66, 67, 69, 70, 112, 114, 115
Wednesbury, 140
Welsh main, 25, 73, 157
Welshing, 85, 137
Welshpool, cockpit at, 60
Wesley, John, 57

West Indian cockers, 52
Westmorland, 31, 96, 172
Whitehall Palace, 58
Whites, 20, 23, 24
Wild, Dr. Robert, verses of, 82ff
William III, 102
Wiltshire, 67
Wilson, George, 16, 82
Wings, clipping of, 47
Worcestershire, 69, 114
Worship of fighting-cock in ancient world, 87ff
Wounded cocks, care of, 48, 50
Wright, Thomas, 119

Yellow birchens, 24
Yorkshire, 32, 66, 68, 103, 108, 116, 172

Printed by C. Tinling & Co., Ltd.,
Liverpool, London and Prescot